CAMBRIDGE LIBRARY COLLECTION

Books of enduring scholarly value

Classics

From the Renaissance to the nineteenth century, Latin and Greek were
compulsory subjects in almost all European universities, and most early
modern scholars published their research and conducted international
correspondence in Latin. Latin had continued in use in Western Europe long
after the fall of the Roman empire as the lingua franca of the educated classes
and of law, diplomacy, religion and university teaching. The flight of Greek
scholars to the West after the fall of Constantinople in 1453 gave impetus
to the study of ancient Greek literature and the Greek New Testament.
Eventually, just as nineteenth-century reforms of university curricula were
beginning to erode this ascendancy, developments in textual criticism and
linguistic analysis, and new ways of studying ancient societies, especially
archaeology, led to renewed enthusiasm for the Classics. This collection
offers works of criticism, interpretation and synthesis by the outstanding
scholars of the nineteenth century.

Classical Scholarship and Classical Learning

John William Donaldson's 1856 essay tackles the topic of university reform,
a hotly debated political issue in his day. Donaldson presents a series of
suggestions for the improvement of university teaching, and argues for
the value of a classical education. Drawing upon his experience both as a
headmaster and as a scholar at Trinity College, Cambridge, he considers
himself well-placed to address the subject of education, maintaining that
there are 'not many who can claim a better right to speak without one-sided
prejudice and narrow-minded partiality to some hackneyed system'. He
discusses many aspects of the subject, including the meaning of the term
'university', the college system at Cambridge University and the merits of
studying classics in comparison to mathematics. Donaldson also addresses
the class system, emphasising the need for all classes to be educated. This
lively and approachable book foreshadows the debates of our own century.

T0381678

Cambridge University Press has long been a pioneer in the reissuing of out-of-print titles from its own backlist, producing digital reprints of books that are still sought after by scholars and students but could not be reprinted economically using traditional technology. The Cambridge Library Collection extends this activity to a wider range of books which are still of importance to researchers and professionals, either for the source material they contain, or as landmarks in the history of their academic discipline.

Drawing from the world-renowned collections in the Cambridge University Library, and guided by the advice of experts in each subject area, Cambridge University Press is using state-of-the-art scanning machines in its own Printing House to capture the content of each book selected for inclusion. The files are processed to give a consistently clear, crisp image, and the books finished to the high quality standard for which the Press is recognised around the world. The latest print-on-demand technology ensures that the books will remain available indefinitely, and that orders for single or multiple copies can quickly be supplied.

The Cambridge Library Collection will bring back to life books of enduring scholarly value (including out-of-copyright works originally issued by other publishers) across a wide range of disciplines in the humanities and social sciences and in science and technology.

Classical Scholarship and Classical Learning

*Considered with Especial Reference to
Competitive Tests and University Teaching*

JOHN WILLIAM DONALDSON

CAMBRIDGE UNIVERSITY PRESS

Cambridge, New York, Melbourne, Madrid, Cape Town, Singapore,
São Paolo, Delhi, Dubai, Tokyo

Published in the United States of America by Cambridge University Press, New York

www.cambridge.org
Information on this title: www.cambridge.org/9781108012386

© in this compilation Cambridge University Press 2009

This edition first published 1856
This digitally printed version 2009

ISBN 978-1-108-01238-6 Paperback

CLASSICAL SCHOLARSHIP

AND

CLASSICAL LEARNING.

CLASSICAL SCHOLARSHIP

AND

CLASSICAL LEARNING

CONSIDERED WITH ESPECIAL REFERENCE TO COMPETITIVE
TESTS AND UNIVERSITY TEACHING:

A PRACTICAL ESSAY

ON

LIBERAL EDUCATION.

BY

JOHN WILLIAM DONALDSON, D.D.

FORMERLY FELLOW AND CLASSICAL LECTURER OF
TRINITY COLLEGE, CAMBRIDGE

CAMBRIDGE:

DEIGHTON, BELL AND Co.

LONDON: BELL AND DALDY, FLEET-STREET.

1856.

PREFACE.

VERY few words will suffice by way of Preface to the
following pages. Although this Essay is incon-
siderable in extent, and intentionally written in a
familiar and informal style, it contains the results of
no slight experience and reflexion on the subjects of
which it treats. Indeed, I have had many opportunities of discussing these matters before now, and I
have often had to repeat in the present Treatise the
thoughts, sometimes the very words, which I have
used in fugitive publications or in public speeches
and lectures. But the confidence, with which I
bring forward this advocacy of the old basis of liberal
education, does not spring merely from the maturity
of my own convictions. I know also that most of
those, who have paid adequate attention to the questions mooted by me, take the same view, either wholly
or in part, and I have often, for obvious reasons,
quoted passages from the writings of others, instead
of endeavouring to enforce the same opinions by
words of my own. One of my chief objects has been
to correct prevalent, especially recent, exaggerations.
And I venture to hope that, while those, who have
not considered all the bearings of the questions raised

in these pages, may be induced, by a few candid and dispassionate arguments, to abstain from a precipitate depreciation of learning in general, and of Oxford and Cambridge learning in particular, those, who have it in their power to make our School and University teaching all that it ought to be, will not, for the want of the necessary corrections and additions, allow the whole system to suffer judgment before the tribunal of public opinion.

Although I am quite independent of any professional reasons for maintaining the old basis of education, it would have been the height of affectation if I had attempted to dissemble my literary concernment in the subject under discussion. There may be some little disadvantage in this personal implication. But on the other hand, it must be remembered that no one can defend classical studies with a lively interest in the subject and a full knowledge of the case, unless he has acquired an adequate experience in these pursuits. And I have shown that I am not likely to be swayed by any narrow partiality or educational prejudice.

J. W. D.

St Peter's Terrace, Cambridge,
Feb. 4, 1856.

CONTENTS.

	PAGE
Introduction	1
University Reform, its result ought to be improved University teaching	1
The questions raised respecting this improvement mainly refer to the value of classical education: the three propositions stated	2
Adequate experience and immunity from educational prejudices necessary for a proper discussion of the subject . .	3
Conclusions to be maintained respecting University teaching, competitive tests, and scholarship and learning as connected with them	6
Mode of treating the subject	7

I. *University Teaching* . . . . . | 8
Prince Albert's opinion . . . . *ib.*
Classics and mathematics not arbitrarily selected or exclusively studied in the great Universities 10
Education, information, knowledge, and science . . . *ib.*
Mr Dickens' exposure of the fallacy that information is education 11
Liberal education commensurate in extent with bodily growth . 12
Epochs of life: Luther's saying . . . . . . *ib.*
Ancient Greek identification of beauty and mental accomplishment 13
Boy-training and humanity 14
Education should be general, not multifarious . . . . *ib.*
Döderlein's remarks 15
The opinion of Frederic Jacobs 16
Postulates assumed 17
Intellectual education the present subject, and other questions waived 18
The discipline of the mind confines itself to the development of deductive habits—*i. e.* practically to Grammar and Geometry 19
Universities originated in a recognition of this principle . 20
The school of liberal arts was the foundation of modern Universities . . . . *ib.*

PAGE

The *Trivium* and *Quadrivium*   21
Partial cultivation of the seven arts or of one of the two branches   22
Intimate connexion of the faculties with the arts   . . .   24
All doctors considered as regents   25
The Universities include professional as well as general training   26
Meaning of the term *University*   27
It implies joint action and equal rights . . . . .   *ib.*
Hence the school of arts and the faculties stand on the same
    footing   28
A training in the former presumed as antecedent to the latter   29
How this is shown in the different applications   . . .   30
The functions of a University ought not to be unduly narrowed .   31
This is alleged to be the case at Cambridge   32
And attributed to the Colleges by a College tutor   . . .   33
Predominance of examinations over lectures alleged by another
    writer   34
Actual effects of the College system   35
The old method of lectures and disputations . . . .   *ib.*
Subsequent appointment of professorial teachers   . . .   37
A similar substitution has taken place in the Colleges   . .   *ib.*
Gradual establishment of examinations at Cambridge   . .   38
These examinations have virtually restored the old school of arts   39
They are not the cause of any imperfections in the Cambridge
    University system . . . .   *ib.*
The Colleges narrow the University   40
But their merits must not be overlooked   . . . .   *ib.*
The University ought to be one community, not a collection of
    communities   41
College distinctions partly remedied by private tutors   . .   *ib.*
A College attempt to interfere with their legal independence   .   42
Necessity for a University examination at entrance   . .   43
Urged by two tutors of Colleges   44
And by the Master of Trinity . . . .   *ib.*
Mr Martin's objections   46
The author's view of the case . . . .   *ib.*
Difficulties of detail obviated   47
Candidates for holy orders . . . .   *ib.*
Immediate preparation for the University   49
Duties of schools and their relations to the Universities . .   *ib.*
Proposal for shortening the period of compulsory residence   .   50
Nature and extent of the entrance examination   . . .   53
What should be required of the ordinary B. A.   54

CONTENTS.

PAGE

The examiners for entrance and ordinary degree examinations to be provided by the resident M. A.'s 54

University teaching 55

Small amount of work done in the College lecture-rooms . *ib.*

Good private teaching necessarily correlative to a system of competitive tests 56

All really good teaching implies that time and attention are bestowed on the individual pupil 57

Private tuition at public schools . . . . *ib.*

General distinction between professorial and College lectures 58

Special exceptions 59

University teaching consists in private tuition and professorial lectures, or one of these methods of instruction . . . 60

How and when the professorial lecture is profitable . . 61

Advantage of allowing a free choice of higher studies . . 64

Separation of triposes 65

Proposal for connecting the honorary triposes with the degree of M. A. 66

The professorial faculties should require public disputations in Latin from the candidates for their highest degrees . . 68

Value and importance of disputations 70

II. *Competitive Tests* 72

Arguments for the preponderance of classics derived from the gradual concessions at Cambridge and from the Civil Service scheme . . . . *ib.*

Objects of examination at the Universities and for the Civil Service are similar rather than identical 74

Principles laid down in the report on the East India examination 75

Reasonableness of the plan proposed 77

It not only gives the most important place to the old basis of liberal instruction, but, in this, prefers classics to mathematics 79

The author holds this view,

(1) Generally, because classical studies are more beneficial than mathematics ;

(2) Specially for India, because classical studies are more immediately useful in such appointments ;

(3) Specially for the Universities, because classics contribute more than mathematics to their progressive studies . . . 80

(1) Literature more humanising than exact science . . *ib.*

Steinthal's generalisation 81

The scholar's contemplation of nature 82

                                                                    PAGE
Literary culture alone can free men from the trammels of their
      material interests   82
Necessity for this   83
Civilised man a slave to the increased conveniences of the age .   84
Illustration furnished by the railroad . . . . .   ib.
Liberal education of the upper class is the great panacea for
      present and future evils   85
All classes must be educated . . . .   ib.
Beneficial influence of the aristocracy 86
Prejudices and slavishness of the middle class . . , 87
The lower classes owe their improvement not to the middle but
      to the upper class   90
Importance therefore of maintaining the literary cultivation of
      the latter . . . .   ib
Comparison of the educational results of classical as opposed to
      mathematical studies is favourable to the former . . 91
Dr Whewell's opinion examined   92
Mathematics not exclusively the education of the reasoning
      powers   93
The mere mathematician is less completely educated than the
      mere classical scholar . . . .   ib.
Cambridge scholarship exercises the reason only too much and
      too exclusively   95
Logical effort demanded of the classical scholar at Cambridge . 96
Inferior and ancillary place of mathematics in the partnership of
      liberal arts   97
Sir W. Hamilton's opinion on this point . . . . .   ib.
Intellectual defects of mathematicians   98
Their inability to understand conjectural criticism . . . 99
Their pretensions inadmissible   101
Longer time required for classical and literary study should also
      be taken into consideration   102
(2) A training in language more useful than mathematics to the
      civil servant of the East India Company 104
Importance of Arabic and Sanscrit   106
Especially of the latter . . . .   ib.
Arguments for this study quoted from the Times . . . 107
How classical philology contributes to the study of Sanscrit . 116
(3) Classical learning contributes more than mathematical science
      to the studies which should be cultivated in a great University 121
Increase of literary culture in the case of Cambridge mathema-
      ticians   122

PAGE

Applications and literary influences of classical training . 124

III. *Scholarship and Learning* 126

The account between scholarship and learning ought to be more
equally balanced in this country . . . . . *ib.*
Invidious comparison between England and Germany . . 127
Necessity for an answer to this exaggerated depreciation . *ib.*
Mr Horsman's speech 128
Professor Conington's exaltation of German scholarship . 131
Scholarship not tested only by literary productiveness . . 132
Mr Goulburn's vindication of English as compared with German
scholarship 133
English writers on Roman and Greek history, antiquities, or
literature 135
Philological treatises 136
English editions of Greek authors 138
Latin editorship 142
Lexicography 145
General contributions to classical learning . . . . *ib.*
English scholars who are not University men 146
Grammatical works . . . . . . ' . . . 148
The scholar 149
The learned man 151
Porson 152
Pye Smith . . . . *ib.*
Process of scholar-making in England 153
Proofs of scholarship 155
German scholars—Hermann and Lachmann were exceptions to
the general rule 156
Ordinary career of a German philologer 159
General comparison of English and German scholarship . . 162
Their mutual relations 163
Why the latter is exaggerated 166
English and German theology 167
Why Biblical criticism is backward in England 168
Privileges and obligations of the Anglican Divine connected
with his academical and professional character . . 170
Marsh and Möhler 177
Proposals for the increase of classical learning in England 179
That German education requires an increase of skill is admitted
by Germans 180

PAGE

That the English scholar requires an increase of knowledge is
    allowed by distinguished Englishmen   181
Learning is not adequately encouraged in this country . .   182
How the classical examinations might be conducted at Cam-
    bridge   184
Alphabetical order and brackets   185
Essays to be required from the best scholars   188
Practical equality of the most successful competitors . . .   190
Selection of examiners   191
New linguistic professors would be desirable   192
Functions of the professors of Hebrew and Arabic ought to be
    defined and prescribed   193
Professorships of Latin, Sanscrit and English to be created .   194
Duties of private teachers might become more important   197
An historical and philological society might be instituted   198
Corresponding improvement of schools would lead to a saving
    of time   199
How early education ought to be conducted   201
Plan for the management of grammar-schools . .   202
Conclusion   204
Longer notes and authorities . .   207

CLASSICAL SCHOLARSHIP

AND

CLASSICAL LEARNING.

———◆———

INTRODUCTION.

THE delay, which has interrupted the progress of
the Cambridge University Bill, and which seems for
the moment to have placed us in the rear of Oxford,
will in all probability be productive of results ultimately, if not immediately, beneficial. Various opinions
and expectations will be entertained in regard to the
advantages which will, it is hoped, be secured to us,
without any mischievous qualification, by the measure
which has been delayed only to make it more complete
and more generally acceptable. But it seems eminently
desirable that the interval, which has thus occurred
between the attempt and its consummation, should be
employed in the calm and dispassionate consideration of
another subject, which has always been freely and openly
discussed at Cambridge, which does not immediately
invite the restorative interference of the Legislature,
and without which the readjustment of our University
machinery will not produce its proper effects on the work
to be done here. I refer of course to the great question
of improved University teaching.

For, after all, the main object in any attempt to
reform or restore our system of University government,

1

and to obtain the full development of the University constitution, must be to improve and extend University education, and to connect it more and more with its natural continuations and enlargements into learning, literature, science, and professional training. A full examination of this great and important subject involves the discussion of many questions, which have often been argued from different points of view in the war of speeches and pamphlets occasioned by the desire to promote or resist University Reform. And some of these questions have obtained a value independent of their University interest, from the institution of competitive tests to determine the appointments to civil and military offices in England and in India.

The questions most frequently raised in regard to University teaching, and the competitive tests, which are likely to give a new impulse to the educational training of the whole country, may be stated, like Abelard's *Sic et Non*, in the following propositions :

1. That the University system is wrongly confined to the basis of a liberal education—that is, specifically, to classics and mathematics—to the exclusion or neglect of professional training and many branches of literature and science : *et contra.*

2. That at the Universities, and in the competitive examinations, which have just been instituted, an undue importance is attached to classical even as opposed to mathematical knowledge : *et contra.*

3. That the classical learning of England is not good of its kind, but is altogether inferior to that of Germany : *et contra.*

It will be observed that these three propositions are in a *crescendo* strain—they repeat the same complaint, with successive aggravations. We are first told, that we have too exclusive an addiction to classical and mathematical studies; then, that we unduly prefer classics to mathematics; finally, that we prefer the worse to the better method of classical education. Or to take the propositions in the reversed order, it is urged that even if classical learning were the all in all of University education, we fail to compass it in its best form; that even if we were perfect in this respect, we ought not to bestow so much time upon it, as contrasted with mathematical science, which is so much more useful; that even if classics and mathematics were equally valuable and cultivated at the same expense of time, it is not right that the University and the Government should make these branches of general knowledge the main test in the distribution of the rewards and emoluments and opportunities of professional activity, by which they propose to stimulate the industry and encourage the ability of young Englishmen, and to obtain for the public service in Church and State the flower of our youth, or, as Pericles beautifully called it, the spring of our year *.

In the title-page I have proposed to discuss these questions with especial reference to the last proposition; but I shall not neglect the two antecedent complaints by which it is intensified. Now I feel that any value, which may attach to the opinions of a writer on a subject of practical importance, must result from the opportunities which he has had of making himself practically acquainted with it in all its bearings. And perhaps there are not many who can come to the discussion of classical scholarship, as it is in England, and at Cambridge in particular, after such a long and complete apprenticeship in

* Aristot. *Rhet.* I. 7, 34.

varied fields of labour, or who can claim a better right to speak without the imputation of one-sided prejudice and narrow-minded partiality to some hackneyed system. There is no reason why I should, from mere habit, prefer general to professional training, or *vice versâ;* why I should be prejudiced in favour of the tutorial as opposed to the professorial system of teaching ; why I should exalt the public at the expense of the private tutor ; why I should prefer scholarship to learning, or classical learning to mathematical science ; why I should extol English and depreciate German learning; or why I should undervalue any of the advantages which properly belong to the College system. It has been my lot to learn by experience the faults and the merits of every method of training and discipline. Educated myself at a good private school of the modern type, I was for fourteen years the head master of an old-fashioned grammar school, hampered by the most exclusive limitations, and in this capacity I endeavoured, as far as I could, to secure for mathematical acquirements their due proportion of encouragement. Introduced, while still a boy, to the study of the law, and having made some progress in it long before others have generally commenced this pursuit[1*], I was able to convince myself that a much larger amount of classical learning than I had brought with me from school was necessary for the English lawyer, or at least for such a lawyer as I wished to be. From the London University, where the professorial system flourished at that time in its best form, I passed to Trinity College, Cambridge, at a time when the lecturers were confessedly among the most eminent men in England ; and

[1*] The numbers refer to the longer notes and authorities at the end.

it would be strange if there were any prejudice against
College lectures in the mind of a man who attended,
either at the same time or in succession, the lecture-rooms
of Whewell, Hare, R. W. Evans, and Thirlwall—to say
nothing of the fact that I was eventually a college lecturer myself. It was also my good fortune to read privately during my undergraduateship with some of the
most accurate and accomplished of those scholars in this
University, who have devoted themselves to this employment; and having always acknowledged the benefits
which I derived from their tuition, it would be surprising if I joined in the indiscriminating outcry against
this mode of instruction. As I resided ten years within
the walls of Trinity College, and was during the greater
part of that time a recipient of the bounty of that mag-
nificent and illustrious foundation, I am not likely to be
blind to the important functions of well-endowed colleges
in a great University. As I professedly belong to the
German school of philology, it would be a strange incon-
sistency if I did injustice to my teachers and fellow-
labourers across the water; and as I have made contributions, such as they are, to almost every department
of literature connected with classical learning, I should
stultify my own procedure if I maintained that classical
learning was not the natural and expected fruit of classical scholarship. With these manifold experiences, I think
I may trust myself to attempt an impartial solution of
the difficulties raised in the propositions which I have
recited. And if I allow myself to believe, that those
who have studied the subject will accept my premises as
true, and acquiesce in my conclusions as valid, I am supported by the fact that every step, which has been taken
of late in the improvement of the two Universities, was

briefly and explicitly recommended in a paper which I contributed to a London periodical immediately before the appointment of the two University Commissions, so that I am not unlikely, on this occasion also, to enjoy the blessedness of thinking as every man thinks, and of finding that my thought keeps the road-way of general convictions *.

For the sake of distinctness, it will be convenient that I should state beforehand the conclusions, at which I have arrived respecting the three propositions enunciated above, and the manner in which I propose to discuss them in the following pages.

Taking the propositions in the order already given, I am prepared to show :

1.   That although it is the business of a University to provide for the expansion of a liberal or general education into science, literature, and professional knowledge, the Universities do not arbitrarily or erroneously make classics and mathematics the basis of all the instruction which they give, and the object of those rewards and emoluments which they are enabled to bestow ; but that, on the contrary, their mode of proceeding is a result of their original constitution, and recommended by the practical experience of many generations.

2.   That there is good reason why, in the University system, and in the competitive tests, which have been recently instituted, classical learning and scholarship should receive a larger amount of encouragement and reward even than mathematical attainments, which form their necessary supplement in any complete course of liberal education.

3.   That although classical scholarship flourishes to a

* Shaksp. *Henry* IV., *part* 2, *Act* II. *Sc.* II.

much greater extent in England than in Germany, and though our classical learning is in some respects superior to that of our fellow-labourers on the continent, there are some obvious methods of improving our University teaching and our competitive tests, so as to increase our classical learning without diminishing the classical scholarship, which has long been the chief ornament of the English gentleman.

It will thus be seen that I have proposed to myself three main subjects, namely, those which are indicated in my title; 1. The proper functions of University teaching. 2. The best subjects for competitive tests. 3. The relations of classical scholarship and classical learning to both of these important topics. And those who remember that the title of a book, though printed at the beginning, does really, like the preface, take a retrospective view of its contents, will not be surprised to find, that I treat of these three questions in the order in which I have here stated the intended results of my inquiry, rather than in accordance with that general description which stands in front of my essay.

I. UNIVERSITY TEACHING.

THE common opinion, that our great Universities arbitrarily, and therefore perhaps erroneously, confine the main
part of their studies and examinations to the two departments of classics and mathematics, which form the basis
of liberal education in this country, has recently found an
exponent no less able than influential in the person of
His Royal Highness the Prince-Chancellor of Cambridge.
In a speech delivered at Birmingham, on the 22nd No-
vember, 1855, when he laid the foundation of the Midland
Institute, after arguing, with his usual felicity of thought
and language, against the vulgar depreciation of scientific
as contrasted with practical knowledge, Prince Albert
said :—

"The study of the laws by which the Almighty go-
verns the Universe, is therefore our bounden duty. Of
these laws our great academies and seats of education
have, rather arbitrarily, selected only two spheres or groups
(as I may call them), as essential parts of our national
education—the laws which regulate quantities and proportions, which form the subject of mathematics, and the
laws regulating the expression of our thoughts through
the medium of language—that is to say grammar, which
finds its purest expression in the classical languages. These
laws are most important branches of knowledge ; their
study trains and elevates the mind. But they are not the
only ones ; there are others which we cannot disregard,

which we cannot do without. There are, for instance, the laws governing the human mind and its relation to the Divine Spirit—the subjects of logic and metaphysics. There are those which govern our bodily nature and its connexion with the soul—the subjects of physiology and psychology. Those which govern human society and the relations between man and man—the subjects of politics, jurisprudence and political economy, and many others. While of the laws just mentioned some have been recognised as essentials of education in different institutions, and some will, in the course of time, more fully assert their right to recognition, the laws regulating matter and form are those which will constitute the chief object of your pursuits; and as the principle of subdivision of labour is the one most congenial to our age, I would advise you to keep to this speciality, and to follow with undivided attention chiefly the sciences of mechanics, physics, and chemistry, and the fine arts of painting, sculpture, and architecture*."

As His Royal Highness recommends the members of the Midland Institute to adopt the principle of the subdivision of labour, as one most accordant with the spirit of the age in which we live, it might be urged that the old seats of learning, even if they had arbitrarily selected the classical and mathematical studies, to which they devote so much attention, as essential parts of our national education, would be justified on the very principle, which

* It is right to mention that Sir W. Hamilton agrees with his Royal Highness in the use of the term "arbitrary." He says, "Oxford and Cambridge are now what they were at first, schools exclusively of liberal instruction, but of liberal instruction, it should be added, not in all, but only in certain arbitrary branches."—*Discussions on Philosophy, &c.*, p. 673.

Prince Albert suggests to the new foundation at Birmingham, and might be left to do their part in the great work, which is given out to be done, piece by piece, in the different sections of the community. The fact is, however, that the Universities did not make an arbitrary selection of these studies, nor do they profess or intend to limit their functions to the successful prosecution of certain branches of study or even to the completion of a liberal education as such.

It is not necessary that I should here repeat all that I have written on previous occasions respecting education in general or a liberal education in particular. But I will briefly state, in what sense I have always used the terms, on which the discussion is made to rest, and from the definition of which it must start, if it is to be generally intelligible. If we confine ourselves to the province of the intellect, *Education* is properly a cultivation and development of those faculties, which all men have in common, though not all in the same degree of activity. *Information*, when it is nothing more, merely denotes an accumulation of stray particulars by means of the memory. On the other hand, *Knowledge* is information appropriated and thoroughly matured. We speak of knowledge of the world, knowledge of our profession or business, knowledge of ourselves, knowledge of our duties—all of which imply a completeness and maturity of habit and experience. And when knowledge extends to a methodical comprehension of general laws and principles, it is called *Science*. It is the natural and proper tendency of information to ripen into knowledge, just as knowledge itself is not complete until it is systematised into science. And as intellectual education necessarily presumes a certain increase in the information or acquired knowledge of the person

under training, it is clear that, while the main object of
education, namely, the gradual development of the faculties, should never be neglected, the information conveyed
and the method of imparting it should be such as to lay
the foundation and pave the way, for the superstructure
of knowledge and science, in the case of those persons
whose capacity and tastes render such an enlargement of
the future field of study either probable or desirable.
From this it follows, that the great object of education is
utterly ignored by those teachers, who, when the mind is
unformed and undisciplined, force upon the memory a
crowd of unconnected and unprolific recollections, which
can neither be digested nor retained, and which, if retained,
produce no results on the healthy action of the understanding. That keen observer, Mr Charles Dickens, has
admirably described the process and its results in his
account of poor little Paul Dombey's progress under the
cramming and forcing exertions of Dr Blimber and his
daughter Cornelia,—that mother of modern British Gracchi.
Our "little friend's" library comprised "a little English,
and a deal of Latin—names of things, declensions of articles" (if there are such things in Latin, Mr Dickens!)
"and substantives, exercises thereon, and preliminary
rules—a trifle of orthography, a glance at ancient history,
a wink or two at modern ditto, a few tables, two or three
weights and measures, and a little general information.
When poor Paul had spelt out number two, he found he
had no idea of number one ; fragments whereof afterwards
obtruded themselves into number three, which slided into
number four, which grafted itself on to number two.   So
that whether twenty Romuluses made a Remus, or *hic,
hæc, hoc* was troy weight, or a verb always agreed with
an ancient Briton, or three times four was *Taurus* a bull,

were open questions with him *." This picture, though
sufficiently humorous, is neither out of drawing nor too
highly coloured, and there are many parents, who estimate
the proficiency of their children by the number of stray
particulars, which are tumbled together in the confused
store-house of an unreflecting mind.

But even in cases, when this process is postponed
beyond the period of earliest boyhood, even when it is
adopted after a certain course of real mental discipline,
its effects are prejudicial to the ripening mind, and unfavourable to the confirmation of those accurate habits
without which information seldom settles into knowledge
or rises into science. And it is always desirable that the
process of liberal education should be carried on as long
as possible, and that the acquirement of special knowledge,
whether tending to science or applicable immediately to
professional practice, should be postponed until the youth
has accomplished more than half of the third septennium
of his life. That periods of seven years constitute a real
element in the life of man is acknowledged by the tacit
consent or familiar language of all nations. At any rate,
our own experience teaches us that at seven years old the
child passes into the boy, by a change of dentition ; that
at 14, the age of puberty is attained ; at 21 the age of
manhood ; at 42 the age of maturity ; and at 63—the
grand climacteric as it is called—the period of senility.
Nor is this subdivision at variance with Luther's celebrated enumeration of the four decennia, in his pregnant
statement, that if a man is not handsome at 20, strong at
30, wise at 40, and rich at 50, he will never be handsome,
or strong, or wise, or rich. Such a subdivision presumes
that while growth of body is completed at 20, strength of

* *Dombey and Son*, p. 115.

body must be reached, if at all, at 30, and strength of mind, when we have well passed 35, which Dante calls "the midway of our life." And taking this view of the matter we might maintain with great confidence, that the education of the reasoning powers cannot really terminate before the body has attained to maturity ; that no man can be set free from the duty of forming and invigorating his mind before the period at which he reaches a full development of his material growth ; that while his frame is still unformed his understanding cannot have reached its completion, and that his intellect cannot be perfect as an instrument of thought until nature has set the stamp of manly beauty on the young man's brow.

This necessity for a commensurate progress in mental and bodily growth, this presumption that accomplishment of the mind and beauty of person are attained at the same period, namely, when the boy has grown into a man, is involved in the language of that nation which understood better than any other wherein beauty consists, and by what means the graces and refinements of body and mind can best be imparted and secured. The Greeks had only one word to express personal beauty and mental accomplishment. The adjective καλός, in its primary sense, denotes "furnished with outward adornments" in general ; that of which the outward form or the outward effects are pleasing and grateful. "But," as I have said elsewhere *, "to the Greek idea of κάλλος something beyond mere outward garnishing of the person was required ; it was not a languishing beauty, a listless though correct set of features, an enervated voluptuousness of figure, to which the homage of their admiration

* *New Cratylus*, § 324, p. 509.

was paid. It was the grace and activity of motion, which the practice of gymnastic exercises was calculated to promote—the free step, the erect mien, the healthy glow, combined with the elegances of conversation and the possession of musical accomplishments; it was in fact the result of an union of the μουσική and γυμναστική of which their education was made up." The name, which the Greeks gave to the process of making the mind and body both elegant or handsome and clever, implied that the business was not complete till a fulness of stature and a maturity of understanding had been attained. They called it παιδεία, or "boy-training," and the word also denoted the period of life during which this bringing up or education was to be carried on.

With the Greeks, then, I believe that a liberal or general education—that which the Romans called *humanitas*, because the pursuit and discipline of science is given to man only of all the animals *—ought to be carried on as long as the mind and body are still immature, that is, nearly till the twentieth year if possible; and while I believe with Plato that the boy-training, which alone is worthy of the name, is that which is pursued for its own sake without reference to extrinsic objects †, I think also that we import into the legitimate province of the teacher that which does not belong to it, when we crowd a mass of multifarious acquirements into the period of life allotted to the growth and improvement of our reasoning powers and our physical energies.

That this view of the case is not the narrow prejudice of an English teacher, but fully shared by those con-

---

* Aulus Gellius, XIII. 16; cf. Cic. *pro Archia*, 1; *de Oratore*, I. 9.

† *Legg.* I. p. 643 B.

tinental scholars with whose greater versatility and learning we are so often and so scornfully contrasted, will be
inferred from the following passages.

The true object of a liberal education is thus described
by Döderlein * :

" Even at the present day, one hears voices which tell
us that the school forms a more appropriate preparation
for the business of life when it encourages such employments as are most subservient to this and most connected with it. For example, the medical man will be
best trained by the earliest possible study of the physical
sciences. But reason has prophesied, and experience has
fulfilled the prediction, that this sort of education (the
infallibility of which has always found the quickest acceptance with the most narrow-minded, and which appears
to the most superficial the only road to an adequate training) is calculated only to debase every one of the more
intellectual occupations to the rank of a better sort of
trade. Accordingly, all public schools, unless they mistake their destination, hold this as an unassailable principle : that although a classical education presumes that
all its pupils are designed for some intellectual employment, it does not trouble itself to inquire what particular
sort of employment this is to be. The future physician
and lawyer, as well as the future clergyman and teacher,
essentially different as their contemplated employments
may be, are trained precisely in the same manner, having
regard only to that which they have in common, namely,
that their ulterior occupation, whatever it may be, will
demand the most practised exercise of the intellectual
faculties.

* *Reden und Aufsätze*, p. 6.

"It is the primary object of the education of classical schools to impart to the mind of every pupil a capacity for learning that business of which the Universities and other higher institutions profess to convey the definite teaching. The schoolmaster therefore is not deterred by the thought, that so much of the learning which he has, with great pains and infinite labour, conveyed to his scholars, and which they have acquired with no little exertion of their own, has been learned by many of them only to be forgotten sooner or later. As the sculptor, when he has finished his statue, does not hesitate to break up the model (the most troublesome part of his work), so the grown-up man does not forget or lay aside what he was taught at school, until he has derived the full advantage from these studies. He may fail to recognise their unseen fruits, but he cannot eradicate them; for his lessons have strengthened his mind in learning and thinking, just as his exercise in the playground braced and invigorated his body."

And Frederic Jacobs has protested in language equally forcible against the erroneous notion that multifarious acquirements may be allowed to take the place of a liberal discipline of the mind. He says * :

"It has been repeatedly said, that it is of less consequence in youth what a man learns, than how he learns it, and that the saying of Hesiod, 'The half is often

---

* *Vermischte Schriften*, III. § 27, p. 254. He quotes to the same effect a passage from Lord John Russell's History of the English Government and Constitution, which is not before me in the original, and which I will not attempt to reproduce by the counter-process of a retranslation from the German. Sir W. Hamilton too has some good remarks on "superficiality (better expressed by the Greek πολυπραγμοσύνη, by the German *Vielwisserey*)," which, he says, is now the order of the day.—*Discussions on Philosophy, &c.* p. 684.

better than the whole,' admits of an application here. The heaping up of knowledge for the sake of knowledge brings no blessing; and all education, in which vanity bears the sceptre, misses its object. The young are not called upon to learn all that may by possibility be useful at some future period; for if so, as Aristotle facetiously remarks*, we should have to descend to learning cookery; but only such particulars as excite a general activity of mind, sharpen the understanding, enliven the imagination, and produce a beneficial effect on the heart. Not only on grounds of science, but also, and especially, on moral grounds, it is more important to be master of one subject than to be superficially acquainted with many. Knowledge strengthens; superficial acquaintance with many branches of knowledge puffs up and produces a pedantic arrogance; and this is perhaps the most unhappy endowment which a youth can carry with him from school into the world. It is hated because it is illiberal. Illiberality, however, with regard to knowledge and art, always prevails in those who know neither the root nor the summit of the tree of knowledge."

To attempt to support by arguments a view of liberal education, which has been held by enlightened men from the days of Plato and Aristotle down to our time, would be only to waste words. And I shall consider myself entitled to start from the postulates, that, wherever it is possible, that is, in all cases which fall within the scope of University teaching, the discipline of the mind should be carried on to the end of the period of adolescence; that this discipline should be general and not professional; and that it should not consist in sciolism or a smattering of miscellaneous acquirements.

* *Polit.* VIII. 5.

2

As I am speaking only of intellectual education, or the discipline of the reasoning faculties, it is not necessary for me to enter on other questions of equal importance, which lie beyond the scope of my present argument. Accordingly, I do not intend to inquire how we ought to conduct the social and moral training of youth, or how we should combine with the lessons of secular wisdom that spiritual education which emanates from the higher schooling of Christianity. Nor do I speak now of the extent to which it may be desirable, especially in certain cases, to employ the memory of youth in learning modern languages with foreign masters or abroad. It is not part of my business to determine whether musical accomplishments are desirable to every man or capable of attainment by all. And I leave it to be settled in individual cases, whether riding, dancing, fencing, and other graceful or manly exercises should be diligently taught in academies, or left to those occasions and opportunities which generally occur when these accomplishments are most necessary. To those, who prefer the continental to the English school, on account of the greater advantages which the former possesses in these respects, I will only give the warning of my own experience. It has been my lot to receive pupils into an English grammar school, who had previously learned French and German on the banks of the Rhine without acquiring that habit of manly straightforwardness, which is a frequent, if not a general, characteristic of English boys, and who had omitted the third and most important accomplishment of the ancient Persians—that of speaking the truth. But waiving these points of detail, what sort of instruction is the best basis of intellectual training, as such ? What is the best nurture for the ripening intelligence of youth ?

Referring to what has been said on a former occasion for a fuller discussion of the subject*, I will merely state that mental culture, or the discipline of the mind, depends entirely on that system of logical teaching, which gradually imparts the habit of methodically arranging our thoughts, and exercises the reasoning faculties in the practical processes of deduction. Beyond this, intellectual education cannot advance. Knowledge may be gradually matured, experience may be enlarged, observation may widen the field of scientific induction, reading may bring into the hive the sweetest treasures gathered from the undying gardens of the Graces; but the groundwork must ever remain the same. Educational training will attempt what does not belong to its own province, if it does not confine itself to the development of deductive habits,—in fact, to teaching the method of language; for in man, the only reasoning and speaking creature, the thought is necessarily completed in the expression. Now, as far as the world has hitherto advanced, there are only two forms under which this instruction is possible—on the one hand it appears as Grammar, which deals with the expression of our thoughts in language; and on the other hand it presents itself as Geometry, which applies the rules of language to a methodical discussion of quantities, magnitudes and proportions, or, in Kant's phraseology, to a development of the intuitions of space and time. Future ages may reach a wider field of elementary training; but up to this time the known materials of deductive reasoning are exhausted in Grammar and Geometry.

Such being the case, the two Universities would have stood justified even if they had deliberately selected these branches of human knowledge as the basis of that system

* *New Cratylus*, pp. 8 sqq.

of intellectual training, which they undertake to carry on
and complete—for this has been done by a recently founded
University[2]. In point of fact, however, they have had no
opportunity of making such a choice. So far from being
arbitrarily selected by the Universities, the fundamental
studies of Grammar and Geometry, with their necessary
adjuncts, were the causes rather than the effects of the establishment of Universities in Europe; and with regard to the
particular form, which grammatical teaching has assumed—
namely, the study of the Greek and Latin languages and
of the authors who have written in them—the Universities
are not responsible for a literary basis, which is the necessary result and the inevitable condition occasioned and imposed by the important parts assigned to Greece and Rome
in the historical drama of European civilization.

It may be desirable to show this, however briefly, by
a survey of the circumstances to which the great Universities of Europe owe their origin and their present form.

There can be little doubt that the University of Paris,
and the other similar institutions, which either claim a
contemporary foundation or are content to trace back
their system to an early adoption of its forms and usages,
sprung up in the twelfth century, and were the offspring
of the intellectual excitement occasioned by the first
crusade[*]. "It was universally allowed," says Professor
Malden, "that the most ancient part of the University of
Paris was the faculty of arts or philosophy. This faculty
originally constituted the whole University; and the faculties of theology, law and medicine, were not added
till a later period. In consequence of this superior anti-

* In the text I have followed here and there Professor Malden's
clear and accurate little book, *On the Origin of Universities and Academical Degrees.* London, 1835.

quity, the rector of the University was always chosen from the *artistæ*, or graduates in 'arts ; and a doctor of the higher faculties was ineligible." Now the arts or branches of philosophy taught in the schools of the twelfth century were, in accordance with the practice of the times, which attached a mystical reverence to the sacred number seven, obliged to correspond to the seven cardinal virtues, the seven deadly sins, the seven sacraments, the seven planets, and the seven days of the week ; and it was also a result of the same love of symmetry that they were sub-divided into two classes of three and four, answering to the two sides which included the right angle in the nup-tial diagram*. The first course, consisting of three arts, was called the *Trivium ;* the second, which contained four liberal accomplishments, was designated as the *Quadrivium.* The arts of the *Trivium* were Grammar, Logic or Dialectic, and Rhetoric ; that is to say, the method of language was taught in the first of the two courses. The arts of the *Quadrivium* were Arithmetic, Geometry, Astronomy and Music ; meaning by the last, not the science of harmony, which afterwards became a distinct faculty with doctors of its own ; but a branch of arithmetic, according to the form in which the subject is treated by Aristoxenus and other Greek writers ; so that the second course of arts dealt entirely with numbers, quantities, and proportions, or the intuitions of space and time. These seven liberal arts were enumerated, like the forms of the syllogism, in barbarous hexameters ; thus :

> *Gram.* loquitur ; *Dia.* vera docet ; *Rhet.* verba colorat ;
> *Mus.* canit ; *Ar.* numerat ; *G.* ponderat ; *As.* colit astra.

---

* The γαμήλιον διάγραμμα of the Egyptians was the right-angled triangle, of which the sides were 3 and 4, and the hypothenuse 5 ; for $3^2 + 4^2 = 5^2$. (Plutarch, *Is. et Osir.* p. 373 E.)

These seven arts, which were supposed to require seven
years' study, really correspond to those two elements of
liberal education, which have been ever since the basis of
the teaching at Oxford and Cambridge—namely, philology
and mathematical science. Of course, both in amount and
quality, the knowledge possessed and imparted in the
twelfth century was very different from that which now
passes under these names ; but the intention was the
same—to lay a solid and broad foundation of liberal accomplishments. The great ambition was to be a *Sophista
generalis,* or skilled in all the arts*; and degrees, as a
general rule, were given to those only who had passed an
examination in all the seven branches; but the majority
of students were well contented to have mastered the *Trivium,* and it was mentioned as a proof of extraordinary
accomplishments in regard to Alan of the Isles, a famous
scholar and teacher of the University of Paris, that " he
knew the three, the four, and all that could be known :"

Qui tria, qui septem, qui totum scibile novit.

It is remarked by Professor Malden that " Oxford has
shown a disinclination to rise above the *Trivium ;* and
that Cambridge, while it does not neglect the *Trivium,*
has manifested a peculiar predilection for the nobler *Quadrivium.*" Without inquiring as yet which is the nobler
of the two courses, it seems not impossible to find an explanation of this partiality. The certificates of proficiency
were called *degrees* or steps (*gradus*); and this shows that
the successive stages of proficiency were marked by cor-

---

* Sir William Hamilton says (*Discussions on Philosophy and Literature, Education and University Reform.* Lond. 1852. p. 393) : "The
General Sophist was a special degree in Logic, but subordinate to
the general degree in Arts." But the term seems too extensive for
such a specialty.

responding titles. The inferior or preparatory degree in
arts was that of *Bachelor, baccalaureus,* a barbarous title
derived from the French *bas Chevalier,* which primarily
denoted a knight bachelor, one who sat at the same table
with the Bannerets, but, being of inferior rank, was *mis
en arrière et plus bas assis;* hence, it came to signify the
unfinished apprentice, the unmarried man, and the demi-
graduate. The fact, that the arts were divided into two
classes, shows that this degree must have distinguished
originally those who had accomplished the *Trivium* only,
and as the title of *senior soph* or *sophista generalis* is
anterior at Cambridge and Oxford to that of "bachelor
of arts," and as special degrees were anciently given in
grammar, rhetoric and music*, it may be inferred that
the latter University borrowed from Paris, with many
other usages, the practice of acquiescing in the *Trivium*
as a representative of both branches of the seven arts, and
did not exact a corresponding study of the *Quadrivium,*
whereas the University of Cambridge, which originated
in the lectures on the *Trivium* only, delivered by the three
associates of Gislebert†, probably endeavoured to crowd
into the period of study required for the bachelor's degree
a portion at least of the business of the *Quadrivium,*
which should have been reserved for the interval between
the first and second degrees ‡.

Be this as it may, it is clear that in theory at least
the "master of arts" was a professor of both classics and

---

* Sir W. Hamilton, *Discussions,* pp. 393, 483, and for the
degrees in Grammar see Dean Peacock, *On the Statutes,* p. xxx.

† Malden, p. 92.

‡ There is some analogy to this substitution of the part for the
whole in the fact that *humanity* in the Scottish Universities means a
study of Latin only.

mathematics ; and the object of the original Universities was limited to the production of such teachers and professors—the *Magistri*, or master-workmen of the school. At what period the three professional faculties of theology, law and medicine were added to the school of arts cannot be certainly determined. Originally the great teachers of theology at Paris belonged to the school of arts, and taught divinity as the highest application or exhibition of the artistic faculty. Even to the present day, the graduate in divinity at Oxford and Cambridge is presumed to have passed through his curriculum in arts, with the exception of that debasement of University distinction at Cambridge, which Queen Elizabeth sanctioned in the case of the ten-year-men, as they are called. It appears that the other faculties were also included in the arts' school until the latter half of the thirteenth century, when "in consequence of a dispute with the Dominican friars, who wished in fact to intrude themselves into all the chairs of the University, the faculty of arts consented that the doctors in theology should separate themselves and form a distinct body. This example was followed by the teachers of law and medicine ; and thus the three faculties were formed, which were represented and governed by their deans. The University was thus divided in an anomalous way into the four nations of the faculty of arts under their procurators, and the three superior faculties under their deans. But it must be borne in mind, that the doctors only constituted the higher faculties : the bachelors and scholars of theology, law and medicine were included in the four nations*." At Cambridge in particular it cannot be said that the faculties have been formally or theoretically separated from the school of arts. There are,

* Malden, pp. 24, 25, quoting from Savigny.

on the contrary, evident indications of the fact that the
doctors in the faculties are still regarded as belonging to
the same class with the *Regents* or junior masters of arts,
that is, with those who are still engaged in the public
teaching of the University. As Mr Blakesley observes*,
"every doctor in divinity, law or physic, may, if requisite,
perform any University function which the several regius
professors in those faculties are competent to perform."
In the proceedings of the senate the doctors of any standing may, if they please, vote in the *Regent*, or *Upper*,
House, because they, like the public orator, are considered
to retain or resume their functions without any enabling
grace. At Cambridge, the vice-chancellor was originally
elected in open poll by the regents alone†, and though
this was altered by the system of nomination subsequently
introduced, the doctors of all faculties have still a right to
concur with the heads of colleges in the nomination of
two persons ‡, an invidious distinction which they have
practically relinquished, being quite contented with their
ancient and legitimate rights as regents of the University,
or actual *Artistæ* and *Professores*.

From this it appears, that the original functions of a
University were those of a "school of arts," out of which
the three professional faculties were subsequently developed. It was a *studium generale*, and could send forth
sophistæ generales, and *magistri artium*, with reference only
to the acknowledged elements of a liberal education, and
without any regard to the professional destination of its
students. It is clear, then, that Oxford and Cambridge
have not acted arbitrarily in making the representatives of
the *Trivium* and *Quadrivium* of the middle ages the basis

---

* "*Where does the evil lie?*" London, 1845. p. 12.
† *Stat.* p. 26, § 52, and p. 155.   ‡ *Stat.* p. 354.

of their educational system, but that in so doing they are true to the principles of their original constitution.

It cannot however be doubted that, although University teaching has always rested on a liberal or general education,—on that *humanitas* which implies a training of the human mind as such, and which presumes a cultivation of our habits of thought, without any reference to the specific occupation or profession for which we are destined or which we may be led to embrace,—the business of the University cannot now be limited to the cultivation of the individual mind for its own benefit, and without reference to any special work or vocation. At the present time, the age at which students enter the Universities presumes that they have completed the business of a liberal education; and a proper system of matriculation would relieve the University from the necessity of doing what ought to be done at school. Besides, the professional faculties have coexisted with the school of arts in every University since the end of the thirteenth century; and though it is not true that a University *is so called* because it professes to teach *universal* learning, or because, in the words of Mr Blakesley *, "it is a point of union for the maintenance and promotion of all the branches of human knowledge to which a liberal character attaches, —that is, which are not merely technical qualifications for a lucrative profession or trade,"—it may be maintained that the University, as such, presumes the existence of the professional faculties as well as of the school of arts, and does, now at least, involve the necessity of a wider field of teaching.

The term *universitas* denotes a combination and union and common action of all the members of a body politic

* *"Where does the evil lie ?"* p. 6.

or corporate, possessed of congruous rights, by which they are distinguished from other societies amenable externally to the same civil government. Whether we refer to the classical meaning of the adjective *universus*, or to the more modern usage of the derived word *universitas*, we shall see that the real signification of this term must point to the body of men as distinguished from the individuals of which it is composed, and to their general consent in one inclusive work as distinguished from their subdivision into different classes, contributing by their separate functions to the joint action of the whole[3]. Thus, in classical Latin, the word *universi* is properly opposed to *singuli* and *unusquisque*, and distinguished from *omnes*, which implies the separability of the collection. And in the language of the middle ages, *universitas*, as Sir William Hamilton has truly said [*], "was applied either loosely to any understood class of persons; or strictly (in the acceptation of the Roman law) to a public incorporation, more especially (as equivalent with *communitas*) to the members of a municipality or to the members of a *general study*. In this last application it was, however, not uniformly of the same amount; and its meaning was, for a considerable period, determined by the words with which it was connected. Thus it was used to denote either (and this was its more usual meaning) the whole body of teachers and learners, or the whole body of learners, or the whole body of teachers and learners divided either by faculty or by country, or both together." Primarily, then, both in its etymology and in its usage, the University was so called with reference to the collected members of the body which it contained, and to the union of the

---

[*] *Discussions on Philosophy and Literature, Education and University Reform.* Lond. 1852. p. 479.

different classes of which it was composed. As predicated
of a public seminary of higher education, it denoted the
combination of teachers and learners, masters and scholars;
or, if there was more than one faculty or department of
learning, it included them and supposed them all invested
with equal rights, and placed on a similar footing, just as
I have shown that Regent Masters and all Doctors have
joint votes in the Upper House of Convocation. But as
such a seminary, though complete and united in itself,
was generally established in some municipal town, which
was itself an *universitas*, the term had necessarily its
sense of separation from other communities and its implication of exclusive privileges. This is of course the
natural result; for those, who are equal among themselves,
are necessarily to the same extent unequal as distinguished
from those not belonging to the particular body. The
distinction between " gown" and "town" in the English
Universities is shown in a variety of ways, of which not
the least significant is the mention of "the civil incorporation of this town," as distinct from the University,
in the bidding prayer before the University sermon. If,
however, we speak of the University in reference to itself
only, it is clear that the name implies a complete union
of all that the body corporate contains; and while the
distinctions of the degrees sufficiently mark the relative
status of the individual members, they are all equally
members; and if there is more than one school, or faculty,
or department of study, they are equally parts of the
system, and entitled to their share of consideration. As,
then, the Universities of this land have professional faculties in addition to the original school of arts, and as there
is nothing to prevent them from creating new branches of
study to any extent, it cannot be said that their functions

are limited to an indoctrination in the liberal arts which form the basis of education both in the Universities and in the schools preparatory to them, or that we have arbitrarily confined ourselves to certain branches of knowledge.

The fact is, that the principle of union, which makes the University one within itself, and at the same time distinguishes it from other bodies, presumes that the original basis of *humanitas* or a school of arts will never be forgotten, though its applications will be gradually and progressively extended: and the whole system is or ought to be so constituted that, in every application, the reference to the original training in liberal arts should be equally marked and conspicuous. The University student, who really carries on the work of the place, is continually widening the empire of his acquisitions, but he never forgets the starting point in his operations. He does not, when he builds his Constantinople, allow his Rome to fall into ruin and oblivion. While University teaching provides for the continuance and completion of that which has been begun at school, while it conducts the boy to manhood, while it converts scholarship into learning, and knowledge into science, while it provides the young man, who is exactly taught and liberally instructed, with that additional apparatus which will enable him to become a teacher of others, while it qualifies the student to enter into life as a physician, a lawyer, or a divine, or to contribute to the existing store of information as a philosopher or man of letters, it not only rests on the original foundation of the liberal arts, but asserts, or tacitly implies, in every subsequent development, the necessity for that basis of sound learning and liberal accomplishment. The true University-man cannot be an unscientific scholar, or an illiterate mathematician, or a merely modern

dogmatizer in moral philosophy. The classical student, who
is properly imbued with academical principles, will write
over the portals of his school, as Plato did, μηδεὶς ἀγεωμέ-
τρητος εἰσίτω, "let no one enter here who has not cultivated the intuitions of space and time;" for independently
of the intellectual training which this supposes, the student of ancient literature is without one of his keys, if he
cannot sometimes act as a *palmoni* or mystic numberer *.
How else will he deal with Philolaos and Manetho? how
else will he be able to read and understand Scaliger's treatise *de emendatione temporum*, that master-work of modern
philology? how else will he comprehend the works of the
Agrimensores, and those principles of limitation on which
so much of the old Roman literature depends for its
complete elucidation? The mathematician, who is a true
University-man, will not be a mere calculating machine,
profoundly skilled in analysis, and ignorant of every thing
besides. He will be, at least, acquainted with the history
of his own science ; he will not forget that Euclid was a
Greek ; and if he does not read the works of that prince
of geometers in the original language, he will be able to
refer to his text and those of the other geometrical and
gromatical writers, whenever such an illustration may be
necessary. The moral philosopher, who has passed through
our schools, will not talk fluently of categories, and syllogisms, and enthymemes, without knowing something of the
language in which these words are significant terms : he

---

* This word, which occurs only in *Dan.* viii. 13, is generally
rendered "a certain one ;" but the other rendering given in our mar-
gin—"the numberer of secrets," or "the wonderful numberer"—is
equally defensible. In this sense it appears on the title of a remarkable book : "*Palmoni*: an essay on the chronographical and metrical
systems in use among the ancient Jews. London, 1851."

will not be disposed to sneer at Aristotle, because he will
know that in some departments of his own science the
best treatises are still those of the Stagirite ; and while he
descants on Scottish and German metaphysicians, he will
remember that Plato's writings are still extant, and that,
for depth and fulness and elegance, they are still unrivalled. And so in other fields, the solid learning of the school
of arts will manifest itself, and no one, who is really entitled to the academical certificate of proficiency in liberal
education, will show that he is unworthy of it by ignoring
the basis of his own acquirements. The physician, who
calls himself an Oxford or Cambridge man, will not have
to be told that his art, like the name by which he calls
himself, is of Greek origin, and that Hippocrates, Galen,
Aretæus, and Celsus are still worthy objects of liberal
study ; the lawyer will not be content with mastering the
details of cases and decisions, but will rest his power of
legal logic and his acquaintance with national jurisprudence on the basis of his general education and on the
suggestions of that Roman law from which the principles
of his own system are in many cases derived ; above all,
the academical divine will scorn the false, puerile, and
dishonest reasoning of religious periodicals, and will resist
the imposition of those fetters which inevitably check the
free play of judgment, good sense, logic and learning.

On the other hand, it is equally the business of a
modern University to take care that its functions are not
unduly narrowed and limited ; that it does not confine
itself to the business which ought to be done at school,
or, it may be, to only a part of that business ; that it does
not merely undertake to teach to young men of 18 years
and upwards, what they might have learned long before,
and what they ought to learn in any place rather than a

studium generale. Even if we consider the rewards and
prizes with which the Universities, and still more the
Colleges, stimulate and encourage young men on first
entering at Oxford or Cambridge, as expressly designed to
test the successful prosecution of school studies, it is quite
clear that the fellowships and other emoluments and
distinctions, which are open to competition on the part of
those who have spent some time at the University, ought
to involve and require on the part of candidates a greater
extent and maturity of knowledge than any mere school
can be expected to impart. And if this extended range
of acquirements is not exacted and produced in the
examinations of second and third year men, and still more
in the degree examinations at Cambridge and Oxford,
there must be a fault somewhere, perhaps a degeneracy of
the system, which will give good grounds for animadver-
sion, and perhaps cry aloud for immediate correction and
amelioration.

The first inquiry is as to the *fact;* the second as to
the *cause;* and the *remedy* may then be considered.

The *fact* that the system of education is too narrow
both at Oxford and Cambridge, that classics and mathematics—the former occupying the first rank at Oxford,
the latter still predominant at Cambridge—are practically
cultivated exclusively, or to the discouragement of all
other branches of study, is alleged by all who have written
on the subject of University reform, and is known to
be slightly, if at all, qualified by the institution of new
triposes. And the *cause* is as confidently and unanimously
alleged to be the College system, or, immediately, that
substitution of competitive tests for University teaching
which is referred to the influence of the Colleges. The
case, as far as Oxford is concerned, has been stated re-

peatedly and with great ability by Sir William Hamilton*, who has also treated of the undue pre-eminence given to mathematics in particular at Cambridge†. With regard to Cambridge, I will quote a passage from a pamphlet published by a tutor of one of the smaller Colleges, in 1850, which, however, is still applicable to the question‡.

"Mathematics, and under certain restrictions the Greek and Latin languages, are almost the exclusive studies of the University of Cambridge. Almost all the public instruction which the student receives,—certainly all that he has the slightest encouragement to attend to,—is derived from the tutors and lecturers of his own College. And College lectures are neither more nor less than mere schoolboy lessons, attended by mixed classes of ignoramuses and proficients. Lectures properly so called exist but in one large College, and there only as the exception, and not the rule. The lecturers are mostly very young and very ill paid, and when possessed of any ability, usually soon betake themselves to situations where they are better paid, and can look to obtaining a *permanent* settlement. In the large Colleges, it is true, there is pecuniary inducement, in the one case for three, and in the other for two tutors to remain for a considerable period; and perhaps most of the smaller Colleges can offer a tolerable pecuniary recompense to a single tutor. But upon all alike weighs the incubus of celibacy. The tutors of small Colleges, if there be more than one, and the lecturers of all Colleges both large and small, have

* *Discussions, &c.*, Appendix III. pp. 651 sqq.
† *Ibid.* 257 sqq.
‡ *Observations on the Cambridge System*, by the Rev. A. H. Wratislaw, M.A. pp. 14, 15.

3

no inducement whatever to continue their exertions beyond the mere fact of not having yet provided themselves with satisfactory permanent situations in other quarters. There exists also, not unfrequently, a great accumulation of subjects upon the shoulders of a single tutor or lecturer. There will probably, in most cases, be several mathematical lecturers, but Latin, Greek, and Theology are often accumulated upon the shoulders of a single individual; and how the Colleges are to adapt their system to the addition of the moral and natural sciences, I have never even heard suggested. Under such a system how can the students receive the lectures and education they have a right to expect? How can the *higher instruction* be otherwise than dependent upon private tuition? The fact is, that the College system is not capable of further extension; and if other branches of learning besides Latin, Greek, and Mathematics are to be pursued here, extensive organic changes must open the way for an extended University system, of which the Colleges in their several spheres may form a most useful and beneficial portion."

Another writer*, whose name I do not know, but who is obviously a man of ability, in a pamphlet published at the time when the new triposes were instituted, attributes the narrow basis of the Cambridge system to the predominance of examinations over lectures, and for some reason does not allude to the part which the Colleges have played in making the examinations what they are. As, however, it is clear that the lectures, to which he refers as having become subordinate to examinations, were connected with the old constitution of the University as

---

* *The next step respectfully suggested to the Senate of the University of Cambridge by one of its Members.* Cambridge, 1849. pp. 6—10.

distinct from the Colleges; and as the main stimulus to the competition, which has given examinations their importance, is undoubtedly furnished by the College fellowships, this argument also, if it were valid, would make the College system responsible for the narrowed field of University teaching.

For my own part, I am bound to express my conviction that, so far as education is cramped and narrowed and degraded at Cambridge in particular, the cause is to be sought in the subordination of the University to the Colleges, and in the admission to the latter of a great number of students who are not duly qualified for University teaching, and that the first and main remedy would be a genuine University matriculation. At the same time, I think, that the case with regard to the Colleges has not always been fully understood and fairly represented, and that the important functions, which they will perform even when the University is restored to its proper independence and authority, are not duly appreciated, but frequently undervalued.

Now the writer, whom I have just referred to, is mistaken in supposing that the narrowed circle of Cambridge studies is due to the predominance of examinations and the abeyance of lectures. Examinations have not superseded lectures, but have taken the place of the disputations in the schools, which bore the same relation, that examinations have always borne, to the teaching of the University. The lectures of the schools were originally substitutes for books; for before the invention of printing, "the great majority of students," as Dean Peacock has observed*, "had no other means of becoming

* *Observations on the Statutes of the University of Cambridge*, by George Peacock, D.D. Dean of Ely. Lond. 1841. pp. 30—32.

acquainted with the subjects of their study, but by hearing the manuscripts read (with or without the glosses or comments which generally accompanied them) in the public schools, a duty which furnished a daily and principal employment to the bachelors of arts and regent masters of the University. The method of reading was usually sufficiently slow and deliberate to enable the student to copy the actual words, or at all events the import of what was read, which formed the only manuscripts, to which they commonly had access; for the complete manuscripts of the classical or other authors were much too costly articles for a poor student to purchase, and the libraries were in general very scantily stored, and were only accessible under restrictions and conditions, which confined them almost exclusively to the regents only. Towards the close of the fifteenth and the beginning of the sixteenth century, printed books had become so greatly multiplied, and their prices so much reduced, as to be placed within the reach of ordinary students, and the practice of reading authors *cursoriè* became less and less necessary; and we consequently find that before the middle of the latter century, it had almost disappeared. The revolution which was thus effected in the mode of conducting academical instruction does not appear, however, to have led to any immediate alteration in the statutes of the University, though it contributed not a little to render some of their provisions antiquated and little adapted to the times. But we find that the increased study of the originals of the classical authors, which had hitherto been generally known in the form of translations only, adapted to the barbarous Latinity of the middle ages, whilst it rapidly improved the taste, and extended the sphere of speculation, both of readers and authors, in no respect tended to diminish the profound reverence for the logical and other works of Aristotle, and for the scholastic philosophy founded upon them, which had characterized the three preceding centuries; and the further progress of academical legislation will show that disputations in the public schools of all faculties, conducted *scholastico more,* were more frequently held and more strictly enjoined, than they had been during the prevalence of the system of *cursorian* and other readings, properly so called, in the more barbarous ages which preceded the discovery of printing."

From this it appears that the lectures in the schools were preparatory to the disputations and substitutes for private reading in the want or scarcity of books. They were not professorial, but were given by the graduates at large, who have still the right to teach in their different faculties. " It was only," as Professor Malden says*, "by a slow change that this practice fell into disuse. The chief cause of its discontinuance and final cessation was the general appointment of public and authorized professors and lecturers." The employment of these professors was, like the liturgies of the ancient Greeks, regarded in the first instance as a work done for the faculty to which they belonged; but the substitution became so general that at last "this method of providing public teachers became general in all the Universities of Europe." And "in those Universities which were founded by sovereigns and governments, after the first age of such institutions was gone by, the business of instruction was from the beginning committed to a body of professors, as in almost all the Universities of Germany; and in those of Scotland the case was much the same." In Germany

* *Ubi supra,* p. 115.

this professorial teaching was so exclusively the system, that the power of exercising the functions of a teacher was not given to the graduate without a qualification, similar to that imposed upon the deacon's preaching by the English ordination service, namely, that the doctors should have the *facultas legendi, docendi*, &c. *si modo ad ejusmodi munus rite vocentur.* "However," adds Professor Malden*, "in most of the German Universities there are facilities by which a graduate, who wishes it, is enabled to lecture as an extraordinary or temporary professor. In this way teachers are exercised and trained to fill the regular chairs ; and the ordinary professors are not left to slumber in the secure possession of a monopoly."

The same substitution of special lectures for the general employment of the graduates has taken place in the Colleges. Originally every fellow, being Master of Arts, was a College tutor, and received a certain number of pupils, who are now assigned to one or more tutors appointed by the Master. And as long as these private teachers—corresponding to the *privat-docenten* and extraordinary professors of the German Universities just referred to—adequately performed the work of preparing the students for the disputations in the schools, the gradual extinction of the school teaching produced no inconvenience. The professors appointed from time to time were designed to give a new start or fresh impulse to certain branches of study, and some of the most important of them were connected with the foundation of the principal Colleges.

The predominance of the *Quadrivium* at Cambridge over the *Trivium*, and of mathematics, as such, in the

* *Ubi supra*, p. 117. See also Peacock, *On the Statutes*, p. 34.

Quadrivium itself, naturally led to the substitution of examinations,—in which the relative merit of mathematical students was more accurately tested,—for the school disputations, in which the logic of the *Trivium* played a prominent part; and the influence of Newton, Cotes, and Smith, not unassisted by the more general scholars, Barrow and Bentley, paved the way for the establishment of the mathematical tripos in the middle of the 18th century. The literary tendencies of Trinity College, and the great scholars produced by that institution, began about the same time to assert the claims of classical learning to similar encouragement in the examinations. First, Chancellor's Medals were instituted for the two best classical scholars in the first mathematical tripos list. Then, Bishop Monk, the immediate successor of Porson, after improving the classical examinations of Trinity College and of the University at large, contrived, with great difficulty, to effect in 1824 the establishment of a classical tripos open to all Bachelors whose names had appeared in the mathematical tripos. And, at last, the students of classical literature are about to be allowed to compete for places in a tripos of their own, without the previous necessity of appearing as class-men in mathematics.

By these examinations a broad foundation has been laid for the re-establishment of the school of arts at Cambridge ; and the *Trivium* and the *Quadrivium*, appearing in a modern dress as learning and science, literature and philosophy, grammar and geometry, philology and physiology, may now be regarded as receiving, or about to receive, equal encouragement. If the studies of the University of Cambridge are still too elementary or too circumscribed, if they are still confined to the school of arts, if they prolong the business of education beyond the time when it ought to become

available to the business of life, or to the promotion of
literature and science, the fault is not to be sought in the
machinery of the examinations, or in the theory of the
University ; but in certain phenomena connected with the
practical working of the College system and the influence
which that system exerts on the University at large.

There is unfortunately a tendency, in all discussions
on reform, to extenuate the merits and exaggerate the
defects of the object which is supposed to require amelioration. And the serious mischief, which has resulted from
the system of College absorption at Cambridge, has led
some, who have been properly anxious for improvement,
to overlook the meritorious administration of the Colleges
and the great services which they have rendered and will
continue to render to the University. Nothing can be
farther from my intention than to detract from the high
character, which, in many respects, they deservedly enjoy.
As far as my knowledge extends, they are distinguished
by the admirable conscientiousness with which they
manage the funds placed at their disposal, and in some
instances they have exhibited a magnanimous and self-
denying liberality which is above all praise. It would be
well if all possessors of property and church patronage in
England were equally anxious to discharge the duties of
their stewardship. The tutors of all the Colleges, so far
as I know, spare no pains in endeavouring to promote the
moral and intellectual education of their pupils, and in
many cases their efforts are attended with eminent success.
In regard to the University, the College fellowships and
scholarships, and the fairness with which they are awarded,
have contributed in no slight degree to make the scholarship and mathematical reputation of this country what they
are. And while the other Colleges are generally content

to abide by the decisions of the University examiners in selecting their fellows, Trinity and St John's, the one completely, the other partially, require the candidates for the lucrative positions at their disposal, to pass an additional examination, which, in the case of the former College, is the most complete and extensive in England. Indeed if Trinity College were the whole University, there would be comparatively little reason to complain of the narrowness of our system, and not so much room for improvement in any respect.

But the very fact that the best Colleges are the largest, and the smallest generally the worst, seems to furnish an argument in favour of the opinion, that the desired object would be obtained, if the University were, what its name denotes and what it once was, one community and not a number of different communities. At any rate there is no doubt in the minds of those who have studied the subject, that, in spite of their various merits and the importance of their endowments, the Colleges interpose the greatest obstacles to the free play of our academical agency. While they do not spend any part of their revenues on the education of the undergraduates, they oblige all undergraduates to pay for such education as they furnish by becoming members of some College, and, by virtue of the revolution forced upon the University by the Elizabethan Statutes[4], usurp the rights belonging to the University as such. Much of the mischief occasioned by the narrow and unprofitable lectures delivered in most of the Colleges, which the resident undergraduates are obliged to attend and pay for, is corrected by the system of private tuition, which has prevailed for so many years, and which is an approximation to the ancient practice, when all graduates prepared pupils for the exercises of the schools. From the days when Jones of Trinity assisted the studies of Marsh of St John's with such effect that tutor and pupil appeared as first and second wranglers of the same year (1779), until the present time, when for more than 25 years Mr Hopkins has sent forth from his own private teaching all the best mathematicians of the University, there has always been an active staff of private tutors ready to lend their aid to all aspiring undergraduates without reference to the distinctions of College. And it is a remarkable proof of the completeness with which the Colleges have superseded the University, that a rather presumptuous proposal was made some years ago by a tutor of one of the smaller Colleges to bring even the private tutors under College supervision; and a tutor of Trinity was obliged to remind him that * " whatever defects there may be in the present practice of private tuition, there can be no doubt that every one who is created Master of Arts has precisely the same University sanction for exercising it, as the Proctor himself has for creating him : and whether a University Grace for preventing such exercise by other than College officers be or be not expedient, to pass it would be in principle exactly identical with forbidding a Regius Professor to lecture except he were also a tutor of a College, or under the direction of one."

But it is not only by obliging all members of the University to be members of Colleges also, and then compelling them to attend and pay for a sort of school-boy lessons, that the College system cramps and trammels the University teaching. The Colleges are also responsible for the admission and matriculation of a very large proportion of members quite disqualified by their existing knowledge from any intelligent participation in a course

* Blakesley, " *Where does the evil lie ?*" pp. 13, 14.

of genuine academic teaching. That this should be a
natural result of the limitation of the University to the
Colleges and their members must appear to any one who
reflects. The Colleges are really a collection of rival
boarding schools. The interest and credit of each of them
make it desirable that they should have the largest possible number of entries. Can it be surprising then that
they should be unwilling to reject any candidate for admission, who comes to them with a plausible recommendation ? In most of the Colleges the plan has been to place
on the books the name of any student, who can procure
from a M.A. of the University a certificate to the effect
that he has been examined in Greek and Latin, and is, in
the examiner's judgment, competent to commence residence at Cambridge. How insufficient such a test is to
secure even moderate proficiency in the whole body of
freshmen, is notorious to every one moderately acquainted
with the University. According to Mr Blakesley *, " at
least one fifth of the numbers matriculated every Michael-
mas term " may be described as " quite inadequately prepared for profiting by instruction of such a quality as
every College, which will not be content to degenerate
into a mere school, is bound to maintain." A first step
towards remedying this cardinal evil was taken some years
ago by Trinity College, which introduced and has since
carried on a matriculation examination. That this has
produced some effect, I cannot allow myself to doubt.
Indeed, I have heard that on the very last occasion a good
scholar was rejected because he was totally ignorant of
mathematics. And, as I have said before, if Trinity
College were the whole University, there would be much

* *Ubi supra*, pp. 16, 17.

less cause for complaint on many accounts. As, however,
the University is not identical either with the largest
College or with all the Colleges taken together, it is clear
that the remedy will not be fully applied until it is undertaken by the University as such.

A proposal to this effect was brought under the notice
of the Senate by a tutor of Caius College some time ago,
and was advocated by Mr Blakesley in his pamphlet of
1845. He says*, "I think it a great dereliction of duty
that the University does not take some step towards preventing the admission of this class of students in such
numbers. To throw the ungrateful duty of rejection upon
the particular Colleges is a course as ungenerous as inex-
pedient. Its effect is to hold out a bounty to the continual
debasement of the standard of qualification ; and where
there is too much public spirit to be affected by this bane-
ful influence, still a most painful and invidious task is laid
upon the very last persons who ought to be saddled with
it. If an University examination were to take place
once a year, and no College were allowed to place any
person on its boards who had not passed it to the satisfaction of the examiners, a vast portion of the evils at present
complained of would be removed, and, I am inclined to
think, a means furnished of gradually raising the education
throughout the country to a much higher pitch. All
temptation to adopting a low and unworthy standard of
qualification would be thus removed ; and the power of
resisting temptation will never be considered by a wise
man as a reason against its removal."

About the same time a similar argument was advanced
by Dr Whewell, who distinctly proposed an *Initial Ex-*

---

* "*Where does the evil lie?*" pp. 21, 22.

amination *, for the following reasons, which appear to me conclusive : " If such an examination were placed at the beginning of the pupil's residence, it might be made to answer the valuable purpose of securing the means of a progressive education by a system of which School-teaching, College-teaching, and University Examinations, should form coherent and successive parts. The University may very reasonably require to be satisfied that the pupil brings from school, or from other teaching, a correct and familiar acquaintance with Latin, and a power of construing ordinary Greek : and along with this, as I have also said, a familiar acquaintance with Arithmetical working. When students possess such a knowledge as this, College lectures and examinations, may, by a proper selection of classical subjects, as well as of mathematical, (to which the Progressive Sciences ought also to be added,) be made to carry on a system of education, which, at the end of three years and a half, shall leave all the students with their minds more cultivated, more expanded, and more instructed, than they were when they entered upon their residence. But if there are many of the students who do not, on commencing their residence, possess the above described amount of knowledge, their labours, and those of their tutors, must be employed, in a great measure, in repairing the defects of their school education, and all attempts at a good combined education at College, will be interrupted and frustrated. If the University were to institute such an *Initial Examination* as I have suggested, the Colleges, having to deal with better and more consistent materials, would be encouraged to

---

* *Of a Liberal Education in general, and with particular reference to the leading Studies of the University of Cambridge,* by W. Whewell, D.D. Master of Trinity College. 1845. pp. 212, 213.

improve their systems of instruction. Moreover if there be anything with which the University has reason to be dissatisfied, in the state of instruction in which pupils are sent to College by grammar schools and early teachers; such an examination, steadily enforced, offers an effectual means of producing the requisite improvement : for it cannot be supposed that the schools would long be content to turn out their scholars in a state of instruction in which they should be rejected by the University."

The objections to this plan are stated, from the College point of view, in a paper by Mr Martin, of Trinity, which is quoted by Dr Whewell, in the second part of his book on University Education*. Mr Martin's objections are classed under four heads. 1. The differences of system, &c., in the different Colleges. 2. The inapplicability of the precedent furnished by the preliminary examinations at Trinity. 3. The difficulties of detail in carrying out the plan, and the College jealousies which would ensue. 4. The chance of excluding deserving persons, who might wish to use the University as an access to holy orders.

My own view of this question was stated some years ago, and I have only to repeat the form and substance of what I then wrote on the subject. To me Mr Martin's objections, and all others that I have heard, appear to assume the necessity for a continuance of that subjection of the University to the Colleges, which I regard as the cause of all that is wrong in the practical working of the Cambridge system. It appears to me preposterous to argue against a measure, which would exclude imperfectly qualified persons from all the Colleges, by alleging the differences of College lecture-rooms. There ought to be

---

* *Of a Liberal Education*, &c. Part II. 1850. pp. 139—141.

no College for irreclaimable dunces or perversely idle
spendthrifts; and if a young man cannot learn the elements of Geometry and Grammar at some school or with
some tutor before the age of 18 or 19, he is not likely to
make up for deficiencies in ability or application amidst
the temptations and independence of a College life. The
imperfect success, which has attended the introduction of
a preliminary examination at Trinity, is rather an argument for extending this practice to the University
at large than an objection to the plan; for the imperfect
and partial results are entirely due to the fact that it is
a private and a College examination. The tutors, who
conduct it, cannot, in all cases, divest themselves of the
wish to receive the pupils who have been recommended
to them; and as the examination takes place after the
young men have actually commenced residence, and when
some of them have furnished rooms within the College,
there is of course an additional reluctance to send them
down and check their academical course at its first starting. If there are any positive results from the Trinity
examination on the admission of pupils, it is reasonable
to suppose that all the advantages would be secured in
still greater measure, and that all the drawbacks and
defects would be obviated or avoided, if it were extended
to the whole University. The difficulties of detail, to
which Mr Martin refers, could not exist if the influence
of resident fellows did not control all the operations of
the University. The objection raised on behalf of those,
who wish to use the University as a mere access to holy
orders, appears to me particularly untenable. If there is
any class of students, who especially require a good and
complete education as the basis of their professional studies,
if there are any, to whom learning, as such, is particularly

and immediately necessary, those who are destined for the
ministry of a Protestant Church are called upon, before
all others, to give indications of early proficiency in the
liberal arts. And in the scheme for an examination before matriculation issued by the Prussian Minister of
Instruction in 1834, the students intended for the theological department are placed on the same footing as those
who are designed for the philological branch of study, and
are required to bring up from school a proportionate
amount of previous learning *. The examination, which
I propose and which alone is intended by its other advocates, is such a previous scrutiny as would suffice to
ascertain that a youth, who had arrived at the age of 18
or 19, when a liberal education, as such, is or may be
completed, has made such progress as will enable him to
receive with profit the only description of teaching which
a University can condescend to undertake, and that he
holds out a reasonable promise of successfully prosecuting
the studies proper to a great seminary of learning. If a
lad of 18 or 19 cannot meet such a test as this, I do not
rate very highly his qualifications for holy orders or any
other profession. The Church at all events will not lose
much by the absence of such a minister; and having discovered betimes that he has mistaken his vocation, he
may be employed profitably in some other walk of life.
If the inability to pass the matriculation scrutiny arises,
not from want of industry or capacity, but from early
neglect or bad early instruction, the student has only to
wait a year, as Kirke White did, and betake himself to
some competent teacher. Whatever other effects may be
produced by the restoration of the University system and
the removal of the College monopoly, it can hardly be

* See *Journal of Education*, Vol. IX. p. 156.

doubted that it will tend greatly to increase the number of graduates willing and competent to take charge of private pupils; and as there is no superannuation at Cambridge, it will be no real disadvantage, and may be a great benefit, to constrain some raw and uneducated stripling to postpone the period of his matriculation until he has attained the age at which many senior wranglers have begun their career of university distinction ; and, instead of thrusting him at once into a College lecture-room, to let him pass, what would otherwise be his first academical year, in daily contemplation of the portals, which are, for the present, closed to him.   For those, who have been at good schools, no such probation can ever be necessary.   Every competent schoolmaster can ascertain which of his sixth-form boys are fit for college ; and it is the business of endowed schools at all events to shape their instruction with a special view to the University criterion. The act of 1 Edward VI., A.D. 1547, by virtue of which so many grammar-schools were endowed, expressly mentions the supply of scholars to the University as a principal object to be attained.   And Thomas Lever, in his sermon before the king, on the 14 Dec. 1550, reminded him of this.   "Your majesty hath given and received, by act of parliament, colleges, chauntries, and guilds, for many good considerations ; and especially, as appears in the same act, for erecting of grammar-schools to the education of youth in virtue and godliness, *to the further augmenting of the Universities,* and to the provision of the poor and needy.   But now many grammar-schools, and much charitable provision for the poor, be taken, sold, and made away, to the great slander of you and your laws, to the utter discomfort of the poor, to the grievous offence of the people, to the most miserable

4

drowning of youth in ignorance, and *sore decay of the Universities* *." Although this object is forgotten in many country-towns, where an attempt is made to convert the grammar-schools from their proper office of providing adequate preparation for the Universities, and finding poor students the means of living there, into commercial schools for the purpose of imparting, what the trades-people are pleased to consider as the only useful education, it is obvious that if the University laid down a rule and consistently acted upon it, many masters of these schools, and all the best of them, would shape their course accordingly, and would take care that all their pupils, who were likely to go to Oxford or Cambridge, were well prepared in those subjects which were required for the entrance examination.

Before I venture to make any suggestion respecting the nature and extent of this examination, I must advert to another subject intimately connected with it. If the University consisted only of properly qualified students, we might combine the plan for shortening the period of compulsory residence with some improvements lately introduced into the competitive system at Cambridge. The proposal to make one general examination the access to all or any of the special triposes was, I believe, first put forth in the pamphlet, from which I have made an extract in a subsequent page†, and it was, a few months after, suggested independently by myself; but the proposal to shorten the residence of candidates for an ordinary degree, an important and almost necessary accompaniment of the scheme, which will take effect after the present year, was, if my memory does not deceive me, enforced by arguments in a sermon which Dr Peacock

* Strype, *Ecclesiastical Memorials*, II. 101—103.   † *Infra*, p. 66.

preached many years ago in Trinity College Chapel*. Those arguments are not now before me, but the following are some of the considerations by which it is most obviously recommended.

There has long been a tendency at Cambridge to diminish the number of terms of residence required for a degree in arts, in proportion as the age and supposed qualifications of the students admitted have increased. No residence is required for the second degree, and the first and last terms required of the B. A. are really given to him. At first, no doubt, when mere boys were admitted, the necessary residence was much more prolonged. In those days of boy-bachelors and juvenile masters, it was only reasonable that the student should spend at the University the years which he now passes at school. But even then, as I have mentioned above†, special degrees were given in the separate arts of Grammar, Rhetoric, and Music, which must have involved a shorter residence than that which was required for the completion of the whole curriculum; and if, as has been supposed, logic alone conferred the title of *sophista generalis*, the same abridgment of the number of terms to be kept must have followed from the conferring of such a subordinate degree. As the case now is, since no one comes up until he is nearly nineteen,—until he has attained the age to which nature, as I have said before, points as the period at which education as such should terminate—I cannot see why two years' residence ‡ should not suffice for an ordinary

---

* In his book *On the Statutes*, p. 151, he proposes that the B.A. degree should be taken in the *ninth* term instead of the *eleventh*.

† p. 23.

‡ If the B. A. commencement took place, as it now does, in January, the residence required would be *seven* complete terms.

degree in the case of a commoner, quite as much as it does in the case of noblemen. And this would lead to a further simplification. Supposing that the matriculation test were adequately framed and effectually carried out, there would be no occasion for any previous examination or *little-go* in the second year. The *initial* or *matriculation* examination would, as Dr Whewell suggests *, be placed at the commencement of the student's residence, and then, at the beginning of the third year, a re-examination of the undergraduates in the appointed studies of the University would settle the question as to the propriety of conferring or withholding the ordinary degree of B. A. Those, who passed this second ordeal, ought to be at liberty, either to declare themselves candidates for a place in one or more of the honour lists, which, as now, should depend on examinations of the fourth-year men, or to decline all further competition; in which case they should be discharged from all necessary residence, and allowed to betake themselves to their destined avocations. This saving of a third year's residence would be a great boon to many a parent, by deducting one-third of the cost of a University education, in those cases where the results were least worthy of the outlay; and it would be no slight advantage to the University itself; for it would probably increase the number of those, who take the first degree instead of leaving the University without it, as many do, in the second or third year; and it would greatly diminish the crowd of dissolute young men, who, having three years assigned to them for what is in fact the work of a couple of terms, spend their time in proving by a sort of practical etymology that the seat of the Muses ought to be a place of amusement, and who pursue the vices of man-

* *Ubi supra,* p. 44.

hood with all the precipitation of inconsiderate youth and all the recklessness of unexhausted health and vigour.

There will be no difficulty in determining the nature and extent of the initial examination, and its relation to that for the ordinary B.A. degree, if we really propose to ourselves a clear idea of the studies proper to a University, and the preparation necessary for them. Different opinions will be entertained as to the relative value of classics and mathematics, and some of these opinions will be examined in the second part of the present book; but all persons, who have really studied the subject, will agree that the modern representatives of the old *Trivium* and *Quadrivium* of arts, namely, philology and mathematical science, are still the main ingredients in a liberal education, and the proper basis of an University education. I will here state, as briefly as possible, the results at which I have arrived, after six years of experience as a Cambridge teacher, and fourteen years' practice as the Head Master of an endowed grammar-school.

It appears to me then that every person who applies to be admitted, at the age of 18 or 19, to a course of two years' University study, ought to be able to convince the examiners that he has a sound grammatical knowledge of the Greek and Latin languages—so far as to be able to construe simple authors—that he knows the first four books of Euclid, and possesses a reasonable familiarity with the most important processes of arithmetic and arithmetical algebra. To this I would add, that he ought to be thoroughly acquainted with the English language, and should prove that he can write and spell like a gentleman; and I would also require him to show that he knows the outlines of English history, and the elements of physical and descriptive geography. My experience as a school-master convinces me that every lad, who is fit for a course of University study, may learn thus much before he is 18; with less than this he could not take a part in those studies which are proper to the University. To what extent these University studies may be prosecuted in a course of two years, must depend on the capacity of the student and the advantages of tuition which he is able to command. But their distinctive nature, and that of the probationary examination by which they will be tested, may be easily described. School education is the training of a boy. University teaching is the instruction of a man. The former deals with the groundwork of knowledge. It trains the mind for future acquirements. It prepares the soil for the good seed to be sown in it. The latter sows the seed. It uses the instrument. It does something towards filling the storehouse. If this is so, as the school imparts, and the initial examination would require, a grammatical knowledge of Greek and Latin and the power of constru-ing ordinary passages, the University would assist and the B.A. examination would require the study of a certain number of Greek and Latin authors, with regard not only to their language but also to their subject-matter. As the school would teach and matriculation would exact a familiarity with the elements of pure mathematics, the first degree would presume that this acquaintance with principles and processes had been applied to an acquisition of knowledge in some of those branches of physical science, to which mathematical reasoning is immediately applied. As an educated intimacy with his own mother-tongue would be demanded of every candidate for admission to the University, the incepting bachelor should be required to show that he had read a certain amount of English literature, and that he had paid a proper attention to modern history and political geography.

This scheme of University teaching and University examination, if properly carried out, would occupy a very considerable number of resident graduates. For to say nothing of the teaching, the examinations, to be conducted in a complete and satisfactory manner, ought to involve a large proportion of oral or *viva voce* questioning, which would necessarily consume a great deal of time. Indeed this part of the examination might be publicly conducted, so as to test at once the proficiency of the candidates and the ability and learning of the judge, and his fitness for the office of teacher. I feel convinced too that an attendance on these public examinations would afford no small amount of valuable instruction to the undergraduates in general, and they would prove a modern and fully adequate representation of the exercises in the old schools of the arts. As there are generally some 200 masters in residence, there would be no difficulty in finding a sufficient number to perform the duties of *regency*, and a proportion of the fees would furnish a competent remuneration to those who did the work.

With regard to the teaching, which is to carry on the educational training proper to a University, it presents itself, if we look to the existing practice, under three different forms. At Cambridge, and, I believe, at Oxford also, we have the regular Professorial lecture, the College-lecture, and private tuition. On the supposition that the University system will be fully restored, and that the monopoly of the Colleges will be superseded by the free agency of the Senate, the compulsory attendance on College-lectures will become the least, as it is now the most, significant part of University teaching. At the

best, a College-lecture is only a lesson exacted from young
men of very various diligence and capacity.   By the nature of the case, the amount of reading, which it guides
and illustrates, is very small.   More ground is travelled over
during the year in the sixth-form room of a good school
than even in the lecture-rooms of Trinity College.   In the
yearly business of the school over which I presided, besides
Hebrew, Theology, and general subjects, and independently
of Mathematics, including some of the second-year subjects
at Cambridge, we used to read considerable portions of five
Greek and five Latin authors, and two established works
on classical history or philology.   At the best Colleges,
the first academical year is occupied by three mathematical subjects—Euclid, Algebra, and Trigonometry;
and three portions of classical authors—a Greek play, a
Greek oration, or a book of Herodotus or Thucydides, and
some one extract from the ordinary Latin repertorium.
The whole amount of work occupies one hour a day; and
while the well-prepared reject the small pittance of prof-
fered aid, those, who are most in need of instruction, find
the College lecture-room generally incompetent to supply
their wants.   The fact is, as I have already said, that
private tutors have been in constant demand for a great
number of years, and that most men, who have sought
mathematical distinction, and all classical students, who
have not come up to the University from the head of
some really good school, have been obliged to avail themselves of the aid of those eminent graduates, who, independently of College distinctions, have placed their talents
at the disposal of the whole University.   This general
adoption of a system of private tuition is a proof that this
mode of teaching really meets the demands of the time.
Indeed, it may be shown that it is the necessary correla-

tive of a system of competitive tests. And if evils and
abuses have sprung up, if instruction has been degraded
into cramming, the evil lies in the conventional defects of
the examinations, and not in the teaching which necessarily depends upon them. The proper mode of conducting the examinations, in Classics at all events, will form
the subject of discussion in a subsequent page; but if
teaching is really an efficient agency in education, it must
be influential in proportion to the amount and intimacy
of the intercourse between the tutor and his pupil.
Those young people, who are most likely to make progress
in learning, derive a perceptible benefit from habitual
association with men abler and better, and more experienced and accomplished than themselves. Thus, the son
of highly-cultivated parents has a better start than the
cleverest boy who spends his early days in the midst of
coarse carelessness and rude vulgarity. It was well then
that the clear-headed Greeks used a verb denoting "to
consort" or "keep company" (ξυνεῖναι) to describe the
intercourse of the master with his scholars, and of the
scholars with their master; and with a distinct recognition
of the same principle, the private tutor is said "to read
with" his pupils, and his pupils are described as "reading
with" him. And even if we inquire, why it is that the
boys from public schools are generally better instructed
than most other undergraduates, and why they of all
others can most safely dispense with the aid of a private
tutor, we shall find that the instruction of the upper boys
at a public school is, in spite of the contradiction in terms,
a system of private tuition of the most minute and elaborate kind. In certain large schools this private tuition
is a separate and formally recognised part of the system.
In others the reality exists without the name. The boys

are not merely called upon to construe lessons, and do
exercises, and receive such information as the master may
think fit to deliver *ex cathedra ;* but they are at liberty to
ask any questions and to bring any difficulties for private
solution ; and, as they generally board in some master's
house, they have always at hand an oracle to consult and
a guide to help them through the most devious tracks and
across the most impassable streamlets of juvenile perplex-
ity.   No doubt, this kind of teaching is expensive ; but
so is all good education.   The only just cause of discontent is when it is inefficient as well as expensive.   To
complain that really good private tuition costs more in a
few years than the useless lessons of a day-school, which
are spread over a considerable period, and in which some
single master undertakes to teach a class of 60 or 70 boys,
is as unreasonable as the remonstrance of the country
squire, who, when charged a guinea for the skilful extraction of a molar in Burlington-street, objected that the
provincial dentist had given him twice as much pain for
a shilling.

Those who enjoy, or who for a considerable period
have enjoyed, these resources of private superintendence
and instruction, cannot want anything in addition, except
a sufficient access to books, and the expositions of a
genuine professor on the subjects which they are specially
engaged in studying.   It is by no means difficult to
explain the difference between such expositions and the
lessons of the College lecture-room.   First of all we must
remember, that College-lecturers are generally young men,
who have had no opportunity of learning their business as
teachers, who in fact are still learning it, and who have
not yet extended the reading, which obtained for them
their distinctions and emoluments, so far as to gain a

comprehensive acquaintance with any great department of knowledge. Many of them are men of first-rate ability and possess most exact scholarship or eminent skill in mathematical analysis. And such persons contain the potentiality of future professors. Then we must recollect, that what is called a College-lecture generally does not pretend to be a lecture at all. The classical lecturer hears the young men construe, and construes after them, giving such explanations as the subject may require. Nothing is farther from his intention than to deliver an ἐπίδειξις or regular discourse on a given subject. He is a commentator on a prescribed portion of a particular author, not the original expounder of large views on some great field of philology and criticism. If he ever discourses at length, his remarks are analogous to one of those lengthened notes which are significantly called *excursions*. Similar observations might be made in regard to the College-lecturers on mathematical subjects. Contrast with this the position and performance of a genuine professor. While, as Mr Vaughan says *, the College-lecturers "upon the whole and as a class consist of men between 25 and 35 years of age, who have distinguished themselves in the University," the professors "will be commonly men between 35 and 60, men selected both from the tutors and from all the Masters of the University for ability and attainments acquired during the labours of a life ;" and, it may be added, they will generally be men with whom teaching is the chosen vocation, not an incident to the possession of a fellowship, and who have, as College-lecturers and otherwise, served an adequate apprenticeship to their calling as oral instructors. In drawing this distinction between the University and the College teacher, between the Professor

* *Oxford Reform and Oxford Professors*, pp. 17, 19.

and the Tutor, I am not unaware or oblivious of the fact
that some of the best courses of real lectures, which have
ever been delivered in Cambridge, have been limited to
the students of a particular College, and undertaken as
part of the work of College-lecturers. The two courses of
lectures on Aristotle, which Dr Thirlwall delivered as
Classical Lecturer of Trinity College in 1833 and 1834,
and which were all that professorial lectures ought to be,
were not accessible to the classical students of the University at large, and would in the regular routine have
been confined to the undergraduates of one of the three
sides or subdivisions of that great College. As a fact they
were attended not only by all the third-year men of the
College, but also by several graduates. Of these lectures,
delivered by a graduate of 15 or 16 years standing, who
had already achieved an eminent literary reputation, and
had thoroughly studied his subject, and expounded it with
the eloquence, accuracy, and philosophical acuteness, which
distinguished him, it can only be said with regret that
they were an exceptional case, and that they were confined to a particular College, that is, to about one-third of
the University. The lectures on Plato, which Mr Thompson subsequently delivered as Tutor of Trinity, were also
those of an original thinker and matured teacher, who
had made the subject his own by prolonged study; and I
rejoice to be able to add, that he is now empowered, as
Regius Professor of Greek, to invite the whole University
to his lectures. But these examples, and others, which
might be cited, in which a full exposition of a congenial
subject is given by an experienced and mature teacher, do
not belong to the ordinary description of College-lectures;
more usually, as I have said, they are lessons in which the
students are called upon to take a part, and which are,

in the majority of instances, conducted by distinguished young men, to whom the business of teaching has not become familiar by long practice.

On the whole then it may be said that University teaching, or the real instruction of the students, must consist in private tuition and professorial lectures, or one of these methods of instruction. And in order to show that a University properly constituted ought to furnish both in the best form, I will endeavour to indicate the manner in which they are necessarily supplemental to one another. I must reserve to the third part a description of the effects of private tuition on classical scholarship, and of professorial lectures on classical learning, as manifested in England and Germany respectively. But it may be said in general that the professor's lecture cannot educate, it cannot supersede study, it cannot impart matured and exact knowledge. All this must result from the independent exertions of the student seconded by the immediate aid of a competent tutor. On the other hand, the beginnings, the suggestions, the stimulants of special study are often to be found only in the lecture-room of the genuine professor; and while he may always give information more or less copious and satisfactory, there are some kinds of information, which cannot be so well derived from books, as from the oral exposition of one, who pours forth his knowledge from the overflowing fulness of his own mind, and with the enthusiasm of a true devotion to the subject. This is particularly the case in regard to those subjects of study which admit or require ocular illustration. Wherever maps, diagrams, specimens, or experimental manipulation are necessary to the full development of a subject, the lecturer cannot be replaced by private tuition or private study, and the name *demonstration*,

which is specially applied to anatomical lectures, might
be given to all similar exhibitions in geography, geology,
ethnology, mechanical science, botany, zoology, chemistry,
and descriptive astronomy. Without converting the
University into a polytechnic institution, or popular-
ising its teaching into that of a Midland Institute or
provincial Athenæum, there is no doubt that in these
days of almost universal illustration the "faithful eyes"
of the learners should be invited in all possible cases to
fix their attention and assist their memory; and there are
more departments of knowledge than is generally supposed,
in which, by a judicious application of these outward
helps, we may "bid the pencil answer to the lyre," and,
with the mediation of a competent draftsman, may see—

> " each transitory thought,
> Fixed by his touch, a lasting essence take ;
> Each dream in fancy's airy colours wrought,
> To local symmetry and life awake."

Even in those cases, however, where the ocular or
pictorial illustration is neither desired nor available, the
professor's lecture may have its advantages over the
chamber-study of the same subject. The mere fact, that
every lecture is a number of pages illustrated by the voice
of one who has a right to speak, gives it a peculiar access
to the mind of the listener. The contrast between the
dead book and the living lecturer has been well developed
by an Oxford professor. "The type," says Mr Halford
Vaughan*, "is a poor substitute for the human voice. It
has no means of arousing, moderating and adjusting the
attention. It has no emphasis except italics ; and this
meagre notation cannot finely graduate itself to the needs
of the occasion. It cannot, in this way, mark the heed

* _Oxford Reform and Oxford Professors_, p. 33.

which should be chiefly given to peculiar passages and words. It has no variety of manner and intonation to show by their changes how the words are to be accepted, or what comparative importance is to be attached to them. It has no natural music to take the ear, like the human voice; it carries with it no human eye to range, and rivet the student, when on the verge of truancy, and to command his intellectual activity by an appeal to the common courtesies of life. Half the symbolism of a living language is thus lost when it is committed to paper; and that symbolism is the very means by which the forces of the hearer's mind can be best economised, or most pleasantly excited. The lecture, on the other hand, as delivered, possesses all these instruments to win and hold and harmonise attention; and above all, it imports into the whole teaching a human character, which the printed book can never supply. The professor is the science or subject vitalised or humanised in the student's presence. He sees him kindle into his subject; he sees reflected and exhibited in him, his manner, and his earnestness—the general power of the science to engage, delight and absorb a human intellect. His natural sympathy and admiration attract or impel his tastes and feelings and wishes for the moment, into the same current of feeling, and his mind is naturally and rapidly and insensibly strung and attuned to the strain of truth which is offered to him."

I would venture to say then that, while for all purposes of education in the liberal arts, which are to serve as the basis of University teaching, and for that kind of knowledge which is to be tested by emulous competition and rigorous examination, the tuition cannot be too immediate, or, if you will, too private, personal, and familiar, the superstructure of learning and science, which are to produce their influence on the literature of a generation, cannot be more effectually secured than by professorial lectures, delivered by men of experience and established reputation in their respective departments; for from such men alone can we expect clear notions, apt illustrations, fulness of matter, and hints suggestive and creative of the studies, which we wish to promote.

Now the business of the private tutor properly terminates just where the functions of the professorial lecturer properly begin—namely, at that period when the University is able to give its certificate of a completed education in the form of a B. A. degree. When therefore I propose that the first degree should be conferred at the beginning of the third year, I am far from wishing or expecting that the better class of students—the intellectual aristocracy of the University—should take their departure and terminate their connexion with us. Those, who are contented with an ordinary degree and shrink from a competition for higher honours, should be free to go at once. But the able and ambitious will remain to compete for such distinctions as they most value or find most congenial to their tastes, and to receive from the professors of the University the light and guidance which they require for an enlarged course of study.

And here I must strongly express my conviction that young men seldom attain to real eminence in any study which they pursue against their will. Almost every one is fit for some employment; and parents and teachers may show a great deal of sagacity in discovering the aptitude and natural bent of young children. But the lad, who is growing old enough to think for himself, will not be driven into a course selected for him by others. He knows what his own tastes are. . He can tell whether he

is fit to be a student at all. And, when he has proved to
the satisfaction of a great University, that he is capable
of completing the basis of a liberal education, he may
safely be left to choose, at that gromatic* point, which
road of science or learning he will enter upon and tra-
verse to the end. I cannot therefore refrain from con-
gratulating the University of Cambridge on the progress
which has been already made towards an absolute separation
of the triposes old and new. The plan, which I formerly
proposed and now urge again, will among other advantages remedy an inconvenience which has been noticed
in the present arrangement concerning the classical tripos.
Instead of giving a general B.A. degree as a consequence
of the previous examination, which is exacted from all,
this degree is conferred at the beginning of the fourth
year on those who pass an ordinary examination, or obtain a place in the mathematical tripos. But a place in
the classical tripos will also obtain a B.A. degree. Now the
degrees are conferred immediately after the mathematical
examination, that is, three weeks before the classical examination begins. So that the senior classic may lose a
year in standing as compared with the senior wrangler.
The Board of Classical Studies have noticed this anomaly[5],
and it will of course be remedied ; but surely the best
plan would be that which confers the B.A. degree before
the publication of any tripos list, and which, setting at
liberty all those who do not aspire to honours, leaves the
candidates for distinction on a footing of perfect equality.

In order that the different triposes may not wan
their special encouragement and the corresponding stamp
of University approbation, I feel strongly inclined to
concur in the proposal made by the anonymous author of

* *Varron.* p. 60.

5

a pamphlet to which I have already referred. Merely
placing the general examination for B.A. in the second
instead of the last term of the third year, and omitting
divinity in that examination, I would gladly see the
adoption of all the other details in his plan, which I
here quote in his own words* : "The plan I should
propose is briefly this. That all students be made to go
through a course of instruction in those subjects which
are essential to a liberal education. That this course be
terminated by an examination at the end of the third
year, in classics, mathematics, history, divinity, English
literature, and English composition. That the degree of
B.A. be conferred on all who pass this examination. That
every one who has taken the degree of B.A. be qualified
to compete for honours in any tripos he may choose.
That the examinations for mathematical and classical
honours be at the same times as at present, and those of
the other triposes succeed them singly and at such inter-
vals that students may go in for each with a sufficient
rest between the examinations. I would have the theological examination, which is now rather amusingly called
'Voluntary,' erected into a tripos, and placed on the same
footing with the rest. The Hebrew examination might
form a part of a tripos for Oriental languages. I would
confer the degree of M.A. on those only whose names
should have appeared in some one of the triposes. I would
allow degrading to any extent, only I would not permit
any one who had degraded without a medical certificate
to appear in the first class of any tripos. I would make
a place in the theological tripos necessary for the degree
of B.D., a place in the moral science tripos for that of
LL.B., and a place in the natural science tripos for that

* *The Next Step*, pp. 28, 29.

of M.B., and thus should endeavour to get rid of the farce
of conferring these degrees without any special qualification, or allowing them to be bye-ways by which men may
scramble through the University into the Church. The
present civil law tripos might be merged in that for
moral science, and the medical examinations combined
with those in natural science. I would not lay too much
stress on the part of this plan which refers to the degrees
above that of B.A., being aware that the University is
not very rich, and may perhaps not be in a condition to
endanger the fees which are derived from this source.
I think it, however, by no means to be assumed that
degrees will be less in request, if they are made to mean
something, than now when they mean nothing. It is
perhaps startling at first sight that honours should be
required for the degree of M.A.; but, when we consider
that the qualification may be obtained by an examination
which nearly all clergymen now pass, or by either of two
other examinations which lawyers and physicians respectively ought to be able to pass, the apparent harshness
almost vanishes. The plan I have described might be
carried into effect by a systematic arrangement of examinations, which we already possess either in operation or
in contemplation, and both from the enlightened spirit of
improvement among us, and the difficulty of carrying out
our new measures without some such arrangement, I think
we may fairly hope that something not very unlike it will
soon be done. We shall then, at any rate, act consistently
and fairly as far as we go. But even then, I do not think
we shall have gone far enough. I cannot think our honour
system complete without English literature and composition, and history in its more general sense. These
subjects, with the addition perhaps of modern languages,

5—2

might be included in another tripos, with, I conceive, incalculable advantage to the University. We should thus remove, not only a just cause of reproach, but a defect which is more and more depriving our distinguished men of the place they ought to occupy in the world.

" It is scarcely necessary for me to say, that I would relieve the mathematical tripos examination from the preliminary three days trial which is now somewhat clumsily fastened to it. The five days examination might stand as at present, and those candidates only admitted to honours who acquitted themselves in it with credit."

With regard to the professional faculties of divinity, law and physic, I should be inclined to withhold the highest degree of doctor from all those who cannot prove their affiliation to a learned University by the ability to maintain a disputation in precise and accurate Latinity. It seems desirable that these exercises should be more frequent and more difficult, especially in regard to the theological school, and then I should not be afraid to undertake that the University degrees in divinity would be worthy of the body by which they are granted, and would truly indicate the possession of a large amount of ability and knowledge, instead of being, as is too often the case, a mere matter of expenditure rendered necessary by the previous attainment of some post of scholastic or ecclesiastical eminence. Such disputations, connected with the theological tripos, in accordance with the proposal which has just been quoted, would exercise a salutary influence on the clergy in general ; and, if we are still to have *ten-year-men* at Cambridge, they would thus have an opportunity of proving that they have been properly excused a probation in the faculty of arts. As it is, the existence of such a class of theological graduates seems to

me a total abandonment of the principles, which should
regulate the constitution of a great seat of learning. With
regard to the faculty of civil law, I agree with the writer
whom I have quoted above, that its present examination
might be merged in the moral science tripos. It appears
to me, however, that the study of civil law is an application of one great branch of classical learning, and its
faculty should, I think, be more intimately connected than
it is at present with the faculty of arts; perhaps the degree of LL.B. might be limited to those whose names
have appeared somewhere in the classical and moral
triposes; and it might be desirable to require also a certificate from the Downing Professor of Common Law.
But a satisfactory disputation in the schools ought to
be an indispensable condition for the degree of doctor.
Medical degrees can never have much value in the eyes
of the public unless they are understood to imply regular
and continued study in some great hospital. Sir W. Hamilton seems to intimate that this is not the case at
Oxford and Cambridge. He remarks with some emphasis:
"*Pro tanto* the University has, in fact, illegally abrogated
itself; and it would be difficult to say, whether the English or Scottish Universities have acted more contrary to
law and common sense, in their grant of medical degrees,
the former without professional, the latter without liberal
education*." Whatever may be the case at Oxford, Sir
W. Hamilton is misinformed with regard to Cambridge,
which requires for the medical degree a very sufficient
attendance in some hospital containing 100 beds. At the
Scottish Universities there is no requirement of learning
or literary accomplishments for the highest degree in
medicine beyond a Latin dissertation, which is generally

* *Discussions,* &c. p. 673.

written, in such Latin as would puzzle Celsus, by a *grinder*,
as he is called, who lives by this vocation. The presumption that English doctors of all the faculties will be liberally educated, and especially in classical learning, is
sustained not only by the general theory of the University
and its derivation from a school of liberal arts, but also
by the special fact that all the regius professors—not only
the professor of Greek, but those of Divinity, Law, Medicine, and Hebrew—are examiners for the University
scholarships, which are amongst the most important tests
of classical proficiency, and that they are not allowed to
appoint deputies. To men who are good scholars, it will
matter little whether they are called upon to hold disputations in Latin or in English; but independently of the
guarantee of adequate learning furnished by the Latin of
the schools, the disputation itself is, if properly conducted,
a very important discipline of the highest faculties. "Disputation," says Sir W. Hamilton*, "is in a certain sort
the condition of all improvement. In the mental as in
the material world, action and reaction are ever in proportion; and Plutarch well observes, that as motion would
cease, were contention taken out of the physical universe,
so all human progress would cease, were contention taken
out of the moral. Academical disputation, in fact, requiring
calls out, and calling out educates to, the most important
intellectual virtues;—to presence of mind, to dominion
over our faculties, to promptitude of recollection and
thought, and withal, though animating emulation, to a
perfect command of temper. It stimulates also to a more
attentive and profounder study of the matters to be thus
discussed; it more deeply impresses the facts and doctrines taught upon the mind; and finally, what is of

* *Ubi supra*, p. 680.

peculiar importance, and peculiarly accomplished by rightly regulated disputation, it checks all tendency towards irrelevancy and disorder in statement, by astricting the disputants to a pertinent and precise and logically predetermined order in the evolution of their reasonings."

For these and other reasons which might be adduced, I would strongly advocate the retention of Latin disputations, at least in the exercises for the higher faculties, which presume the groundwork of a completed liberal education. I have heard instances of the beneficial effects of this discipline even in the mathematical schools; but I would willingly leave to the mathematicians at Cambridge the now unmeaning distinction of *Wrangler*, if the reality without the name could be secured for the professional faculties, to which the first-class men of all triposes might contribute their foremost representatives.

II. COMPETITIVE TESTS.

In the discussion which has occupied us hitherto, I have endeavoured to show that Classics and Mathematics, as representing the two departments in the old school of liberal arts, are still the best foundation of University teaching. It is my next business to examine these two departments in their relation to one another, and to prove that, with a view to the competitive tests in the Universities and in the Civil Service, classical literature deserves the preponderance of encouragement, which it receives in general and at Oxford, and which it will, ere long, receive at Cambridge also.

As a first argument in favour of this position, it would be quite fair to urge that, as a fact, it has been found impossible to retain for mathematics the supremacy which they had gained at Cambridge[6]; and classical studies, as I have mentioned above*, have gradually raised themselves to an equal footing, if they have not virtually gained the upper hand. The relative amount of encouragement, which has been given by this University to mathematics and classics respectively, was made a subject of dispute between two eminent writers a short time since. For while Sir W. Hamilton maintained that "the University of Cambridge bestows not only a special, but a paramount, not to say an exclusive encouragement on the mathematical sciences," Dr Whewell, on the other hand, averred that " it is impossible to refer to any record of the prizes which the University bestows, without seeing that there

* p. 39.

is a much greater number offered and given in other subjects than in mathematics *." It cannot, I think, ·be
denied, that, as long as the Classical Tripos was subordi-
nated to the Mathematical, no amount of special prizes
bestowed on classical attainments would affect the proposition that the University of Cambridge gave the preponderance of distinction to mathematical studies. And if
we except the two largest Colleges, it may be said that
the solid reward of the Fellowship was for a long time
dependent on the results of the Mathematical Tripos.
Even at St John's College, and after the institution of the
Classical Tripos, the highest distinctions in this field have
sometimes failed to obtain this ultimate object of academical ambition. Chancellor's Medallists have generally
been Fellows ; but they have been regarded as also mathematicians of the better class. This limitation of the
competition for the highest classical distinction to Wranglers and Senior-optimes must have led occasionally to the
glorification of men who were not the best scholars of the
year ; for, until the year 1841, the medals were always
awarded to the best of the few candidates who competed
for them ; and we may form some idea as to the value of
these prizes as a merely classical criterion, if we picture
to ourselves what would have been the case, if there had
been no Mathematical Tripos, and if the Smith's Prizes had
been given without reserve to the two best mathematicians
in the first and second classes of a Classical Tripos.
Both before and after the institution of the Classical Examination for incepting Bachelors, the literary ordeal
exacted by the electors to the Trinity Fellowships has
been the main counterpoise to the supremacy of Mathematics at Cambridge, and must be regarded as the chief

* Hamilton, *Discussions*, &c. p. 319.

cause of that separation of the Triposes, to which we have
been gradually advancing, and which will be accomplished
in 1857. But we should not have arrived at this state
of things, if there had not been in the minds of an influential section of Cambridge men a growing conviction of
the value of classical studies as compared with mathematical, which is, of itself, a strong argument in favour
of the former.

A second argument of the same kind is furnished by
the preference for classical scholarship exhibited in the
Report, which led to the institution of competitive tests,
as the best means of selecting the most eligible persons
for civil appointments in India; a scheme which will, I
hope, form the basis of a more extended system of adequate and public examinations in the place of private
interest and arbitrary patronage.

Although this scheme is professedly formed on the
model of the University examinations, I hope that those,
who have read the previous discussion, will agree with
me in thinking, that the objects, to be attained by the
University and by the Civil Service examinations respectively, are similar rather than identical. The object
of the University examination is or ought to be the
selection of those persons who are best qualified, by
their abilities and previous acquirements, for the ulterior prosecution of what Dr Whewell terms progressive
studies, and for an unlimited advancement in learning
and science, to the extent at least of their residence in
the University, a residence for which the higher emoluments of the Fellowship or Professorship immediately and
effectively provide. On the other hand, the object of the
Civil Service examination is to determine which of the
candidates, for certain lucrative and responsible employ-

ments, exhibit the largest amount of intellectual power and activity, and are therefore most likely to discharge the duties imposed upon them with credit to themselves and benefit to the public service. This object, and not the advancement of science and learning, is distinctly proposed in that able Report, bearing the signatures of Mr T. B. Macaulay, Lord Ashburton, the Rev. H. Melvill, Professor Jowett, and Mr Shaw Lefevre, which was issued in December, 1854, and constitutes an epoch in the educational history of England. This Report distinctly maintains the great principle of liberal education, on which I have more than once insisted—namely, that the education which is to prepare young men for the higher business of life, must begin with a general discipline of the intellect, and that special or professional training ought to be reserved until this process has been brought to some satisfactory stage or landing-place. Their views will be most clearly displayed by means of a few extracts from the Report itself.

They thus speak of the importance of making a general education an approach to the special business of life in its higher walks :—

"We believe that men who have been engaged, up to 21 or 22, in studies which have no immediate connexion with the business of any profession, and of which the effect is merely to open, to invigorate, and to enrich the mind, will generally be found, in the business of every profession, superior to men who have, at 18 or 19, devoted themselves to the special studies of their calling. The most illustrious English jurists have been men, who have never opened a law-book till after the close of a distinguished academical career; nor is there any reason to believe that they would have been greater lawyers, if they had passed in drawing pleas and conveyances the time which they gave to *Thucydides,* to *Cicero,* and to *Newton.*"

Of the Mathematical portion of the Examination they say :—

"We think it important that not only the acquirements, but also the mental powers and resources of the competitors should be brought to the test."

Speaking of the Moral Sciences, as included in the scheme of the examination, they remark :—

"Whether this study shall have to do with mere words or things, whether it shall degenerate into a formal and scholastic pedantry, or shall train the mind for the highest purposes of active life, will depend, to a great extent, on the way in which the examination is conducted...The object of the examiners should be rather to put to the test the candidate's powers of mind than to ascertain the extent of his metaphysical reading."

With the same reference to the immediate objects of a competitive test, they recommend that eminence in classical composition should have a considerable share in determining the issue of the competition :—

"Skill in Greek and Latin versification has, indeed, no direct tendency to form a judge, a financier, or a diplomatist. But the youth who does best, what all the ablest and most ambitious youths about him are trying to do well, will generally prove a superior man ; nor can we doubt that an accomplishment, by which Fox and Canning, Grenville and Wellesley, Mansfield and Tenterden first distinguished themselves above their fellows, indicates powers of mind which, properly trained and directed, may do great service to the state."

And with regard to the Examination in general they observe with perfect truth :—

" Experience justifies us in pronouncing with entire confidence that, if the examiners be well chosen, it is utterly impossible that the delusive show of knowledge, which is the effect of the process popularly called cramming, can ever be successful against real learning and ability."

It is clear, from these explicit statements of their views, that the able and eminent persons, who framed the scheme for the civil service examination, had no wish to send out to India clever smatterers, feeble bookworms, scholastic pedants, and one-sided mathematicians; but to select the most energetic and vigorous young men from the crowds who were likely to offer themselves as candidates for a share in the administration of our most important Satrapies. The particular kind of knowledge, which would be most serviceable to them in the presidencies, was to be prescribed to those selected by the first test, and this subsequent course of study was to be stimulated by a second examination. But, for the preparatory selection, it was only necessary to test existing methods of education, and to discover the best men they could produce. The reasonableness of this procedure was manifest. On the one hand, as the candidates would come from schools and colleges, which had long pursued fixed systems of instruction, differing in different parts of the country, it was necessary that the touchstone should be applied fairly to them all. On the other hand, as only a limited number of the candidates could be successful, it was essential that the whole body of applicants should not be drawn away from their general studies by specialties, which might be of little or no use to those who would not ultimately proceed to India. But, independently of these considerations, suggested by the distinctive peculiarities of the appointments themselves and the means of filling them,

the framers of the scheme of examination could not but
foresee that such an object of competition would soon
produce an effect on the educational system of the whole
country, and that teachers would address themselves to
the immediate preparation of candidates. They, therefore,
wisely laid down some general principles, applicable to
the future no less than to the present. They have declared unreservedly that they want the fruits of real
mental discipline, that they desire habits of exact thought,
and not a wide range of diversified information; and thus
they give their adhesion to the old rather than to the
new form of education, and would prefer the solid groundwork of the old school of arts rather than the showy
stucco-work of modern sciolism. They indicate, that, up
to a certain time of life, it is of much less consequence
what we read than how we read it*; and that the young
man, who would prepare himself for future distinction,
must be frequently less anxious to advance than to know
the route which he has already traversed. The student,
who is worthy of the name, must be willing to acquiesce
in those teachers, who, in the older Universities, were
called *repetents*—a sort of intellectual drill-serjeants; he
must often remind himself of the words of the Platonic
Socrates: "Perhaps it would not be amiss to go over this
ground again; for it is better to accomplish a little
thoroughly than a great deal insufficiently †." In the
words of a modern philosopher, he will thus learn that
"as the end of study is not merely to compass the knowledge of facts, but, in and from that knowledge, to lay up

* See above, p. 16.

† Plat. *Theætetus*, p. 187, E: ὀρθῶς ὑπέμνησας. ἴσως γὰρ οὐκ
ἄπο καιροῦ πάλιν ὥσπερ ἴχνος μετελθεῖν. κρεῖττον γάρ που σμικρὸν εὖ
ἢ πολὺ μὴ ἱκανῶς περᾶναι.

the materials for speculation; so it is not the quantity read, but the degree of reading which affords a profitable exercise to the student. Thus it is far more improving to read one good book ten times, than to read ten good books once; and *non multa sed multum,* 'not much perhaps but accurate,' has, from ancient times, obtained the authority of an axiom in education, from all who had any title to express an opinion on the subject*."

Adopting these principles and thus confining the competitive test to the results of a liberal or general education, these exponents of the newest demands upon intellectual culture have not only given the most important place to the old basis of instruction, namely, classics and mathematics, but have even declared their preference for the more old-fashioned of these two departments of study. For while mathematics have only 1000 marks assigned as the maximum of credit, 1500 marks are allotted to Greek and Latin. And thus in our newest educational stimulus we have, as in our oldest academical institutions, a premium for the cultivation of classical scholarship even as compared with mathematical science.

Many have, from time to time, complained of this preponderance as it is manifested in the great schools and universities of England; and some letters have more recently appeared in the newspapers protesting against the application of this time-honoured preference to the competitive tests, by which we are to select, from the whole kingdom, the ablest civil officers for our Indian Empire. Although, then, I fully admit that mathematical knowledge is a necessary ingredient in any complete course of liberal education, I feel myself called upon to show, that there is good reason why classical attainments

* Hamilton, *Discussions*, &c. p. 682.

should receive a larger amount of encouragement both in these new examinations for Indian appointments and in those which determine the distinctions and emoluments awarded to successful industry at Oxford and Cambridge.

With this view I shall first attempt to prove that, in regard to the merely educational results, and as a discipline of the human mind in general, classical and philological studies exercise a more beneficial influence than the pursuit of mathematical science.

It will be my object to point out, in the next place, the greater practical utility of classical as compared with mathematical knowledge, in the particular case of one who is to fill an official position in British India.

And, lastly, I shall try to recommend to others my own conviction, that, as ancillary to the progressive, ulterior, and wider studies of a great University, the acquirements of the classical scholar and philologer are more desirable and important than even the practised ingenuity and analytical skill of the accomplished mathematician.

In regard to the educational results of the two branches, the general truth was recently stated by Professor Blackie, at a public meeting in Glasgow, namely, that literature produces more humanising and civilising effects than science; and a writer in one of the weekly journals has well remarked, that despotical rulers know what they are about when they suppress the study of moral philosophy, history, and classical literature, and encourage only the exact discipline of mathematics. There can be no doubt, that, if it be our object to train man as such, to develope all that is noble and divine in him, without reference to his use as a mere instrument in the hands of others, his best nurture is the contemplation of that which is peculiar to man—his reason and language—and the examination of the general mind and speech of man as recorded in the written memorials of present and past generations. All human study, according to the German generaliser, is divided into two great departments—the retrospective and the prospective—the known and the unknown—philology and physiology. "It appears to me," says Steinthal *, "that it is the business of the human understanding or of literature in general to comprehend those simple and absolute laws, which appear in the *world* or in *nature* on the one hand, and in *the history of the human race* on the other hand. As therefore there are two forms of literature, one *the history of nature* or *physiology*, the other *the history of the human mind*, philologers undertake the examination of all that the λόγος or human reason has produced. Now whatever the human reason produces is some idea, something recognised and discerned by the mind, although it may be clothed in some outward form, whether it be a form of government constituted by human society, or some monument of hewn stone, or some type of mythology and religion, or some demonstrative result of philosophical acuteness, or some outpouring of poetical genius or oratorical eloquence. So that even the history of philology belongs to philology—with this limitation, that *e. g.* the history of classical philology is the specialty of those who consider modern life from a philological point of view. Accordingly, the only true definition is Böckh's, that *philology* is the *teaching and learning of that which is already discovered* (*philologiam esse cogniti cognitionem*). Which is not to be understood, as though philologers were always doing over again the work done to their hands; but all the products of the human mind,

* *De Pronomine Relativo, commentatio philosophico-philologica:* scripsit H. Steinthal. Berolini, 1847. pp. 4, 5.

which remain as recorded facts, have to be submitted
afresh to the crucible of human thought, to the end that,
being recognised, not as the arbitrary acts of individuals,
but as sprung from the necessary laws of minds individu-
ally free, they may be regarded as a mirror or picture
of the human reason in general." Without waiting to
inquire how far these sweeping statements ought to be
qualified by special modifications, there is no doubt that
they are generally true; that human speculation is either
conversant about the laws impressed on visible nature, in
which case induction leads to discovery, or else busied
with the records of human thought, or with literature in
its various forms and applications. The former may be
the employment of man's reason, which is most useful to
his generation. The latter is certainly the employment
most profitable to himself. Doubtless the contemplation
of nature is in itself a delightful occupation; but who are
those who read with most intelligence and pleasure the
great open pages of the world's book; who are those
whose eyes see the infinite articulations of visible phenomena, who thus discern the symmetry and beauty of
the universe, and proclaim it to be a *cosmos* or perfect
order of things? Is it the man whose eyes are only
guides to his working hands, who is labouring at details,
who is a tool or machine engaged in some material task
of practical utility; or is it the scholar and philosopher,
who, like Alexander Humboldt, surveys the present and
the past at once, and enjoys and expands the prospect,
because he both feels himself and knows what men from
olden times have felt and thought about it? In proportion as the material interests of the present moment
become more and more engrossing, more and more tyrannical in their exactions, in the same proportion it becomes

more necessary that man should fall back on the common interests of humanity, and free himself from the trammels of the present by living in the past. As Dr Johnson says very truly*, "Whatever withdraws us from the power of the senses,—whatever makes the past, the distant, or the future predominate over the present, advances us in the dignity of thinking beings." Imagination and its correlative, faith, are the functions of the human mind which most of all insure and exemplify its freedom from the body, and so set at nought the thraldom of time and space. And man has a right to claim as his own the grand definition of liberty, namely, that he is without any let or hindrance which does not arise out of his own constitution. The great additions, which have been made to our material comforts by the scientific ingenuity of modern times, induce men to think that time is misspent when it is not employed either in adding something to these advantages, or, at least, earning the largest possible share in them. There cannot be a greater mistake. Every concession on this account is a sacrifice of the mind to the body, of our intellectual liberty and spiritual happiness to our personal enjoyment now or some years hence. In this England of the 19th century we seldom allow ourselves to reflect on the manner in which the individual becomes merged in the mass by means of those very improvements, which the genius of individuals has discovered by a noble employment of unfettered intellect. How few there are who understand the absorbing centralisation and monopoly, which has resulted from the formation of railroads†, and, instead of complaining that

---

* *Journey to the Western Islands, Works,* x. p. 501.

† Ficquelmont has made some striking remarks on this subject. *Lord Palmerston, l'Angleterre et le Continent,* Vol. I. pp. 97 sqq.

their position has been injuriously affected by this revolution, apply themselves to a discovery of the best practical
course under this change of circumstances! To say
nothing of the absorption into one vortex of a hundred
little scattered trades, of the drainage of a morass of
industry into one great canal leading into the ocean of
commerce, the railway affects the social and commercial
freedom of every man in the community. Neither for
the personal traveller nor for the transport of goods is
there now any free choice or alternative: as a general
rule we become slaves to the necessity of taking the
cheapest and most expeditious route. And this feeling has
led men to the admission that, when we have once discovered the best way of doing anything, we necessarily
sacrifice liberty to equality, and freedom of action to
increased convenience. Thus we may say that the Great
Exhibition of 1851 was a celebration of the triumph
of the material interests of man over his moral independence. The world is becoming a great manufactory in
which each individual is employed mechanically according
to his abilities; and the division of labour seems likely to
end by reducing each man to the rank of a tool or the
integral part of a machine. Consequently the great
moral question of the day is to examine and ascertain
the relation between our material conveniences and
our freedom. It is only by a liberal education, and
by that part of it in particular which belongs to literary culture, that we can really see the road by which
we are travelling, and avoid falling into the pit from
which there is no return. And although it is true that
a liberal education is only attainable by those who are
able to devote their youth to the business of improving
their minds, it is not less true that the education of the

whole community depends upon the culture of the upper classes.

The importance of education is fully appreciated among us at present. It is indeed the great question of the day; and no one, who is not blind to the signs of the times, can fail to perceive that the future destinies of this country must depend in a great measure on the success with which we carry out the indispensable undertaking of educating the whole community. But although this is generally admitted, I think it is often supposed that this problem is confined to the duty of providing school-training for the children of the lower orders. This supposition, whenever it is productive of any effect on the conduct of individuals, must be regarded as a mischievous error; for it induces a forgetfulness of the reasons which make it desirable that the mental and moral cultivation of all classes should be duly regarded. Now we must educate the *upper classes*, if we would not deprive rank of its brightest lustre, and wealth of its greatest charm; we must educate the *middle classes*, if we would furnish them with the inducements for shaking off the selfishness of indolent respectability, if we would enable them to resist the aggressions of intrusive bigotry, if we would break down the party-walls of class prejudices, if we would inspire every one of those, who have virtually a large share in the government of England, with an enlightened regard for his own and his country's welfare; and lastly, we must educate the *lower orders*, if we would make the labouring man feel that he is a responsible and rational being, not a mere tool for doing work, or an echo for propagating opinions, which he does not understand; we must educate the lower orders, if we would give them that reverence for law, that sense of truth and justice,

that habit of self respect and self-control, without which
we cannot ensure the gradual amelioration of our institutions from the risk of revolutionary disturbances, and
save this country from the alternative so sternly proposed
to many nations on the continent—the alternative of
choosing between despotism or anarchy.

If the man of rank and fortune is not properly educated, we have either the rude sportsman, who despises
literature, or the voluptuary, who scoffs at morality, or
the town dandy, who dawdles away the brief and precious
hours of existence in the pursuit of contemptible frivolity.
All these, and others more or less like them, are lost to
their country and their age.   They live and die without
having effected anything, except so far as they have succeeded in making their order odious or contemptible in
the eyes of those beneath them.   Fortunately the aristocracy of this country have always been distinguished,
in the majority of instances, by their endowments of mind
and character, no less than by the nobility or opulence to
which they are born.   In this country, as in Greece, the
gentleman is accomplished and good, as well as rich or
highly-connected ; and while we may often add that he
is the true knight, who bears the cross on his shield, on
his sword-hilt, and in his heart, who exhibits the spirit
of Christianity in the unsullied brightness of his honour,
in the unselfish devotedness of his personal courage, and
in the unaffected benevolence of his demeanour and conduct, we may now and then point to some well-born lady,
who, when war is raging in a distant land, tears herself
from the undisturbed tranquillity of a luxurious home,
and travels to the far East to combat the squalid disorder
of a military hospital, and with gentle books and dulcet
words to alleviate the poignant sufferings of ill-fated and

prostrate valour. We find also many instances, in which
young Englishmen of rank and fortune are, like Sir Philip
Sidney, not only soldiers or statesmen, but literary men
and scholars. A long list might be formed of books
written by men moving in the highest circles of English
society; and if a new Athenæum or other educational
institution is to be founded, or encouraged by lectures,
addresses, and other forms of sympathy and co-operation,
it will generally be found that, though men of the middle-
class may sometimes stand aloof or interpose obstacles,
the voluntary services of those who belong to the aristocracy of rank or education may always be commanded.
It is on account of this real superiority and this active
sympathy that the English noble maintains his ascendant
position in this half democratic country; it is for this that
he is loved, respected, and imitated by his inferiors ; it is
for this that he is permitted, while still a stripling, to lead
the stern discipline of our embattled array; it is for this
that his success, in equal competitions, to which all are
admitted, is always greeted with expressions of cordial
good will and general approbation.

Of the education of the great middle class at the present day it is somewhat difficult to speak. Divided as it
is into a number of different subsections, it is perhaps
impossible to say anything which does not require a great
deal of special qualification. But if we define the middle
class as consisting of those who do not belong in any way
to the aristocracy of education, who are engaged in making
money by some kind of trade or business, and who enjoy,
by virtue of their exertions, all the comforts, and a varying proportion of the luxuries of life, the following picture
may be maintained as generally true in its outline and
colouring. The man of business as such is generally prone

to acquiesce in the consciousness of his own respectability. This, in some of its outward manifestations, is the idol of his heart. If he is ambitious to be fashionable or aristocratic, it is mainly for the sake of appearances, and he is generally found to imitate rather the expensiveness than the refinements of the class above him. If he lays down the law in politics or religion, he is the unconscious mouth-piece of some short-sighted utilitarian or canting bigot, whom it is respectable to follow. When he sends his boys to school, he cares less for their improvement than for the credit which redounds to himself from their educational advantages. But when most satisfied with his own position, he seems to care for little beyond the uncontradicted maintenance of the sentiments which he has adopted from his newspaper or his preacher, his personal and domestic comfort, and the decencies of his outward appearance. Abundant meals, and good clothes, and a well-furnished parlour are the extent of his wishes. And he measures things without his immediate circle by the ideas which suffice for his own narrow world. Hence he is too often the tool of bigotry, the echo of stereotyped opinions, the victim of class prejudices, the blind or obstinate advocate of measures which have no connexion with his own or his country's better interests; and he has too frequently no wish that his sons should be more cultivated or enlightened than himself, though he has no objection to spend his money in procuring ornamental accomplishments for his daughters. If this is a true description, the middle class must be very difficult to educate. Indeed, I am inclined to regard them, as practically the great stumblingblock in the way of a general diffusion of higher cultivation in this country: for though they have really no opinions of their own, it is almost impossible to induce them to listen to any argument which runs counter to their inveterate preconceptions : while therefore I would take all means to wake them from their self-complacent dreams, and to rouse them to the necessity of enlightening their own minds, or at least of seeking a better kind of education for their children than that in which they too generally acquiesce, I place my hopes of an improvement in their intellectual condition—an improvement on which, as I have said, the prospects of this country very much depend—in the lateral pressure of the upper and lower classes, when the ameliorated condition of the latter shall combine with the daily increasing condescension of the former, and both together will break through that crust of comfortable indolence in which our tradespeople and professional men so often envelope themselves.

The intellectual improvement of the lower orders is the most practicable and most immediately influential, though neither primarily nor ultimately the most important department in the great work of national education. It must result from the increased enlightenment and awakened discernment of the higher order among us, and will, in the end, combined with this and directed by it, react on the more inert mass of the middle classes. It is not my business, on the present occasion, to discuss the general question of education, or to show how we ought to deal with the masses. There is no form of communicating instruction which is not calculated in some degree to forward the great business of leavening the crude mass which sinks to the bottom. Every kind of school and educational institution should receive that amount of encouragement and support which it deserves and requires. Ragged schools and respectable schools, endowed schools and self-supporting schools, Sunday-schools and week-day schools, infant-schools and working-men's colleges, Athenæums and public reading-rooms and free libraries, are all, in their different ways, worthy of consideration and assistance. But all these depend for their existence and successful action on the proper mental cultivation of the higher and best-educated classes in the community. The legislative enactment, the pecuniary subscription, the occasional lecture or address, the regular superintendence of a class, are all due to that power of discerning the path of duty, and that earnest desire to follow it, which is created in the aristocracy by their superior intellectual and moral enlightenment. We look in vain for a spontaneous manifestation of these qualities on the part of the non-independent middle classes, who live in subjection to the claims of their immediate interests. Men are not free to speak or even to think, if they are oscillating between the thraldom of class prejudices and commercial gains.

If then the education of the whole community is so dependent on that of the upper classes, and if these owe their normal influence to the circumstances which enable them to escape the trammels of material interests, it must follow that the liberal education, which is the peculiar attribute of the highest order, ought to consist in the literature which humanises and generalises our views, and not in the science which provides for the increase of opulence and comfort. The higher training of our youth must not be that of a polytechnic school. We want such institutions no doubt; for we need observers and surveyors, engineers and artillerymen to do the work, which can best be performed by such intelligent automatons. But the proper training of those, who are to influence the moral and intellectual growth of their generation, must have for its object the improvement of man as such, and not the mechanical performance of any given task, however conducive to our material comfort and advantage.

But although it seems very clear that the education of civilised man consists rather in literary than in scientific cultivation, it still remains to be considered, whether the basis of literary training, which is furnished by grammar and philology, as illustrated by the classical languages, is or is not better adapted in itself to enlarge and invigorate the mind than the basis of scientific training, which is furnished by pure mathematics. I have already admitted more than once that the latter is, like the former, a necessary part of a liberal education. The question now is, which of the two deserves and requires, for its educational results, the greatest amount of study, and consequently the greatest amount of encouragement in those competitions which test the intellectual capacity of candidates for reward or lucrative employment.

It is not at all unnatural that those, who have addicted themselves more particularly to one of the great departments in a liberal education, should maintain the superiority of their own favourite study, and depreciate the branch of knowledge with which they are less conversant. As the old proverb says,

> The ploughman will despise and scoff
> The thing he is not skilful of.

And classical and mathematical students are too often only rustics and barbarians in the estimation of one another. For myself, I claim an immunity from any such prejudice in favour of philology as would lead me to undervalue mathematical knowledge. During the fourteen years which I passed in the management of a public school, I endeavoured to keep the mathematical training of the boys proportionally on the same footing as the classical, and, by the testimony of competent examiners, with very adequate success. But I am the more bound to uphold the superior importance of classical scholarship, because the most eminent writer on liberal education, being himself a great mathematician, has been led, as it seems to me, to form an unduly favourable opinion of the intellectual results of mathematical as opposed to classical studies.

Dr Whewell tells us *, that language and reason, the conjoined attributes of humanity, admit of independent cultivation; and that while classical and grammatical studies furnish us with the means of education in regard to the former faculty, we must go to mathematics for the best cultivation and development of the reason. This distinction is placed in a still stronger light when he says†, that " inasmuch as, in a good education, we must educate the reason as well as the literary taste, we must require of our students a mathematical combined with a classical culture." Admitting, as I have always done, the conclusion, I dispute the terms of this assertion, which implies that the reason could not be educated—that the literary taste alone would be cultivated—if we did not add mathematical to classical discipline. And I am still more disposed to protest against the disparaging tone in which, after speaking of the " vast preponderance of encouragement to classical reading which the condition of English culture offers," he says, it will be seen " how important it is for those, who know that mere classical reading is a narrow and enfeebling education, to resist any attempts to add to this preponderance by diminishing the encourage-

* *Of a Liberal Education,* §§ 10—18.
† *Ibid.* § 183.

ment which the University gives to studies of a larger
or more vigorous kind *." Now in all this, I am obliged
to dissent entirely from Dr Whewell's view of the matter.
The reason, I contend, is as much educated by grammatical, and, what is the further stage, by logical studies, as
it is by geometry—and certainly a great deal more than
it is by analytical mathematics. The full cultivation of
the reasoning or logical faculty does, no doubt, require
geometry as well as grammar or logic. And so far I
agree with Dr Whewell. But I do not admit, what he
implies, that a classical education is confined to the cultivation of our literary taste, or that the cultivation of the
reasoning faculty is the exclusive province of the mathematician. And if I were asked which of the two, if exclusively pursued, was the "more narrow and enfeebling,"
and which "the larger and more vigorous kind" of education, I would undertake to prove by abundant examples
and testimonies the very reverse of what Dr Whewell so
plainly intimates. I feel assured that although the classical scholar, as such, would be ill provided for the full
discharge of his important functions, if he were not also,
to a certain extent at least, a mathematician, and though
a liberal education would be incomplete, if it did not add
geometry to its grammatical training, the mere mathematician stands in an infinitely lower position, in regard
to the cultivation of his intellectual powers, than even the
merely classical scholar. The latter has done something—
nay, something considerable—for the development of his
reasoning faculties. Grammar and logic, and perhaps even
the higher departments of criticism, have been laid open
to him; and he has, besides this, surveyed some of the
most important fields of moral and literary speculation.

* *Ubi supra*, § 311.

But the mere mathematician, if he is an illiterate man, is not at all educated in the higher sense of the term. He is a mere tool or instrument for the performance of certain operations. For the laborious calculation of almanacs, for the rigorous demonstration of problems in geometry or in the higher processes of symbolical analysis, he is a wonderful piece of intelligent mechanism ; he is an automaton in the strictest sense of the term, and his higher perceptions and nobler tastes are often so blunted, that he either disbelieves everything that he cannot prove by the rules of his craft, or, on the other hand, superstitiously adopts everything which his imperfect education will not allow him to investigate. To insist that the classical scholar should also be in some sort a mathematician, is undoubtedly a reasonable demand; for it is requiring the less from those who have accomplished the greater task. But it would be better far if the University would begin to require that all mathematicians should be competently advanced in literary education, and that up to a certain point the claims of philology and exact science should be accurately balanced.

Whatever may have been the case in the middle of the last century, whatever may be the case still at Oxford and in certain great schools, no one who is really acquainted with the facts will suppose that the studies of the classical scholar at Cambridge cultivate his taste at the expense of his reason. On the contrary I shall be obliged to admit, before I come to the conclusion of this essay, that the scholarship of Cambridge, without relinquishing any of the ground which it has already secured, ought to be more directed than it is to the cultivation of a literary taste in general, and less exclusively confined to those grammatical and critical studies which occupy the attention of so many hard-headed reasoners. Mr Blakesley's description of the modern Cambridge scholar is in most of its features strictly accurate. He says * : " The acquisition of classical accomplishments at present is anything but a mere cultivation of the taste, and requires, if any, a totally different corrective from one which the study of a pure science is calculated to furnish. We must not think of the scholar of the present day as a being of the same kind with the scholar of thirty years back. He is no longer the walking Horace, the capper of lines from Virgil, running over with classical allusions, tossing everything that strikes his fancy into a Greek saw or a Latin epigram, ready with an illustration from ancient manners for every incident of the day, a composer of verses which Ovid might have claimed, and which he himself is quite unable to construe. This is no longer his generic description. He may be best defined as a hard-headed, accurate philologer, so far as the empirical study of the structure of three languages in the choicest part of their literature can make him one,—possibly a better thing than the scholar of the last generation, but certainly a different one *." The last report of the Board of Classical Studies †assures us, that the most prominent excellence of the best competitors for classical honours is still the critical accuracy with which the passages set for translation are rendered into English. To those who are acquainted with the refined syntax and complex structure of the classical languages, it is unnecessary to state that this accuracy must be the result of a long course of logical study pursued under the humbler guise of grammar, or else that it involves, in the particular case, a concentrated logical effort.

* " *Where does the Evil lie ?*" pp. 38, 39.
† See note 5 at the end.

The nature of the process, which the Cambridge scholar is called upon to perform, is well described in the following passage by one who has been both examined and examiner within the last twelve years. "The classical student," says Mr Clark *, "is unceasingly employed in collecting and classifying particular examples, and in applying general grammatical rules. In determining the sense of his author, he has to analyse the structure of each period, to select the most suitable out of many significations of each word, and then to regard the connexion of each clause with the sentence, and of each sentence with the context. He is perpetually arbitrating between conflicting probabilities. It would take many pages to write out at length the inductive syllogisms which have to be proposed and solved in determining the true meaning of a difficult sentence in Thucydides or Tacitus. The facility and rapidity with which an accomplished student does this ought really to enhance in our eyes the value of his previous training, not lead us to depreciate it or underrate the difficulties which he is thus enabled to master. Intuitive perception of truth is not a lucky guess, but a masterly condensation of long observation and painful reasoning."

The relation between classical and mathematical studies, as means of cultivating the reasoning powers, is not to be determined by considering separately their respective contributions to this result. The best classical scholars will not deny that the study of mathematics, up to a certain point, is an essential element in a complete liberal training; that classics and mathematics ought to be combined, and that no mental discipline can be more valuable and effective than the study of language, combined with

* *Cambridge Essays.* 1855. p. 303.

that of the laws of number, quantity, and form*. So long
as mathematics only claim what belongs to them—a
second place in the partnership of the liberal arts—no
enlightened writer on University education will seek to
disparage their importance. But when it is attempted,
not only to exaggerate their share in the work of mental
cultivation, but even to claim for them exclusive functions in the education of our reasoning powers, when
invidious comparisons are drawn between classical and
mathematical pursuits, and the former are described as
narrow and enfeebling, it becomes necessary to reduce the
pretensions of the mathematician by indicating the inferior and ancillary office of the acquirements for which a
paramount importance is claimed. This has been done,
and with especial reference to Dr Whewell's advocacy of
his favourite pursuit, by one of the greatest logicians of
the present day, Sir William Hamilton †, who, not content
with showing that other mental exercises are more profitable, plainly declares that "of all our intellectual pursuits
the study of the mathematical sciences is the one whose
utility as an intellectual exercise, when carried beyond a
moderate extent, has been most peremptorily denied by
the greatest number of the most competent judges ‡."
He shows that, since mathematical reasoning is practical
logic as specially applied to necessary matter, whereas
philosophy and general reasoning are practical logic as
specially applied to contingent matter, and since the reasoning faculty of men is, in all principally, in most altogether,
occupied upon contingent matter, mathematics cannot be

---

* Dr Kennedy's *Sermon at Bath,* in Dec. 1853, p. 14.

† " *On the Study of Mathematics as an exercise of mind,*" *Edinburgh Rev.* Jan. 1836. *Discussions,* &c. pp. 257 sqq.

‡ p. 260.

the best instrument for educating men to a full development of the reasoning faculty, or that we cannot come best
trained to the hunting-field of probability, by assiduous
locomotion in the railroad of calculus and demonstration*.
He thus travels to the conclusion that mathematical
studies are unimproving†, and neither conduce to genera-
lisation‡ nor aid us to detect and avoid the fallacies which
arise in the thought of the reasoner himself§. As Sir W.
Hamilton elsewhere says ‖ : "Mathematical, like all other
reasoning, is syllogistic; but, here, *the perspicuous necessity of the matter necessitates the correctness of the form:*
we cannot reason wrong. Logic, whether natural or acquired, is thus less exercised in mathematics than in any
other department of science; and on this account it is
that mathematical study is the very worst gymnastic of
the intellect—the very worst preparative for reasoning
correctly on matters (and these are only not all the objects
of human concernment), in which the mind must actively
precede and not passively follow the evolution of its
objects." With regard to the moral effects of mathematical studies Sir W. Hamilton maintains the conclusions,
at which I had arrived independently, which I stated some
years ago, and which I have repeated above, namely, that
an excessive study of the mathematical sciences leads to
the alternative of blind credulity or irrational scepticism.
"Alienated, by the opposite character of their studies, from
those habits of caution and confidence, of skill and sagacity, which the pursuit of knowledge in the universe of
probability requires and induces, mathematicians are con-
strained, when they venture beyond their diagrams and
calculations, *either* to accept their facts on authority, if

* p. 263.   † pp. 267 sqq.   ‡ pp. 276 sqq.
§ p. 278.   ‖ *Reid.* 2nd Ed. 1849. p. 701.

not on imagination,—*or* to repudiate altogether, as unreal, what they are incapable of verifying*." This tendency is especially manifested by those mathematicians, who set up as theologians; who dogmatise with the utmost confidence on the mechanical process of the argument, quite unconscious of the precarious foundation of their premisses; and who cannot recognise the truth of any criticism which rests, as all literary criticism must, on a balance of probabilities. Not to speak of those whose faculties are limited to the acquirement of mathematical knowledge, and who are, in other respects, childish or fatuous, I have met with more than one man, who, having studied mathematics with success, has arrived at such a pitch of general self-confidence in his limited power of mere deduction, that he charges with a neglect of all the laws of evidence any one who builds on the basis of conjecture or hypothesis; and yet all the discoveries in natural philosophy, in which mathematicians claim the lion's share, essentially involve, as Professor Baden Powell has reminded us †, "*a certain amount of hypothesis*—a certain assumption of more than the bare facts themselves seem strictly to warrant." "The curious, the inquiring spirit of man," says Humboldt, "must be suffered to make excursions— still to surmise what cannot be positively known‡." Again, in Mr Powell's words: "It is by the peculiar capacity for seizing *sound analogies* in these first hypotheses that the highest philosophical genius is mainly characterised; could this be reduced to fixed principles it would constitute no unimportant branch of mental science—the logic of anticipation, the philosophy of the

* p. 294.
† *Essays on the Spirit of Inductive Philosophy.* Lond. 1855. p. 6.
‡ *Cosmos*, p. 252.

unknown*." To the same effect, the able writer, who gave the name of anticipation to "this power of divination, this sagacity, which is the mother of all science," says very forcibly: "The intellect with a dog-like instinct will not hunt until it has found the scent. It must have some presage of the result before it will turn its energies to its attainment." And thus "philosophy proceeds upon a system of credit," for "if she never advanced beyond her tangible capital, her wealth would not be so enormous as it is †." This mode of proceeding is familiar to the classical critic; his corrections of the text, his restoration of mutilated passages, his rejection of spurious documents and unhistorical facts, and his reconstructions of lost literature and annals from the disconnected fragments which the wreck of time has spared, all depend upon that divination which proclaims a truth before it can be proved; and too often this is far beyond the ken of the dim-eyed mathematician, who is not also a philosopher. As contrasted with philological studies, Sir W. Hamilton assigns a very low place to mathematics. He says ‡: " The study of language, if conducted upon rational principles, is one of the best exercises of an applied logic. To master, for example, the *Minerva* of Sanctius with its commentators is, I conceive, a far more profitable exercise of mind than to conquer the *Principia* of Newton." And to the same effect he quotes from Cajetan von Weiller §, who says: "Mathematics and grammar differ essentially from each other in respect to their efficiency as general means of intellectual cultivation. The former have to do

* Baden Powell, *u. s.* pp. 89, 90.
† Thompson, *Outlines of the Laws of Thought.* Lond. 1849. pp. 309—312.
‡ p. 262.   § p. 269.

only with the intuitions of space and time, and are therefore, even in their foundation, limited to a special department of our being; whereas the latter, occupied with the
primary notions of our intellectual life in general, is coex-
tensive with its universal empire. On this account the
grammatical exercise of mind must, if beneficially applied,
precede the mathematical." The utmost concession which
Sir W. Hamilton will make in favour of mathematics is
contained in the following passages: "That their study, if
pursued in moderation and efficiently counteracted, may
be beneficial in the correction of a certain vice, and in the
formation of its corresponding virtue. The vice is the
habit of mental distraction; the virtue, the habit of con-
tinuous attention. This is the single benefit, to which
the study of mathematics can justly pretend, in the cultivation of the mind; and it is almost the one only or
the one principal accorded to it by the most intelligent
philosophers *." "Although, therefore, the inscription over
Plato's school be but a comparatively modern fiction, we
are willing to admit its truth, nay, are decidedly of opinion, that mathematics ought to be cultivated, to a certain
extent, by every one who would devote himself to the
higher philosophy †."

With the general tendency of these remarks I entirely
agree. By all means, let mathematics be cultivated as a
subordinate branch of the liberal arts. Let this study
contribute, as it has always done, to form habits of delicate
accuracy and elegant analysis. But let us not, for one
moment, concede its claims to paramount or exclusive
importance. Let us not allow it to arrogate to itself the
name of philosophy, or to dub with the name of a philosophical society an association chiefly confined to the

* p. 303. † p. 311.

prosecution of mathematical and physical science*. Let
us rather think with shame of the time when an illiterate
mathematician—a man, who, in the words of Aristo of
Chios†, had contented himself with a handmaid of Pene-
lope because he could not win the mistress—when a man,
who knew nothing except the branch of knowledge which
is difficult only because it is too easy‡, when such a man
not only obtained from the University of Cambridge the
certificate of a completed education, but might perchance
be presented personally in the Senate-House before all his
brother-bachelors, or have his name read first in the
schools, while the representatives of the faculty of arts
solemnly declared that they reserved to him his seniority!

As far then as examinations are educational tests, or
touchstones to prove the amount of intellectual qualification, there cannot, I conceive, be any reason to doubt
that classical scholarship deserves a larger proportion of
encouragement and reward than the co-ordinate accomplishments of the mathematician. It is also proper to
recollect that classical proficiency involves a much longer
course of study than mathematics. Connecting itself, as
it does, with the growth and development of the intellect
in general, grammatical training may be commenced, and
often is commenced, at a very early age, and is allowed to
be combined with those many branches of instruction
which it rather facilitates than impedes. Mathematical
teaching, except in rare instances of precocious talent, is
generally deferred till the period of adolescence has well
begun, and a very few years suffice for a complete attainment of all that can be learned, in the case of those who
are qualified to make any real progress in these studies.

---

* See the Note in Sir W. Hamilton's *Discussions*, &c. p. 272.
† Stob. *Floril.* IV. 110.   ‡ Hamilton, *u. s.* p. 281.

Many Cambridge students, who have gained the highest honours of the mathematical tripos, were unacquainted with algebra when they came up to College; and I have heard of one instance where a pupil of the great private tutor, Mr Hopkins, obtained the rank of Senior Wrangler with only fifteen months' study of mathematical science. In classics, on the contrary, the majority of successful candidates for high honours have been under tuition in Greek and Latin for at least ten years. I am disposed to think that with proper teaching this period of probation might be very much abridged; but I am quite certain that no man, though born with literary tastes and tendencies and naturally endowed with the instincts of philological criticism, could pass a first-rate examination in classical scholarship without spending at least four years in a previous course of energetic study. The separation of the triposes at Cambridge will probably produce some effect on the numbers of the candidates for mathematical and classical honours respectively. Hitherto the average number of wranglers or first-class mathematicians has been thrice that of the first-class classical scholars. To a certain extent, this may be accounted for by the fact, that the mathematical tripos has hitherto conferred the B.A. degree by itself, whereas the classical scholar has been obliged to submit to some previous ordeal. But making allowance for this, we must admit that, as most Cambridge men were taught Greek and Latin at school, whereas most of them did not begin to learn mathematics till they came into residence, there must be some intrinsic grounds for the fact that some thirty or forty men every year have been dubbed Wranglers, while only ten or twelve have obtained places in the first class of the classical tripos. Having myself introduced into a public school perhaps the largest proportion of mathematics ever taught in such an institution, I can bear my testimony to the fact, that, while five or six hours a week were amply sufficient for the mathematical studies of the highest boys, twenty-two hours at the very least were expended on their classical and general or literary studies and the exercises in composition necessarily connected with them. If then it were only as representing a longer course of study, classical acquirements should command a larger number of marks than those attainable by mathematics in an examination intended to serve as a general or educational test of mental development.

Supposing, however, that the two branches of a liberal education were entitled to equal weight in examinations designed to test the amount of intellectual culture and general capacity, it would still remain to be considered, which of the two accomplishments is more likely to form a useful basis for the ulterior employments of the successful candidates, in the two great fields of competition now open to the youth of England—the Civil Service in India, and the emoluments and honourable sinecures of the great Universities. These supplementary considerations shall be treated separately, as I have proposed them above.

The framers of the scheme for the examination of candidates for the Civil Service in India have expressly, and for good reasons assigned, repudiated the idea of making the examination special or professional in regard to the future employments of the successful competitors. Notwithstanding this, the test of general capacity must have some reference, however tacit, to the demands of the service, on the staff of which these young men aspire to be placed. And if there is a chance or reasonable prospect that the progressive development of a training in

language will be more useful than the progressive development of a training in mathematical science, this, at least,
should add some force to the other reasons for giving a
greater encouragement to the former. In the examinations for the military service of this country, especially
in those which open an access to appointments in the
artillery and engineers, the accomplishments of the polytechnic school deserve special encouragement. A knowledge of pure mathematics and many applications of
that knowledge are much more important to the young
soldier than a facility in writing Greek iambics and Latin
alcaics. And yet the case of Colonel Rawlinson, not
to mention other instances, is sufficient to show that,
while a soldier does not fight the worse at Candahar
because he has written on the site of Ecbatana, or is engaged in decyphering cuneiform inscriptions, he may be
placed in positions where early scholarship may enable
him to render good service to literature and do credit to
his country in the arena of learned competition. The
civil servant of the East India Company, on the other
hand, is not called upon by his functions, whether finan-
cial or judicial, to know more of mathematical science
than is necessary as an element in liberal education, or to
possess more skill as a calculator than is involved in that
familiarity with the principles and processes of compu-
tation which is expected from every man of business.
But he does require, like all who hold office in India,
whether they be soldiers or civilians, to have cultivated
the faculty of language so as to be able to acquire a familiarity with the native idioms of the country in which
he is about to reside. General as the civil service examination is in other respects, it has a specialty suggested by
this demand for a linguistic apparatus. In addition to

the elements of a liberal education and besides the French, Italian, and German languages, a certain amount of marks are assigned to an examination in Sanscrit and Arabic. These two form a sort of practical basis for the chief spoken dialects of India and its conterminous states. For the Arabic, as the most completely developed and copious of the Semitic languages, furnishes the classic groundwork for a study of all the branches of that family, and the establishment of Mohammedism in the East has made the Koran a sacred book, and the Arabic characters the established form of writing, in many countries in which the language itself is still mainly Tartaric or Indo-German. Thus the Turkish, Persian, and Hindustani are written in Arabic characters, although the structure of these languages is not at all Semitic; and the Persian language, owing to twelve centuries of Mohammedan domination, has been deluged with Arabic words and phrases, though the basis of the language and its general organisation are still entirely Indo-Germanic. A knowledge of Arabic, therefore, could not fail to be of great practical use to any one holding office in India, especially if his duties called him to the north-westerly provinces. But whatever may be the utility of Arabic, the Indian official is especially called upon to acquaint himself with Sanscrit, which is the classical foundation or main element in the dead languages of India and Persia, namely, the Prâcrit, Pâli, and Vaidik of the former, and the Zend, Pehlevi, Parsi, and Cuneiform of the latter—and which furnishes a groundwork for the most complete study of the living dialects. Every one, therefore, whose occupations oblige him to converse in Bengali or Hindustani, would have reason to congratulate himself, if his previous studies had introduced him to the classical Sanscrit, and, as a competent authority has well remarked*, "even a judge who is sent to India will not find occasion for regret if he has read the laws of Manu in the original language, and acclimatised his mind to that intellectual atmosphere in which he is henceforth to live and act."

The reasons, which especially recommend the study of Sanscrit to the candidate for Indian employments, and which show that it may be more advantageously pursued in Europe than in the East, have been fully stated in an able paper, which appeared in the *Times* of the 18th and 20th October, 1855 †, and from which I will take the liberty of making a few extracts.

"While the great variety of the spoken dialects of India creates a difficulty which it might seem almost impossible to overcome, a remedy has been found in one language which, though no longer spoken, except by the learned, is really the source of all the modern languages of India, and will be as useful to the civilian in learning any one of the spoken dialects as Latin is to us in learning Italian, Spanish, Portuguese, French, and Wallachian; nay, almost as much as ancient Greek in learning modern Greek—I mean the Sanscrit.

"Sanscrit supplies the dictionary of all the spoken languages of India, even of those which, like Telugu and Tamil, belong in their grammatical system to another family of speech. The proportion of Sanscrit words in Hindostanee, Bengalee, Hindee, Punjabee, Mahrattee, Guzeratee, Scindee, &c., has been variously stated at between three-fourths and nine-tenths of the vocabularies of each of these dialects. It is in reality impossible to fix it exactly, because every day new Sanscrit words, whether

---

* Max Müller, *Languages of the Seat of War*, p. xiii.
† *The Second Examination for the Indian Civil Service.*

by derivation or composition, are added to the stores of
the modern dialects. 'Every person acquainted with the
spoken speech of India knows perfectly well that its elevation to the dignity and usefulness of written speech has
depended, and must still depend, upon its borrowing
largely from its parent or kindred stock ; that no man
who is ignorant of Sanscrit can write Hindostanee or
Bengalee with elegance, purity, or precision.' New ideas
which are brought before the Hindoo mind by the intercourse with Europeans must invariably be expressed by
Sanscrit derivatives, and all expressions relating to religion, and Christianity in particular, can be obtained from
that source alone.

"Sanscrit, again, offers the key to the grammatical
system of all Indian dialects, with the exception of the
Deccan languages, such as Tamil, Telugu, &c. Although
the grammar of the modern vernaculars of India is by no
means perplexing, yet it becomes far easier and more intelligible if we know the original Sanscrit, from which all
the grammatical forms of the modern dialects are derived
by means of abbreviation, corruption, and composition.
The grammar of French is not difficult ; yet it is embar-
rassing to explain some of its peculiarities to persons
ignorant of Latin, and there are certain mistakes to which
such persons are liable in speaking French or Italian,
which a Latin scholar would avoid as if by instinct. The
same applies to the modern languages of India. What
can be more puzzling to a person unacquainted with the
origin of the grammar of Hindostanee and Mahrattee
than to find that in them the genitive of every substantive takes the signs of the masculine, feminine, and neuter
genders; that if we say the King of England, England
must take the masculine gender, while, if we speak of the

Queen of England, the genitive takes the feminine sign of
the genitive! To a Sanscrit scholar this peculiarity has
nothing strange or irregular, because he recognises in what
is called the termination of the genitive the same syllables
by which Sanscrit adjectives are formed, and which are
liable to the changes of gender on the same principle as
adjectives in Latin, where we may say *Rex Romanus* and
Regina Romana, in the sense of *Rex Romæ*.

"Here, then, we have a language which will prove
equally useful to all civilians, whatever their presidency
or station may be. It can be learnt with greater advantage in England than in India, because our grammars and
dictionaries are composed on a more rational plan than
those of the native grammarians. To learn Sanscrit from
a Pundit in India, according to the native system of
grammar, takes at least five times as much labour as in
Europe.

"The difficulty of acquiring a knowledge of Sanscrit
is generally much exaggerated. Fifty years ago Sanscrit
was a difficult language, because there were no good
grammars and dictionaries from which it could be learnt.
But at present we have both, and the ancient classical
language of India may now be learnt by anybody, whether
he has a turn for language or not. Industry alone is
required for it and perseverance, but neither talent nor
genius.

"Now, although Sanscrit is no longer spoken by the
population of India, yet I know from experience that a
person who knows Sanscrit may learn Bengalee in one
month. Evidence to the contrary effect as to Sanscrit
being a dead language and useless for learning the modern
dialects comes invariably from persons who, not having
mastered even the rudiments of Sanscrit, find to their

surprise that their knowledge, or rather their ignorance, of Sanscrit, is of no assistance to them in learning Hindostanee.

"Nor is Sanscrit altogether a dead language. The Brahmins, the most influential and highly educated class of people all over India, learn it, speak it, and write it. A well-educated Brahmin shuns the use of the modern dialects, and he writes Sanscrit more correctly than Bengalee or Mahrattee.

"These are some of the practical advantages which recommend the study of Sanscrit, and for which it has held hitherto—and it is desirable that it should hold in future—a prominent place among those subjects a study of which was considered obligatory for all civil servants before their departure from this country.

"In most countries the study of the living language would at once be the key to the literature, and, through it, to the national, moral, and religious character of a nation. This is not the case in India. The state of literature in India at the present day is about the same as that of Italy at, or rather before, the time of Dante. The spoken language is Hindostanee, or Bengalee, or Guzerattee, but the language of literature, law, and religion is still the classical Sanscrit. It has often been said that the modern languages of India stand to Sanscrit in the same relation as Italian, Spanish, and French to Latin; and it has been argued that, as we do not require our ambassadors and consuls in Italy, France, and Spain to be acquainted with Latin, but only with the modern languages and literature of those countries, it would be exacting too much were the civil servants of India to be required to study, not only Hindostanee or Bengalee, but also Sanscrit. Now, the analogy is true as far as language is concerned, but not with regard to literature. If we know the works of Molière, Voltaire, Montesquieu, Rousseau, La Mennais, and Guizot, we know enough to gain an insight into the national character and the mental peculiarities of the French nation; and, in order to become acquainted with the law and religion of that country, we are not bound to have recourse to works written in Latin. The case is quite different in India. There are, indeed, some popular works written in Hindostanee and Bengalee, and a new literary impulse has of late been given to these vernaculars by translating into them some of the works of Bacon, Mill, and other English authors. But that literature which really exercises an influence on the laws, the customs, the religious and intellectual life of India, is written entirely in Sanscrit—the Latin of that country. Since the time when Sanscrit ceased to be the spoken language of India, there has been no revival in the Indian mind; the classics of India are the same to-day as at the time of Alexander's conquest. The highest authority in religious matters is still the *Veda;* so is *Manu* on questions of law; *Gautama,* on points of logic; the *Mahábhárata, Rámáyana,* and the *Puránas* with regard to the history and traditions of India. The only people who have an influence over the Indian mind—an influence as great as the monks and priests ever had over the people of Spain and Italy—are the Brahmins, and the chief support of their spiritual supremacy is their knowledge of Sanscrit, the sacred language of the sacred literature of India. No national reform will be possible among the great masses of Hindostan before this all-pervading influence of the Brahmins has either been broken, or gained over to a better cause. Most attempts which have hitherto been made in this direction have

been made at random, and without a due appreciation of
the difficulties which have to be encountered. In order
to conquer or to win over an enemy, we must first know
his position, his defences, and his weapons, and we must
be able to convince him of the superiority of our own
arms for intellectual warfare, or to make him feel it.
Again, if European civilisation is to benefit the natives,
it must be made palatable and digestible, and this can
only be done by men who have studied the intellectual
diet of the Hindoos. A German book, turned into English, is frequently repugnant to English taste; but if a
man like Dr Arnold, who knows what the English public
requires, clothes the results of foreign learning in the
form of clear English argument, the effect is widely different. This is what the civil servants in India ought,
to a certain extent, to be able to do in their daily intercourse with the natives; they ought to be able to accom-
modate their thoughts and feelings, in form at least, to
the capacity of those with whom they have to deal. There
is much that is bad, but also much that is good in the
different systems of law, philosophy, religion, and morals
in India. If the natives perceive that their governors
are able to appreciate what is good in Indian literature,
that they can tolerate much that is indifferent, they will
be ready to listen to them when they point out frankly
what is vile and pernicious. Hitherto much that is positively bad, and of which even the more enlightened
Hindoos are ashamed, has been tolerated, not to say encouraged, by the English, while occasionally violent on-
slaughts have been made on harmless prejudices. In the
daily intercourse between English and natives the most
sensitive parts of man's nature have been unnecessarily
and unintentionally wounded, and, with one or two

exceptions, there has never been a *confidential intercourse
or a real friendship* between an Englishman and a Hindoo.
Yet a Hindoo is not a barbarian or a savage. According
to all accounts, even the poorest Hindoo has something
of the gentleman; his manners are simple, his appearance
pleasing. But the advances towards a mutual understanding and a feeling of fellowship must be made by the
stronger party. A civilian, who feels it his duty to keep
up a more than merely official intercourse with those of
his fellow-creatures among whom the greater part of his
life will be spent, must be able to show his native friends
that he understands their manner of looking at things;
he must be able to use their expressions, to adopt to a
certain extent their mode of arguing, to avoid what would
unnecessarily offend them, and to sympathise with what
they consider as grand and beautiful, of which there is
much more in their literary works than we should expect.
He ought, as much as possible, to see with their eyes and
to feel with their hearts, if he wish to exercise in turn a
beneficial influence on their views and their feelings, and
to improve gradually their social, moral, and religious
state. How much can be effected in this manner has
lately been proved again by the successful and most meritorious exertions of Dr Ballantyne at Benares. It is of
no avail to introduce trial by jury, and to import London
barristers conversant with all the quiddities of English
law, if the natives cannot be taught first to have confidence in their judges and respect for themselves. What
was trial by jury even in England at the time of Charles
II. ? What is it even now in Ireland whenever political
or religious questions are involved? In spite of the
respect which the Hindoos cannot help feeling for the
achievements of European civilisation and science, and

for the military superiority of their rulers, they have not
yet been taught to look upon the English as their friends
and benefactors, and they still listen with implicit faith
to their spiritual instructors, who tell them that all
Europeans are *mlechas*, or outcasts, sent to govern the
twice-born race of India during the Kaliyuga by way of
punishment for national iniquity. How easy would it be
to remove these prejudices if it was done in a kindly and
respectful spirit ! But this can only be expected from
men who take a lively interest in the people of India,
and this living interest, unless it is roused by Christian
charity, is best awakened and kept up by a careful study
of Indian—that is, Sanscrit literature.

"It is in human nature that we take an interest in
matters to which we have devoted much of our time and
about which we know something. A student of art will
learn to admire pictures which to the unschooled eye are
simply repulsive. A student of history will spend many
days in searching for a document which to others might
seem valueless. It will be the same with those who have
paid some attention to the study of Sanscrit language
and literature. As a classical scholar is moved when he
sees the unchanged shores of Greece rising on the horizon
—as he feels an interest in hearing for the first time the
spoken Greek, with its living accent—as he is pleased
when reminded by what passes before his eyes of the
customs, the legends, and the poetry of the classical past
—nay, as he cannot altogether withdraw his sympathy
even from the degenerate descendants of an ancient and
noble race, the Sanscrit scholar also will look to the shores
of India and its dark inhabitants with an interest unknown to those who go there unprepared or full of prejudices, and are wont to speak of the natives as ' a parcel

of black fellows.' A study of Sanscrit and an acquaintance with the classical works of the Brahmins nerve and
tune the mind for the most important part of a civilian's
duty—that of gaining the goodwill, the confidence, and
ready co-operation of those whom he is sent to govern.
He will be anxious to meet those who still speak the
language to which he has devoted so many hours; he will
have questions to ask, and his hours of leisure will not be
hours of idleness. Conversation with the natives will
soon become a pleasure to him, because his knowledge of
Sanscrit will make him feel at home in almost any dialect
of India. At present, 'it is notorious that many of the
company's servants, familiar with the jargon of the courts,
are quite incompetent to carry on conversation with a
native of respectability and education,' and this arises
mainly from their ignorance of Sanscrit. 'Every student
who has gone to India with a respectable knowledge of
Sanscrit has shown himself at home among the people,
and displayed a warm interest in their welfare and improvement.'

"It is impossible to teach in England all the spoken
languages of India; they can be learnt better abroad;
nay, by carrying their study too far in this country, an
Englishman might actually acquire what he would have
to unlearn in India—a bad pronunciation and an unidio-
matic style. Nor is there much in the literature of these
modern dialects which would be of use by supplying a
knowledge of India and its inhabitants. None of these
objections apply to Sanscrit. It can be better taught in
this country than abroad; it will prove equally useful for
all the Presidencies of India, it will give an insight into
the character of the Indian nation, and change very general prejudices against the natives into an interest in

their past, and a sympathy for their present condition. Sanscrit, therefore, should be made an obligatory study for all probationers without any exception, and nobody should be allowed to proceed to India who could not at least construe the laws of Manu.

" Nothing could be a greater mistake than to force every civil servant to make himself a thorough Sanscrit scholar. There may be one in a hundred who, having taste for scholarship, might aspire to the position which men like Sir W. Jones, Colebrooke, Wilson, Dr Mill, Macnaghten, and Muir have held in India. They will be the exceptions. But no consideration should be paid to a clamour raised by men who, professing a want of talent for languages, wish only to avoid the trouble which the learning of a new alphabet and of some pages of paradigms of declension and conjugation entails on the student.

" If all probationers are bound to acquire a knowledge of Sanscrit grammar and to read extracts from the 'Hito-padesa' and 'Manu' during the one or two years between their first and second examination, the study of the modern dialects in this country may almost be dispensed with altogether, or be reduced to a very small amount. With a previous knowledge of Sanscrit, a man may learn on his journey to India enough of Hindostanee and Bengalee to enable him to pass his first examination in India in three months."

Now whatever reasons there may be for encouraging the direct study of Sanscrit in this country, as a preparation for official life in India, these must operate likewise as reasons for encouraging the study of Latin and Greek, in proportion as classical scholarship, and the comparative philology connected with it, are the best access and securest foundation for a complete and accurate knowledge of Sanscrit. For to the same extent as Sanscrit facilitates the study of Bengali, comparative philology facilitates the study of Sanscrit, and the classical languages, especially the Greek, are the best basis of comparative philology. I may speak with some confidence on this subject, after spending some twenty years in developing certain principles, which have been more tardily adopted on the continent[7]. For while the Germans have generally taken the Sanscrit as their starting-point in all their researches in comparative philology, and while they still exhibit, as I have recently said[*], a tendency to find Sanscrit everywhere, and to allow the classical languages no independent development, but rather to make them only the faint echoes of the more distinct utterances, which were heard on the banks of the Ganges, I have been engaged for many years in the task, which I was the first to attempt, namely, the prosecution of comparative philology, and other developments of critical learning, on the safe and ascertained basis of the old classical scholarship; and I have endeavoured to show that the Greek language especially is better fitted than any other to furnish a starting-point for investigations in general grammar, because it stands midway between the oldest form of the Indo-Germanic and the corrupted modern dialects of that family. The same reasons, which qualify the Greek scholar for the successful study of comparative grammar in general, also make it an easier matter for him than for any mere novice in inflected language to grapple with the difficulties of Sanscrit. To those who have had no previous discipline in learning the multitudinous details of form-building, which belong to

* *Journal of Classical and Sacred Philology,* No. VI. p. 349.

the grammar of a highly inflected language, Sanscrit presents an amount of labour from which ordinary minds are too apt to shrink, and it is said that the Pundits occupy themselves for an unheard-of period in learning and teaching the declensions and conjugations, which are mere child's play or matters of course, to those who have gone through the severer effort of memory imposed by the complex structure of Greek. The nature of this effort is well described by C. O. Müller. "We will ask any person, who is acquainted with Greek, to recal to his mind the toils and fatigue which he underwent in mastering the forms of the language, and the difficulty which he found to impress them on his memory; when his mind, vainly attempting to discover a reason for such anomalies, was almost in despair at finding that so large a number of verbs derive their tenses from the most various roots; that one verb uses only the first, another only the second aorist, and that even the individual persons of the aorist are sometimes compounded of the forms of the first and second aorists respectively; and that many verbs and substantives have retained only single or a few forms which have been left standing by themselves, like the remains of a past age*." These difficulties vanish in proportion as the subject is treated in the spirit of comparative philology; and in precisely the same proportion the study of Greek paves the way directly for that of Sanscrit.

The Greek scholar, who, instead of being a victim to the old-fashioned empiricism of the Eton grammar, has his eyes opened, and can really see the anatomical structure of the classical languages, has made some progress in Sanscrit grammar by the regular course of his own studies.

* *Literature of Ancient Greece*, i. p. 7.

When he has learned that the substantive verb was originally ἐσμί, ἐσσί, ἐστί, ἐσμέν, ἐστέ, ἐντί, or in Latin *esum, es, est, esumus, estis, esunt*, he has learned also the Sanscrit *asmi, asi, asti, 'smas, 'stha, santi*. When he has been taught that the conjugation in -μι was antecedent to that in -ω, he is prepared for the whole verb-system of the Sanscrit; and it does not cost him much effort to pass from δίδωτι, φέρω, ὀ-δόντα, πατήρ, μητρί, φρατήρ, θυγα-τέρα(ν), ναῦν, ὀ-φρύς, &c., to *dadâti, bharâmi, dantam, pitâ(r), mâtrê, bhrâtrî, duhitaram, nâvam, bhrû(s)*, &c. Prepositional and other compounds, which are quite novelties to the mere English learner, occasion no surprise to him who has served his apprenticeship in classical Greek. Thus, the intensive force of the prefix in περι-χαρής, &c., appears also in the Sanscrit *pari-tarp-itas*, (περι-τερπ-ό-μενος,) &c., and the compound epithet *un-mârga-jala-vâhini* (sc. *srotânsi*) applied to overflowing streams " out-of-the-margin-carrying-the-cold-water," (*ex-margine-gelu-vehentia*,) is Ovid's phrase concisely expressed[*]. The orthographic laws of *Sandhi*, which constitute a principal difficulty in Sanscrit, are trivial in the eyes of the scholar who is familiar with the Greek rules for contraction, synalœpha, and crasis; and those who know how the final *m* and *s* are treated in Latin are quite prepared to acquiesce in the *anuswâra* and *visargah* of the Indian grammarians.

Still more easy is all this, if the Greek scholar is also an Englishman, and has in the course of his literary culture studied his own language, which, in its primitive Saxon texture, contains many traces of that old Iranian dialect, which was spoken in Sogdiana and Bactriana long before these tribes carried the religion of Brahma to the Ganges

[*] *Fast.* II. 219—222.

and the worship of Wodan to the Baltic, and founded empires in the East and West, which were destined to be fused again into one community, by the countrymen of Clive and Warren Hastings. When Bopp, the great comparative philologer, was engaged at an early age in the combined study of Sanscrit and Gothic, he wrote to his friend Windischmann that "he could fancy he was reading Sanscrit, when he read the venerable Ulphilas, whose language seemed to stand midway between Sanscrit and German, and contained many genuine Indian words, which the German had lost*." As the high German here referred to is much farther removed from Gothic than the Anglo-Saxon, which forms the basis of our own language, it is still more interesting to the English scholar to trace his own mother-tongue in the ancient language, which was spoken by the ancestors of his Indian fellow-subjects.

That Sanscrit editorship and criticism flourishes more in Europe than in the East is shown in a hundred ways; but there is not a more conspicuous proof than that which is furnished by the case of the *Ramáyana*, the great Sanscrit Epic poem. There are two distinct recensions or different texts of this work—one, which is called, not quite correctly, the edition of the commentators, and which is supposed to have been settled at Benares; the other, which belongs to the Bengal school, and is called *Gaudana* from *Gauda*, the ancient name of the central region of Bengal and of its now destroyed capital. Now in the years 1806—1810, two Englishmen, W. Carey and J. Marshman, assisted by native Pundits, published at

* Franz Bopp, *über das Conjugations-system der Sanskrit-sprache herausgegeben von* Dr K. J. Windischmann, Francfurt am Main, 1816, p. x.

Serampoor a considerable portion of the *Ramáyana*, with an English version. Not to speak of their blunders in Sanscrit scholarship, these editors, and the assistant Pundits, jumbled together the two distinct recensions of the book, and so produced inextricable confusion. All this has been remedied in Europe, and we have now the whole or a part of the *Ramáyana* critically revised according to the two texts, the edition of the commentators having been commenced by A. W. Schlegel*, and that of the Gaudana school having been brought to a conclusion by G. Gorresiot†.

The preponderance of encouragement, which is or ought to be given in the great Universities to classics as compared with mathematics, will require only a brief justification after what has been already urged under the head of University teaching. Admitting and conceding most fully all that can be said in recommendation of mathematics as a necessary branch of academical study, I still maintain that the distinctive acquirements of the classical scholar and philologer contribute more directly and more extensively to the furtherance of those objects, which are formally proposed for ulterior pursuit in a great seat of learning. I do not need to be told that there are many branches of physical science, which ought to occupy a foremost rank in the studies of a University, and which not only admit but require a mathematical treatment; I am not disposed to leave the discoveries of practical science entirely to civil engineers, in whose training we can claim no share, or to military men, who

* *Ramáyana : textum codd. MSS. collatis recensuit*, A. G. a Schlegel. Bonn, 1829—1838.

† *Ramáyana: testo Sanscrito secondo i codici manoscritte della scuolo Gaudana per* Gaspare Gorresio. Parigi, 1843, e. s. a.

got their first lessons at Woolwich or Sandhurst, or to
self-taught chemists, who reflect no light on any educational institution ; it is not less a matter of triumphant
gratification to me than to the more scientific members of
the University of Cambridge, when some Cambridge geo-
meter discovers a new planet by working out the problem
in his own study, or when some Cambridge mechanician
developes, as a manufacturer, some new methods of combining and working mineral products.   Nay, I am prepared to admit that the precision of Cambridge scholarship, as distinguished from that of the sister University,
is mainly due to the mathematical character of the University, and to the rigorous system of examinations, which
our mathematical studies contributed to introduce among
us.   But while I concede all this, and more if necessary,
I must still maintain that classical scholarship deserves
more encouragement than mathematical skill in a great
University, not only because its acquisition costs more
time and labour, not only because it represents the larger
and better part of the discipline proper to humanity, but
also because it has more to do with the general business
of the University as such.   That an increasing perception
of this has been observable at Cambridge in particular is
well known to all who are acquainted with the recent
history of the place, and with the tendency of the improvements, which we have gradually introduced into our
system.   The obvious design of the most effective changes,
which have spread from our greatest College to the University at large, has been, not to add to the old preponderance of mathematics, but, on the contrary, to require
of mathematicians a larger proportion of literary culture.
No small contributions to this end have been made by
the eminent Historian of the Inductive Sciences ; for

although, as I have endeavoured to prove, Dr Whewell still claims for mathematics a larger share in the business of a liberal education than really belongs to this department of knowledge, he has done more than any mathematician at Cambridge to create a more literary and learned school of mathematical science, and to give us something above and beyond the dry and technical machinery of instrumental analytics, which, at one time, seemed to be the only delight of our writers on these subjects. Being himself, as every one knows, both a great mathematician and a great man of letters, he has induced many others to take a wider range, and we do not now find many specimens of the same class as the old Cambridge Professor, who would not read Milton because the Paradise Lost did not prove anything! And in thus speaking of the increased cultivation of literature by those who have primarily devoted themselves to the exact sciences, I cannot refrain from a passing reference to that noble mathematician, who though stricken down by the heavy hand of an incurable malady, has not only retained his promised share in the good work of editing Francis Bacon, but has drawn up or rather dictated a masterly plan for one of the most difficult works in philology—a dictionary of the Chinese language—an effort which shows that the unclouded intellect of a man of genius may triumph over all the worst distractions of bodily weakness and suffering. Still, if I may venture to say so, a good deal remains to be done. It would be well if Cambridge mathematicians could be called upon to show their knowledge of the origin and literary history of their own science; if the successors of Newton and Waring were expected to read their capital works in the originals; if the great literary productions of Laplace and Lagrange were made the subjects of professed study and direct examination*; and if it were not still too much the custom to undervalue general discussions and comprehensive explanations of the grounds of pure mathematics. Such a book, for example, on the Differential Calculus, as that which has lately been published at Oxford by Professor Price, seems to me a great improvement on those curt treatises with $d_x y$ and $\int_x$, which I was recommended to read in my undergraduate days. But if mathematicians might fairly be called upon to show that they were worthy members of a learned and literary University, still more would this be incumbent on the graduates of the higher Faculties of Divinity, Law and Medicine. On this point I have already said all that is necessary. I will only add that if music is to have its doctorate at Oxford and Cambridge, I trust it will also conduce to form a school of learned musicians. But independently of ancient faculties, there are many developments of literature, in which the Universities take a part, and which derive great assistance from the ancillary labours of the scholar. History, both ancient and modern, must always depend for a large proportion of its illustration on the labours of the philologer. The great history of Gibbon, as Niebuhr has truly observed†, is a noble masterwork even in a philological point of view; and the same might be said of Milman's *Latin Christianity*. Mr Macaulay's history, modern as it is in subject, style and ideas, owes some of its chief attractions to the classical training of its author. Jomini places Alexander and Cæsar by the side of Frederic on the tribunal before which

---

* Have all senior wranglers even read the treatise, *On Probability?*

† *Hist. of Rome*, I. p. VIII.

Napoleon is cited to defend his strategy *, and Napier's *Annals of the Peninsular War*, though full of modern gunpowder, are dedicated to Wellington in the spirit of a Roman legate. The fine arts cannot be discussed, or their choicest examples appreciated, without some knowledge of ancient literature. The guide-books, written to illustrate the collections in the Crystal Palace, are many of them abridged treatises on subjects belonging to classical literature. If any one would know how far geography is dependent on the old learning, he has only to inspect the bulky volumes of Karl Richter. Even natural history cannot travel on its route of observation without some retrospective reference to Aristotle, Theophrastus and Dioscorides; and the demand for a new edition of Pliny the elder was more strenuously urged by Cuvier and Oken than by any professed student of antiquity. But ethnography, that new-born child of philology, which cannot yet walk without the parent's aid,—ethnography, which is led by its speculations into ages long before the first rise of history, —ethnography alone would be a sufficient excuse for any amount of encouragement to those grammatical studies in which it took its rise; for as man is the apex of creation, "that science, which treats of his origin and growth, and which is now established on a basis as firm as that of physiology, is capable of becoming the end and the goal of all the labours and all the transactions of a scientific and learned institution †."

* Both Frederic and Napoleon were diligent students of the best classical authors, i. e. in French translations; see Hahn's *Friedrich der Grosse*, p. 177. *Mémoires du Roi Joseph*, I. p. 32.

† Bunsen, *Report of the British Association*, for 1847, p. 257.

III. SCHOLARSHIP AND LEARNING.

EVEN among those who have gone along with me in the previous discussion, there will be some, who will maintain that classical learning is not cultivated as it ought to be in this country, and that the amount of time and labour bestowed on classical acquirements is out of all proportion to the results, which we secure. That there is some truth in this view of the matter it seems impossible to deny; and I have long thought that the account between scholarship and learning might be more accurately and fairly balanced; that we might gain somewhat more of the latter without relinquishing what we already have of the former; that the practical skill, on which we pride ourselves, might be retained without any sacrifice of the scientific knowledge, which we might acquire in greater measure; that the educational test might be all that it is without seeming to close the access to a progressive development of the studies on which it rests; and that by a better arrangement of our school training, we might do all we now attempt, and even more, in Greek and Latin without seeming to devote all the years of boyhood to studies, in which only a few can attain to any striking proficiency. I shall therefore conclude this discourse by explaining those improvements in our method of teaching and examining, which seem to me most likely to effect the desired objects. But I feel myself compelled, in the first instance, to vindicate the scholarship of England from a wholesale and sweeping disparagement, which has originated in that tendency to exaggerate deficiencies so common in the zealous advocacy of reforms.

The distinction between scholarship and learning, between the educational and literary effects of philological training, has, in fact, been superseded by an invidious comparison between England and Germany. It is not thought sufficient to tell us, that our scholarship too often fails to ripen into learning. In the most positive and authoritative manner the public has been repeatedly informed that the Germans are infinitely superior to the English in every result of classical study. To some it might appear strange that such admissions or invectives should proceed from our own countrymen. But dissatisfaction, at first only partial, grows wanton in its extravagance; and the odious comparison is often the readiest safety-valve for our indignation. Thus in the Crimea, we were not content with indicating how the English might have managed better—still less did we make the most of their positive merits. It was much more soothing to our disappointed feelings to dilate upon the infinite superiority of our gallant allies; and, to save the trouble of a detailed examination, we effaced the creditor side of the account.

I think that this is a subject, which ought to be discussed on its own merits, independently of any opinions respecting the details of University reform; if for no other reason, because practical injustice is constantly done to English scholars, who are rewarded for the candour, with which they recognise the characteristic excellences of the Germans, by the tacit inference or open reproach that they are themselves fit only to translate and copy the works of their contemporaries. And I grieve to say that, although a cosmopolitan spirit ought to animate the professors of every branch of literature, the narrow and national view is sustained by the arrogant pretensions of some of the Germans themselves[8].

In undertaking to meet the issue, which has been raised, and to show that our classical scholarship is superior and our classical learning not in all respects inferior to that of the Germans, I merely wish to correct exaggeration by stating what I believe to be the truth. I have no prejudice to maintain, for I have been connected with the literary activity of both nations. I have published a work of my own in Germany, and I took a share in translating from the author's manuscripts a work of C. O. Müller's, which appeared first and was intended only to appear in England. This is not the first time that I have attempted to do justice both to English and German philology[*], and though I have expressed my satisfaction that circumstances enabled me to pass through the school of Bentley and Porson before I entered that of Buttmann and Niebuhr[†], I should be truly sorry if German learning lost its value in the eyes of English scholars.

The exaggerated depreciation, to which I have referred, reached its culminating point about two years since. In the debate of Thursday the 27th April, 1854, on the Oxford University Bill, Mr Horsman delivered a long and elaborate speech, in the course of which he made the following remarks :—

" It was objected to every system of reform that it had a tendency to Germanise the Universities; but if there were any such danger it already existed to a deplorable extent, as we had permitted the Germans to surpass us even in those studies which we called our own. The

[*] *New Cratylus*, §§ 29, 30.   [†] *Ibid*, p. x.

German student employed in the study of philosophy, history, and divinity the time which the English student devoted to Greek and Latin; and, therefore, we had at least a right to expect that great works upon the ancient languages would be produced, and that great scholars would be educated at the Universities; but this was not the case, and not only did the Germans monopolise the fields which we neglected, but it was notorious that they surpassed us in classical studies.   All the most improved editions of classical works were German; all the great modern commentators were Germans; and it was the same in ancient history and philosophy, as Niebuhr's work upon Roman history, for instance, was a fountain from which all our knowledge on that subject was drawn. The Germans were now our masters in every branch of philology, although this was not the case in the days of Bentley and Porson, who were the equals of any scholars in Europe of their own time.   So completely was the preeminence of the Germans in these branches of literature acknowledged, that when a scholar, like one who was formerly a member of that house (Mr Grote), gave new interest and threw new light upon Grecian history, this circumstance only increased our surprise, that, for scholarship so deep and for acquirements so vast as were displayed in that great work, our English Universities afforded no welcome and no home."

To this sweeping disparagement, resting, as I shall show it does, on a total misconception or wilful ignorance of the facts of the case, even Mr Gladstone was contented to oppose the very gentle remark that "with a fair and dispassionate spirit, Mr Horsman's observations were pervaded by a tone of exaggeration;" and the representative of Oxford seemed to admit the neglect of learning among

9

us, when he put in a plea for "the active and practical
disposition of the English people, and the tendency of all
men to hurry in early life to the discharge of its active
duties." But although I could have wished that distinguished Oxford graduates, like Gladstone, Cardwell, Lowe,
Phinn, and others, who were or might have been present,
had not been prevented by their political sympathies or
want of interest in the subject, from giving an immediate
and peremptory contradiction to Mr Horsman's extravagant depreciation of English scholarship[9], it would not
perhaps have been worth my while to submit the flimsy
texture of a parliamentary speech to the ordeal of deliberate examination, or indeed to revive a recollection of it
after so long an interval, if the opinions expressed by the
honourable member for Stroud had not been encouraged
by others, who, perhaps, have had better opportunities of
forming an adequate judgment, or were at all events
bound, by the nature of their writings, to observe greater
circumspection than can be demanded of a fluent orator.
Among these, the eminent Oxford Professor, to whose
able pamphlet I have made more than one reference, in
his anxiety to uphold the professorial system has endeavoured to show that "the marvellous fertility of Professorial Universities in learning and talent[*]" is exhibited
in a remarkable manner by the fact that "not only the
familiar, but almost the only books known to classical
literature, are those furnished by a Professoriate[†];" and he

---

[*] Halford Vaughan, *Oxford Reform and Oxford Professors*, p. 58.
[†] *Ibid*, p. 64. To show the careless exaggeration of ex parte
statements, I might call attention to the blunder about Dr Thirlwall
and his *History of Greece*, made by Prof. Vaughan in this page.
"Thirlwall, when banished from his office in Trinity College, solaced
his retirement like Thucydides by composing his *History of Greece*."

favours us with an appendix "on the scholarship of Germany," by Mr Conington, of University College, who has since become Professor of Latin, and of whom, both on personal and on public grounds, I am bound to speak with all respect and friendliness. In this appendix we are told with great confidence and no small affectation of detailed accuracy, but really with the omission of much that ought to have been said on the other side, that the continental method of instruction has produced, especially in Germany, all the good books on classical literature which have appeared for many years.

Now these statements are not only unjust, and, because unjust, offensive to the scholars of Oxford and Cambridge and to all English scholars, with the exception perhaps of Mure and Grote, who are ostentatiously put forward as nurslings of Germany; they are also practically mischievous; they are calculated, if not intended, to throw discredit upon the existing system of our studies and upon the studies themselves. And I feel that I shall be doing a service, not only acceptable to those whose feelings must be hurt by this unfair depreciation or contemptuous disallowance of their labours, but also required of any writer on this subject who is jealous of his country's honour, if I show conclusively that German scholarship as distinguished from learning is not superior, but, on the contrary, essentially and radically inferior to that of England, according to all the tests of relative merit; and that the mode of making scholars on the continent is not

This is to prove by an example that our ancient historians have been "aliens or outcasts from the University System." The fact is, that Thirlwall's *History* was undertaken as a part of Lardner's *Cyclopædia* in 1832, and that the first volume was actually published before the author left College in 1835.

calculated to produce more satisfactory results than those which we have always attained, and may attain, in still higher measure, by our own time-honoured method of classical education.

The assertion, that German scholarship is at this moment superior to that of our countrymen, is made to rest upon the fallacy, that the best test of scholarship is the number of books written on subjects connected with classical literature, in other words, that *scholarship*, as an educational result, is gauged by the amount of literary production on *learned* subjects. If I had any difficulty in meeting Mr Horsman on his own ground, I should begin by showing that this is by no means the only or most important criterion—that, in the strict sense of the term, it is not a criterion of *scholarship* at all. As, however, I deny that England is altogether inferior to Germany, even in regard to the evidence of literary merit and successful literary production, I shall reserve the considerations of those causes and developments of scholarship which are independent of book-making, and shall advert in the first instance to the literary reputation of English scholars.

As the Universities are the primary object of the disparagement, which I desire to rectify, and as the House of Commons was the recipient of the most prominent attack on English scholarship, I shall select my first justification of the learned literature of England, so far as the Universities are concerned, from the records of the same assembly. In a debate on the Universities, which took place on the 10th April, 1845, Mr Ewart anticipated the remarks of Mr Horsman. He entered, says the *Times*, into a statement of considerable length, of which the burden was the depreciation of the English, and the ex-

altation of the German Universities.   To this speech a
reply was made by the late Mr Goulburn, at that time
Chancellor of the Exchequer and member for the University of Cambridge.   He at once met the question by an
enumeration of living writers who had proceeded from
one or other of our Universities.   " If," he said, " he were
to read the whole list of literary men, he should only
fatigue the House with the number; but he could not
but allude to Mr Hallam; Dr Thirlwall, Bishop of St
Davids; Dr Gaisford; Mr Donaldson; Dr Blomfield,
Bishop of London; and Dr Monk, Bishop of Gloucester.
All these, together with the scientific men whom he had
previously cited, were members of one or other of our two
Universities, and were equal, if not superior, to the Professors of any of the German Universities whom Mr Ewart
had praised so lavishly."   This vindication was received
without question by a crowded house, and as the persons,
whose names were mentioned, were still alive, in April,
1854, it is the more remarkable that Mr Horsman should
have repeated the disparagement of Mr Ewart without
receiving any corresponding reply.   The eleven years,
which have elapsed since this former debate, have con-
firmed the truth of Mr Goulburn's answer by an increased
productiveness of learned literature in this country, and
even without this it would be easy to show that the
Germans themselves have virtually admitted what was
claimed for the writers on classical subjects, mentioned by
the late right honourable member for Cambridge.   Mr
Hallam, who is far beyond my praise, belongs to the
glories of our general or modern literature, and there is
no German writer who ought to be mentioned in the
same breath with him, although Mr Macaulay and Lord
Mahon—now Lord Stanhope—deserve a place in the same

niche of our libraries. The classical scholars mentioned
by Mr Goulburn have all written chiefly on those subjects
in which the advocates of University-Reform have claimed
such decided superiority for the Germans; and they have all
received from the Germans themselves the strongest testimony to the inadmissible nature of this claim of superiority.
Dr Thirlwall's History of Greece, a work in eight volumes,
has been, either in whole or in part, translated into
German under the auspices of one of the most original
and learned of the German Professors; a clear proof that
all the bookmaking of Leipsig and Berlin had failed to
produce a similar work; and it is remarkable that an able
and enlightened German scholar, now settled in Scotland,
Dr Schmitz of Edinburgh, has chosen this work as the
materials from which to make an abridgment of Greek
history, rather than any of the histories written by his
countrymen. The late Dr Gaisford's edition of *Hephœstion*
was long out of print in England, and could only be obtained in a literal copy on German paper published at
Leipsig. His splendid and most accurate edition of
Suidas, which is one of the chief glories of the University
Press at Oxford, had no sooner appeared in England,
than Bernhardy proceeded to reprint it in parts for the
benefit of those who wanted the learning without the
typographical beauty of the English edition. And before
this, Bähr had adopted Gaisford's text as the basis of his
recension of *Herodotus*. If any one will read the catalogue of Dr Gaisford's publications, which has been published since his recent death, he will see that no German,
not even Immanuel Bekker, has been more prolific in
editorship. Monk's *Euripides* and Blomfield's *Æschylus*
were similarly adopted in Germany by publishers, who
thought that such valuable and accurate commentaries

ought not to be withheld from students who could not afford to pay for white paper and Porsonian types. With regard to myself, I have no wish to justify or excuse Mr Goulburn's mention of my name in conjunction with those of men who were scholars before I was born; but I have not been afraid at all events to enter into direct competition with my teachers on the continent, and while I am quite prepared, if necessary, to maintain the ground which I have invaded and occupied, I have not discovered on the part of my German contemporaries any unwillingness to receive me into their ranks as a volunteer ally, fighting under their banners against superstition, ignorance, and falsehood[10]. At any rate, as far as the other names in Mr Goulburn's list are concerned, it cannot be said that the Germans have not acknowledged that the scholars produced by Oxford and Cambridge belong to the same class as themselves.

But we are not confined to Mr Goulburn's list: many works, which have appeared since 1845, and are appearing in greater numbers every year, evince in a remarkable manner the solid results of our University system; and I have had opportunities of forming an opinion respecting some labours still in progress, which do not the less establish the learned activity of England, because their authors have exhibited no precipitancy in rushing into print.

Mr Charles Merivale's History of the Roman Empire, of which three bulky volumes are already before the public, has been recognised everywhere as a work likely to form a worthy companion to the immortal labours of Gibbon. In the midst of his political occupations Sir G. C. Lewis has brought out a treatise *on the credibility of early Roman History*, which, for solidity of argument

and comprehensiveness of research, leaves far behind all
the continental writings on the same subject.　If Dean
Liddell's more general history is deficient in those qualities of style, which our scholarship makes us expect and
require in this country, it is not inferior to the common
run of German books in that respect, and is quite equal to
the best of them in sound and accurate learning.　Classical geography has always been pursued with unequivocal
success by Englishmen, and we have lately had a master-
piece of this kind in Mr R. Ellis's work on Hannibal's
Passage of the Alps.　On many questions of Greek
antiquities and art we have excellent essays in Smith's
Dictionary.　Professor Ramsay of Glasgow, who was a
distinguished pupil of Dr Thirlwall at Trinity College,
Cambridge, has published in an unpretending form a
treatise on Roman antiquities, which renders it quite unnecessary for our students to have recourse to the researches of German archæologists.　Professor Browne of
King's College, London, who was a first-class man at
Oxford, has drawn up in three volumes a very popular
and readable history of Greek and Roman literature;
and though, of course, such a work must be more or less
of the nature of a compilation, his acknowledgments are
addressed to English rather than to German scholars.

Mr Horsman has told us that "we have at least a
right to expect that great works upon the ancient languages would be produced" at Oxford and Cambridge.
To this it would be sufficient to answer that—whether
great or little, good or bad—the *only* professed and detailed
treatises of the kind happen to be English; and that
in the University of Dublin, where the scientific philology of the Greek and Latin languages forms one subject
of special study by the candidates for classical honours,

the text-books are not translations from the German,—
and indeed there are no German treatises which could be
used for the purpose,—but two works which were the
fruit of my own Cambridge studies*. I have no right
to complain that Mr Conington, in his glorification
of the Germans, makes no direct mention of these
books. But when he says †, "the vestiges of the
early languages of Italy, the very existence of which has
scarcely been noticed by any English scholar but Dr
Donaldson, have been made the subjects of elaborate
research by an increasing number of German savants, such
as Mommsen, Aufrecht, and Kirchhoff," I really cannot
acquiesce in this exceptional allusion to my labours; for
the German writers referred to are mere collectors of
materials which exist elsewhere, whereas I have subordi-
nated my researches to a comprehensive and consistent
theory, involving some discoveries, or at least new combinations, in ethnography. It seems likely, from some
recent contributions to the further elucidation of the subject ‡, that my hypothesis respecting the ethnography of
ancient Italy will eventually approve itself to others as it
has already done to my judgment; and then it will be
remembered that Dr Freund has excluded his countrymen
from all participation in a discovery, of which the importance cannot be overrated. I am also, as a duty to myself, obliged to protest against Mr Conington's statement

* See Dublin *University Calendar* for 1855, pp. 36, and cxx.

† *Ubi supra*, p. 101.

‡ See especially two papers in the *Journal of Classical and
Sacred Philology*, No. IV. pp. 1—20, No. V. pp. 169—185. Grimm
seems to be coming over to my views; he says, as quoted in this
paper (p. 179), "einzelnes in etruskischen sage und sprache klingt
an germanische." Aufrecht has since noticed some Scandinavian
affinities in the Etruscan (Bunsen, *Philosophy of Univ. History*, I. p. 88).

that "our Greek grammars are either translations or adaptations of foreign works—Matthiæ's, Kühner's, and Madvig's." I have expressly said, in the preface to my own Greek Grammar (p. x.), that it "lays claim to originality in regard to the principles on which it rests, the arrangement of the materials, and most of the characteristic details;" and I am not aware that any German writer has anticipated or superseded either the etymological system, which was put forth in 1839, or the analysis of syntax, which was first published in a Latin form nearly eleven years ago.

But classical editorship is the grand *cheval de bataille* both with Mr Horsman and with Mr Conington. "*All the most improved editions* of classical works are German; *all* the great modern commentators are Germans." This is Mr Horsman's confident exaggeration, which is perhaps based on Mr Conington's one-sided catalogue. I meet this sweeping assertion by a contradiction equally decisive. And first with regard to the Greek authors.

For the last quarter of a century, we were told to expect the *editio absoluta* of Æschylus from the long-continued labours of Godfrey Hermann. This work appeared after the death of the Leipsig veteran, and is universally regarded as a literary disappointment—a feeling which is shared by Mr Conington himself. In the mean time, Mr F. A. Paley, whose religious opinions have disconnected him from the University, where his name, like that of his grandfather, deserves a distinguished place, has given the world a complete edition of Æschylus, in which criticisms and explanations full of learning and good taste are couched in terse, simple, and pure Latinity, such as few of the Germans could imitate*. I am quite

* He has lately republished his *Æschylus* with English notes.

unable to understand why Mr Conington has omitted all
mention of this feat of English scholarship, of which he
had elsewhere recorded his high opinion. My learned
friend, who consents to act as the Oxford *institor* of German merchandize, is contented with placing Blomfield
below Klausen and Müller. I have a high opinion of the
latter of these commentators, an opinion not affected by
the contemptuous tone of Hermann's controversy with
him on the subject of his *Eumenides;* but I think very
little of Klausen ; and among the reasons which prevent
us from giving any great credit to Dr Peile, as an editor
of Æschylus, I must specify his fondness for this German
editor, and the Germanesque cumbrousness of his own
Commentary. Mr Linwood, of Christ Church, Oxford,
has published an edition of the *Eumenides*, and a Lexicon
to the whole of Æschylus. Though inferior, as I think,
to Paley in accuracy, cleverness, and geniality, he is at
least equal to any of the German editors. We have also
from the pen of Mr Linwood an edition of Sophocles, and
a treatise on Greek tragic metres, with the choric parts of
Sophocles metrically arranged. With regard to Sophocles,
I stated in 1848* the undeniable truth that "we find our
starting-point" for all the materials of criticism "in the
labours of Elmsley and Gaisford little more than twenty
years ago;" and from the fact that, out of 110 emenda-
tions which I have introduced or sanctioned in the text
of the *Antigone*, 80 are due to the whole catalogue of previous scholars and 30 to myself alone, it may be inferred
that the numberless German editors have by no means
exhausted this field of research. In Euripides, besides the
anonymous recensions of the two *Iphigenias*, which are
attributed to Bishop Monk, we have Dr Badham's editions

* Introduction to the *Antigone*, p. xlii.

of a few plays, which Mr Conington is pleased to notice as "brilliant exercises." Aristophanes has been under great obligations to English scholarship since the days of Porson and Dobree, who first dealt with his text in a satisfactory manner, and of Mitchell and Frere, who first exhibited his spirit in flowing English rhymes. Mitchell's elaborate introduction is printed *verbatim* in the great German edition of Aristophanes, and the Commentaries, which he published subsequently, though full of faults, are a monument to English erudition. Mr Blaydes, of Christ Church, has published critical editions with Latin notes of the *Acharnians* and *Birds;* we have a good edition and translation of the *Clouds* by Mr B. B. Rogers, of Wadham College; Mr Walsh, of Trinity College, Cambridge, gave us a spirited and accurate version of the first three plays; Mr Holden, of the same College, has published a correct and elegant recension of nearly all the comedies; and Mr W. G. Clark, who has favoured us with a good specimen of his Aristophanic studies in his examination of Süvern's essay on the *Birds*, promises us a complete Aristophanes based on a new collation of the Ravenna manuscript. "For Pindar," says Mr Conington, "those who have done most are Böckh, Dissen and Hermann, as is acknowledged by Dr Donaldson, who himself professes merely to supply a convenient and scholarlike edition for the use of students." This is quite true; but what are most of the modern editions of Greek authors, whether German or English, beyond extensions, improvements, or adaptations of their predecessors? And, as the question is between German and English scholarship, Mr Conington should have shown what the Germans have done towards effecting the object, which I proposed to myself as still necessary, even after what had been done

by my predecessors*. Dr Chr. Wordsworth published
some years ago an edition of *Theocritus* full of the most
ingenious criticisms. Mr Blakesley has recently brought
out an elaborate and original edition of *Herodotus*, in
which, like Arnold in his *Thucydides*, he has directed
attention to the matter rather than to the words, and in
which he exhibits a knowledge of geography in its application to military science, such as no other civilian could
display—unless we distinguish between the *Vicar of Ware*
and the *Hertfordshire Incumbent*. Mr Rawlinson, of Exe-
ter College, Oxford, promises to give us, with the assistance of his distinguished brother, the cuneiform discoverer,
a new translation of the father of history, with an elaborate Commentary. It is known that Mr Shilleto, who
has recently reprinted what the *Journal of Philology* truly
calls "the best edition of the *de Falsa Legatione* which
has appeared in any language," has long been engaged in
a critical recension of Thucydides, in which I venture to
predict that he will surpass Göller, Poppo, and Krüger in
verbal scholarship, as much as Dr Arnold surpassed all
the Germans in liberality of sentiment, practical good
sense, and a wide range of general knowledge. Plato
must wait for his most enlightened expositor until Professor Thompson of Cambridge can be induced to commit
to the press some of that learning which he has long
brought to bear upon his lectures. *En attendant*, we
we have a scholarlike translation of the *Politia* from two
of his pupils, and Dr Badham has brought his usual ingenuity to bear on the difficulties of the *Philebus*. Aristotle
has been studied at Cambridge with great vigour, and in
a very independent manner, since a new stimulus was
given to this revival of the Peripatetic philosophy by the

* *Pref.* pp. viii.—x.

lectures of Dr Thirlwall, in 1832–3.   That there is no
lack of activity in this respect at Oxford is attested by
the contemporaneous publication of two editions of the
Politics by Mr Congreve and Mr Eaton ; and Mr Chase's
excellent translation of the *Ethics* will soon be followed
by Mr Jelf's edition of the same treatise.   Mr Churchill
Babington has edited the recently-discovered fragments of
Hyperides, in such a manner as to obtain from his German
successor Schneidewin the willing admission, "messem
fecit ille, spicas legere reliquit aliis."   No commentary on
a Greek orator could be more instructive than those which
accompany Mr C. R. Kennedy's translations of Demosthenes.   I have been permitted to form some opinion of
what may be expected from the critical version of Athen-
æus, which has long occupied the time of the learned and
accurate Mr Dyce, and can undertake to say, that it will
be worthy of the reputation which he has achieved by his
edition of Bentley, and by his critical recensions of the
old English poets.   In the less classical departments of
Greek literature, the Germans have done nothing superior
to Dr Greenhill's edition of Theophilus Protospatharius,
and to some of the publications of the Sydenham society;
in patristic and grammatical editorship we may point with
just pride to Field's edition of Chrysostom, Humphry's
Theophilus Antiochensis, and the more recent labours of
Gaisford; and Mr Ellicott's Commentary on St Paul's
Epistles has all the qualities of an elaborate effort of classical editorship.

　　But although I think that we are quite able to meet
the comparison with Germany in regard to our Greek
editorship, I willingly repeat the admission which I have
frequently made, and in which other Englishmen have
concurred, that Latin scholarship does not flourish among

us as it ought to do, and that we have done nothing
recently, which can be placed altogether on the same level
with Madvig's editions and *opuscula*, with Lachmann's
Lucretius, Ritschl's *Plautus*, the *Varro* and *Festus* of
O. Müller, Sillig's *Pliny*, Zumpt's *Quintus Curtius*,
Kempfe's *Valerius Maximus*, the *Seneca* of Fickert, the
Macrobius of Janus, the fragments of the Latin tragedians
and of Ennius as edited by Otto Ribbeck and Vahlen,
and the *Agrimensores* as revised and illustrated by Blume,
Lachmann and Rudorff. Still, certain symptoms have
recently made their appearance which indicate an earnest
desire to shake off this reproach. The first volume of
the *Bibliotheca Classica*, a collection of editions, which
does infinite credit to its enterprising publishers, contained
Cicero's Orations against Verres, with notes by Mr Long:
and it has recently been followed by other speeches similarly illustrated. Although this work is blemished by
some grave defects of taste and scholarship, and though it
is more justly characterized in a recent review * than in
the newspaper flourishes of partial friends which heralded
its first appearance, it deserves to be regarded as the most
considerable and independent effort of Latin editorship
which this country has produced for some years. Mr H. Alan,
previously known by his treatise on the Latin particles, has
published in succession, in London and Dublin, a series
of editions of *Sallust* and of various works of *Cicero*, which,
for critical accuracy and exhaustive learning, leave little
to be desired; Mr Merivale too has given us a capital
school-edition of *Sallust;* Dr Twiss of Oxford and Mr
Prendeville of Dublin have edited the whole or parts of
Livy in a most convenient form, and, the latter especially,
with very adequate illustrations of the language; and

* *Journal of Classical Philology*, No. VI. pp. 358, 359.

Mr W. B. Donne, as I have reason to know, is about to give the English student more help towards the real understanding of *Tacitus* than he could obtain from any German commentator. Professor Ramsay's *Tibullus* is an excellent book. Although I cannot say of Mr Paley's *Propertius*

> 'Tis not the hasty product of a day,
> But the well-ripen'd fruit of long delay—"

it will at least save those who wish to understand this poet from the necessity of wading through Hertsberg. Mr Macleane and Mr Mayor have recently published editions of *Horace* and *Juvenal*, which enable the English student to dispense with any foreign commentaries. Mr Munro's elaborate review of Lachmann's *Lucretius*, in the *Journal of Philology*, is a sufficient proof that an English editor might be found to supply what is wanting in Bentley and Wakefield. Messrs Conington and Goldwin Smith promise us an edition of *Virgil*, and then I hope that the former gentleman will not repeat his piteous confession that " even Virgil must be studied in England by the help of Wagner and Forbiger," a confession the more humiliating, because Forbiger is absolutely an object of ridicule to Latin scholars in Germany; "nam Forbigero," says Lachmann*, "injuriam faciat qui eum vel minimam rem per se intelligere postulet." In the meantime one of our best scholars, Mr C. R. Kennedy, has completed his father's elegant translation of *Virgil*, and thus enabled us to prove that we have still men capable of appreciating themselves and conveying to others the characteristic beauties of the prince of Latin poets. Dr H. A. Woodham, whose mastery over the Latin language was proved by the racy and idiomatic

* In *Lucret*. p. 16.

vigour of his University Prize-Essays, has shown, in his
edition of Tertullian, that a man of ability can derive
lessons in philology from the language of the Latin Fathers ; and his example has been followed by Mr Currey,
Mr Holden, and Mr J. E. B. Mayor. As it has been
supposed that a knowledge of juristic Latin is almost confined to the school of Savigny, I am happy to add that
we have to thank Mr Sandars, of Oriel College, for an
English edition of the *Institutes of Justinian,* which
need fear no continental competition.

The honours of Greek and Latin lexicography can
scarcely be claimed by any one country. Henry Stephens,
the French printer, conceived and executed the great
Greek Thesaurus ; the first modern edition of this gigantic
work was completed in London by Oxford and Cambridge
scholars ; the second is now publishing at Paris under
German editorship. Both have been indebted for most
material improvements to writers in an English Review[*].
The great Latin dictionary is still that of the Italian
Professors Forcellini and Facciolati ; and the best edition
is that which bears the name of James Bailey on the title-
page. Mr Conington is pleased to remind us that "the
Oxford Lexicon of Messrs Liddell and Scott announces
itself in its title to be based on the German work of
Francis Passow ;" but he either does not know or has
carelessly omitted to tell us that Passow's was but the
commencement of an improved abridgment of Schneider's,
and that Liddell and Scott have done at least as much as
Passow towards the completion of the work. Indeed, all
that refers to the Attic Greek authors belongs exclusively
to the Oxford editors. Mr Conington also informs us
that "the standard modern Latin Lexicon is Freund's."

[*] See *Quarterly Review,* Nos. XLIV. and CI.

This assertion I venture to deny. The standard modern Latin Lexicon is the English edition of Forcellini already mentioned. If I had a suitable opportunity I could show that Freund's laborious compilation is eminently deficient in the higher attributes of scholarship, and that the English edition or adaptation by Dr W. Smith is very superior to its German original. In fact, as far as original researches into the etymology and meaning of Greek and Latin words are concerned, all that has been done to any extent for the last 15 years has proceeded from English philologers*.

The abridged list which I have drawn up is sufficient to warrant me in a peremptory contradiction of the statements of Messrs Conington and Horsman. As a universal proposition it is not true that all the best books on classical literature, which have recently appeared, are written by Germans. And it is only as a statement unqualified by necessary exceptions that such a stricture becomes either mischievous or offensive; for no one denies that some of the best books have proceeded from our fellow-labourers on the continent. In pointing out the necessary exceptions I have confined myself as much as possible to *the present time*, and I have omitted not only men recently deceased, like Dr Arnold, Dean Cramer, and Fynes Clinton, whose great work stands in its Latin translation as a staring proof of the occasional superiority of English to German scholarship; but also men like Bishop Maltby, who, though still living, have for a long time ceased to contribute to the illustration of ancient literature. It is scarcely necessary to remark that the

---

* Dr L. Schmitz has remarked, in the preface to his translation of Zumpt's *Latin Grammar* (p. xiii.), that "the etymology of the Latin language has been studied by a few scholars in this country more comprehensively than on the continent."

list of English writers on classical subjects might be considerably extended if we added all those, who, like Dean Milman, the late Archdeacon Hare, Sir G. C. Lewis, Professor Malden, Mr E. H. Bunbury, Mr T. Dyer, Sir E. W. Head, Mr E. M. Cope and others, have contributed original essays to learned journals. And there are several books, like Dr Russell's edition of Casaubon's *Ephemerides*, which belong, in part at least, to the domain of classical literature. Besides, all the names, which I have mentioned, belong strictly to the teaching and training of Oxford and Cambridge. As Mr Horsman's disparagement includes all English scholarship, I ought to add the names of Mure and Grote, which are quoted merely to throw some additional discredit, by way of contrast, on University scholarship; I ought to cite Professor Blackie's excellent version of *Æschylus*, and Mr Kenrick's admirable works on *Herodotus, Egypt* and *Phœnicia ;* Professor Pillans would claim respectful mention ; and I ought not to pass over in silence the voluminous editorial and lexicographical labours of Dr W. Smith. Perhaps it will be objected that all or most of these gentlemen are deeply indebted to German literature, and that some of them even received a portion of their educational training in German Universities. I am only stating what is felt by all University men in this country, and what has been publicly alleged with regard to more than one of the eminent writers just mentioned, when I say that in proportion as their scholarship is German rather than English, in the same proportion is it marked by extensive reading rather than accurate knowledge, in the same proportion are they learned men rather than good scholars, in the same proportion are they rather *informed about* the ancient writers than really *acquainted with them.*

10—2

And this brings me back to the fallacy on which all this tirade in favour of German scholarship is made to rest,—the fallacy which assumes that the scholarship of a country is to be tested by the amount of its literary production in regard to learned subjects. I have met my opponents on their own ground, and I have shown, by an appeal to the facts of the case, that some at least of the best books are to be found in England, and not in Germany. Had I thought fit to enter into more minute details, I might have proved that our grammars are generally better than those published on the continent*; that the Germans must learn from English philologers, if they ever learn, the ultimate refinements of Greek and Latin etymology and syntax ; that there is no German grammar of Greek or Latin, which truly explains the distinctive phenomena of either language ; and that, while a perfectly accurate acquaintance with Greek syntax is an essential requisite for success in the classical examinations at Cambridge, the most distinguished German professors cannot teach their pupils, what they do not understand themselves,—the rules for the position of the Greek article in certain predications†. If we are told that the Germans write more books on these subjects than we do, and

---

* Some German scholars, who have had opportunities of making themselves acquainted with the facts, have candidly admitted the superiority of our grammatical literature. Dr Max Müller, in his *Suggestions for the Assistance of Officers in learning the Languages of the Seat of War in the East,* (Pref. p. x.) says, even with regard to the Oriental languages where the number of students is comparatively small in this country, "I believe that where grammars written by Englishmen can be procured they will generally be found the most useful and practical."

† See *New Cratylus,* § 305. cf. *Journal of Classical and Sacred Philology,* IV. pp. 84—5.

that therefore they write better books, it would be easy to find some old saw about the difference between *quantity* and *quality*.   I shall show presently that there are special reasons, which induce literary production on learned subjects in Germany, and so create almost a profession of philological bookmakers.   But the least reflexion must convince us, that, as talent, not to say genius, of the rarest and most peculiar kind, is required for real eminence in classical learning, the demand cannot increase the supply in this respect either in Germany or elsewhere. The contrary inference would be more reasonable, namely, that the standard of excellence is deteriorated by over-production.   But if the learned literature of a country is not the best or only test of its scholarship, where are we to seek the most complete criterion?   In order to answer this question in the most satisfactory manner, I must bestow a few words on the difference between *scholarship* and *learning*, to which I have already adverted more than once.   I maintain then that not all learned men are accomplished scholars, though any accomplished scholar may, if he chooses to devote his time to the necessary studies, become a learned man.   I maintain that it is the business of a liberal education to send forth a maximum number of scholars; that classical education as pursued in England does produce this result, and that a want of the same machinery in Germany leads to a corresponding deficiency.   And I maintain that although a man of real genius may effect a great deal by his own exertions, it is always of the utmost importance that a philological writer should have been made beforehand a classical scholar by education.

The etymology of the word sufficiently shows what we mean when we speak of "a scholar."   We mean, of course, a person who has learned thoroughly all that "the

school" can teach him.   The epithet "scholarlike," or, as
some of our contemporaries prefer to spell it, "scholarly,"
suggests to our minds the idea of complete and accurate
knowledge, as opposed to a smattering of general or diversified information.   When honest Griffith says of Wolsey:

> " From his cradle
> He was a scholar, and a ripe and good one,"

we at once accept the phrases as denoting a certain kind
of knowledge, proceeding from early training, and afterwards completely appropriated, digested, and matured.
Having regard to the results produced by the teaching of
our best English schools, we expect, when we hear that a
man is an elegant and accomplished scholar, that he has
become familiar with all the very best Greek and Latin
authors ; that he has not only stored his memory with
their language and ideas, but has had his judgment formed
and his taste corrected by living intimacy with those
ancient wits.   We should perhaps be disappointed, if we
did not learn on inquiry, that he can write Greek and
Latin, both in prose and verse, with idiomatic correctness
and finished elegance.   If he travels in classic regions, or
surveys at home the relics of ancient art, his scholarship
gives him a new interest in all he sees, and enables him,
if his tastes are literary, to convey his impressions to
others in a manner at once interesting and instructive.
If he is a public man, his classical training exhibits itself
in his oratory, and he is able to enliven with the echoes
of that ancient music even the dry details of fiscal exposition and party controversies.   Even if he is a man of
only moderate abilities, he may say like the perfumed clod
of the Persian poet, " I could not dwell so long with the
rose without deriving thence some fragrance."   If his
tastes and genius incline him to take up philology as a
profession and to become a writer on learned subjects, the

scholar shows himself by the felicity of his illustrations, the wary exactness of his statements, and the liveliness and terseness of his Latin or English style.

The learned writer, the *Gelehrte* or *Savant*, when he is such without being a scholar also, is generally an ὀψιμα- θής, or a self-taught man who has acquired his knowledge late in life. Whatever his own resources may enable him to do, he will always exhibit a marked deficiency in regard to those particulars which especially characterise the well-trained scholar. If, which is rarely the case, he contrives to be accurate, he is almost always conspicuous for un-wieldy and cumbrous diction. If his knowledge is really extensive, it is like an undisciplined host which makes an attack in close column, but cannot charge in line. The difficulty with which he has acquired a large portion of his learning induces him not unfrequently to overestimate its value; and on the *ignotum pro magnifico* principle he often parades a coacervation of details which might very well be taken for granted. He forgets Corinna's caution "to sow with the hand and not with the whole sack," and is often insufferably tedious and long-winded, when he fancies that he is concisely instructive. Above all, if he attempts to disport himself in classical composition, nothing can exceed the infelicity of the effort, except perhaps the respectful admiration with which it is regarded by the author himself and his friends.

An illustration, by way of example, will complete the contrast between the scholar who is also a learned writer and the learned writer who is not also a finished scholar. And that I may avoid any comparison of living men, I will take Richard Porson as a perfect specimen of the former, and John Pye Smith as an adequate sample of the latter. I say nothing about the religious and moral character of the two men, which is not concerned in the present inquiry, and is quite independent of their literary pretensions. But here we have on the one hand Porson, who, though of humble origin, had the best school and college education which could be obtained at Eton and Trinity, and had his vast abilities roused to the highest activity during the whole period of his training by the stimulus of successful competition. A Craven scholarship, the first Chancellor's medal, and a Fellowship of Trinity won after an unprecedently short interval, marked the steps in his curriculum, and showed that he had completed his career of discipline. In all that he subsequently did we trace the fruits of the accuracy and precision which were thus required of him, and the facility and easy management of his own intellectual powers which were the natural consequence; his style, whether Latin or English, is racy, terse, and idiomatic, and he has too much respect for his own command of diction ever to lose himself in verbiage. In Pye Smith, on the other hand, we have a man, with the greatest powers of acquisition, either self-taught, or resting, for the basis of his education, on the slovenly training of the dissenters; he becomes a walking cyclopædia of information, but his ventilation of his learning is cumbrous and excessive, his English style heavy and unattractive, and his Latin, which his friends admire excessively, not only obscure and overloaded, but occasionally full of the grossest inaccuracies*.

* I am obliged to make these remarks on Dr Pye Smith's Latinity, because his panegyrist in the *British Quarterly Review*, (Jan. 1854, pp. 186—188), has made a claim for him in this respect, which, if valid, would overthrow the distinction between scholarship and learning maintained in the text. While we are told that "of all tests of classical scholarship, Latin composition is the most fair and

To return, however, to the subject immediately before us, I assert that it is the tendency of classical education in England not only to produce learned writers, who are scholars also, like Porson, but also to produce a great number of scholars, who, without being learned writers, bring their scholarship to bear in a thousand ways on their own business and on that of the Church and State.   On the other hand I assert that the system pursued in Germany does indeed call forth a great number of learned writers of different degrees of merit, but that it produces an infinitely small number of accomplished scholars.   Let us consider the process in either case.

Every year the public schools of England, including in the number not only the crowded and fashionable institutions known to all the world, but also the grammar-schools, which are scattered over England and managed in many cases by men who are at least the equals in scholar-ship of the Masters of Eton, Harrow, and Rugby [11]—every

conclusive," we are invited to believe that Dr Smith, without the usual advantages of school-training, was at least equal to those who have faced the competitions of a great University. His Latin orations are pronounced to be "written in a pure, vigorous, and elegant style;" and "it is not too much to say that they would do no discredit to any professor of Cambridge or Oxford;" indeed it is thought won-derful (as indeed it would have been) that he should "acquire a power, unattainable by many who have devoted years to the labour, of composing Latin with correctness and facility."   Fortunately some specimens are given, all of which are liable to the objections stated above; and the last passage, quoted from Dr Smith's Latin effusions, concludes with the words : "sic votis omnium bonorum exsequutum erit," a barbarism which would have been avoided by "any professor of Cambridge or Oxford;" for although the later writers now and then use *exsequor* as a passive verb, the only possible construction would be *vota exsequentur;* the dative *votis* would require *satisfiet* or *satisfactum erit.*

year these schools send forth from their sixth form a
number of youths of 18 or 19, who are already, in many
respects, accomplished scholars.   They have a perfectly
exact acquaintance with the grammars of the dead languages and can write Greek and Latin *verse* in a manner
which would astonish a German professor[12].   Some of
these go at once into active life; others proceed to the
Universities, where they find, not only a number of young
men who have enjoyed the same advantages as themselves,
but others too whose education has been neglected or carried on privately, but who, coming into this atmosphere
of competition, and having perhaps brilliant abilities, are
soon enabled to enter the lists with more or less prospect
of success.   The prizes proposed are of enormous value.
It is estimated that the first place in either Tripos at
Cambridge is worth in present value and contingent advantages about £10,000, to say nothing of the effect produced
by the prestige of early success on the career of the young
barrister and statesman.   Accordingly the tests are proportionally rigorous, and the exertions of the competitors
proportionally sustained.   We have thus every year at
Oxford and Cambridge a number of young men, who at
the ages of from 22 to 24 have obtained the last object of
their labours, and are in every sense finished scholars.
That many of these become learned writers is shown by
the long list of commentators, lexicographers, historians,
grammarians, and philologers which I have already cited;
and there are many excellent scholars, who, like Mr Mit-
ford and Mr Dyce, bring their critical abilities to the correction and elucidation of the great English poets.   But
it is a fallacy to suppose that this literary productiveness
is the only test of the scholarship, which exists and may
be ascertained without it.   The fact of the existence of this

high scholarship is attested by the evidence of a large body of competent examiners, some of whose opinions stand on record in the reports of the University commissioners. It is also shown by those collections of classical compositions which have recently appeared, the *Arundines Cami*, the *Anthologia Oxoniensis*, and the *Sabrinæ Corolla**, to say nothing of the prize exercises which are annually printed at both Universities. Then it is notorious that a number of admirable scholars are engaged in classical tuition. Some of these are professors and tutors at Cambridge and Oxford; others, and those perhaps the most eminent, are masters of grammar-schools; a late Fellow of Trinity is Professor of Greek at Glasgow; one distinguished Oxford scholar is Principal of the University of Sydney, and another has organised the public teaching at Corfu. Then again, we have a great number of our accomplished scholars in the ranks of the working clergy, and if they do not bring their learning to bear upon theology, they at least refine the neighbourhood in which they live, and elevate the taste even of the rustics whom they address in their sermons. The bar too abounds in good scholars. Sometimes they have an opportunity of bringing out their Greek or Latin, as may be seen in Alderson's note on *edo* in the report of Burdett's case†. Or a distinguished fellow of Trinity, like Mr Forsyth, may write a book on public pleading, in which the fruits of his Cambridge studies will appear in full force. Travellers in

---

* It is well remarked by Dean Milman, in speaking of one of these collections, that "the exercise of translating poetical English into poetical Greek or Latin is at once the discipline, the test, and the triumph of consummate scholarship."

† *Barnewall and Alderson's Reports*, Vol. IV. p. 129. See also pp. 97—100 of the same Report.

classic lands or in the East show, like Colonel Leake, Sir
Charles Fellowes, Mr Dennis, Colonel Rawlinson, and Dr
Layard, the ease with which an Englishman can deal with
subjects involving learned research.   But it is in the
Houses of Parliament, and in the higher society which
they represent, that we see the distinctest proofs of the
deep roots which classical scholarship has struck in this
country, and of its pervading influence.   Not to speak
of occasional effusions like Macaulay's *Lays of Ancient
Rome*, direct and continued allusions to the language and
literature of antiquity are permitted and encouraged
because they are generally intelligible, and in the heat
of debate a felicitous and well-applied quotation is often
received with the applause due to a successful argument.

On these grounds I am convinced, and I hope I have
convinced my readers, that, while we are able to appeal to
a considerable list of learned writers more distinguished in
many ways than their predecessors, classical scholarship is
still, what it was, a characteristic of the higher classes in
this country.   In order, however, that I may confute the
educational objectors on their own ground, and meet the
invidious comparison with the scholarship of Germany, to
which they provoke us, I must inquire into the system of
classical education pursued in that country ; and I must
examine the means which they possess of producing
scholars, and the causes which create so large a number of
writers on learned subjects.   In such an inquiry it would
not be fair to take as our text-books the biographical
sketches of two scholars recently deceased—Godfrey Hermann, of Leipsig, the greatest Greek scholar among the
modern Germans, who died on the last day of 1848, and
Charles Lachmann, of Berlin, their greatest Latin scholar
and general philologer, who died soon after, though at a

much earlier age, on March 13, 1849. By selecting these two specimens of German scholarship we should indeed adduce the most favourable instances which could be found, but we should not exemplify the general character of the German philologer. For, in their activity of mind and body, Hermann and Lachmann came nearer to Englishmen than 99 out of 100 Germans; and both of them made more progress in classical composition than any *Gelehrten* of their time. In a word, Hermann and Lachmann deserved to be called scholars, and wanted nothing to give a perfect finish to those accomplishments for which nature had so well qualified them, except the advantages of an English education, and the competition of an English University. When Porson scornfully disallowed Hermann's claims to a high place among Greek scholars, he expressed his contempt by a rude parody of a well-known couplet by Phocylides, which, in its original form, is confined to a censure of the metrical knowledge of the Germans; the English version is more general :

> The Germans in Greek
> Are sadly to seek ;
> Not five in five score
> But ninety-five more :
> All save only Hermann,
> And Hermann's a German*.

This squib was written at the very beginning of the present century ; and, having regard to all that Hermann has since done for Greek scholarship, it remains rather as a specimen of Porson's wit than a proof of his prophetic discernment. Still, however, Hermann and Lachmann, and perhaps a few others, remain as exceptions to the remark that German savans are rarely, if ever, good

* *Museum Criticum,* I. p. 332.

scholars, and we might apply this doggerel to the general
run of German philologers by substituting for the last
couplet some such lines as these :

> And when you except
> The Head of the School,
> You find the exception
> A proof of the rule.

The exceptional character of scholarship like that of Lachmann and Hermann is easily shown by the manner in
which their countrymen dwell on their peculiarities. For
although the Latin elegiacs of the former* would not be
considered very first-rate at Eton, and though Hermann's
translation from the *Wallenstein*† might have failed to
obtain the Porson prize at Cambridge, these *Prolusiones*
are considered wonderful efforts in Germany, and certainly
could not be imitated by many of the *doctores umbratici,*
who abound there[13]. They are due in fact to the peculiar
temper of the men themselves, which showed its activity
in other ways, more English than German, besides this
propensity to verse composition. Both Lachmann and
Hermann were little, wiry, and nimble men, full of spirit
and energy—as different, as possible, from the usual type
of German bookworms. The former, just after he had
published his *Propertius* in 1815, must needs march to
Paris as volunteer *Fussjäger;* and though he took no part
in the campaign in Belgium, he was some time under
arms, and it was his favourite joke afterwards to identify
himself with a certain Colonel Lachmann, who distinguished himself in the Russian army during the Polish
war of 1831. Hermann had no actual military experience, but he was devotedly fond of riding *à la militaire,*

---

* Hertz, *Lachmann's Biographie.* Berlin, 1851. *Beilagen,* p. xiii.
† *Opuscula,* v. pp. 356 sqq.

wore long spurs in his lecture-room, and was extremely gratified when on one occasion he was asked by an officer of dragoons, whether he had not served in the cavalry*? This fondness for exercise, as contrasted with the sedentary habits of German professors in general, is particularly noted by his biographical panegyrist, who is pleased to observe that he was "nichts weniger als ein Stubensitzer;" but I fancy that those, who have seen the Cambridge Fellows and Masters of Colleges trotting down Trumpington-street at 2 p.m., would not specify the possession and use of a saddle-horse as a remarkable and distinctive characteristic of some particular scholar. Without being "admirable Crichtons," we are not incapacitated by our studies for any kind of exercise or enterprise; and the "Cruise of the Pet" shows that Cambridge scholars may occasionally be something more than amateur sailors.

Let me, however, leave these exceptional cases of extraordinary men, and trace the ordinary career of one of the best class of German philologers. My imaginary *Bursch* shall have every advantage at starting. He shall not, like Heyne and Lobeck, be obliged to struggle with the inconveniences which result from the *res angusta domi*. His father shall be, if you please, a learned man and *Garnison-Prediger* in some great city, which contains a first-rate *Gymnasium*. His mother shall be the intelligent and accomplished daughter of a field-officer in the Prussian army. With such parents his education will commence at home, and he will not need the *Progymnasium* or preparatory school. I will suppose that he shows at an early age great docility and a considerable power of acquiring knowledge, and that in fact he promises from the first to be a *Philolog*. In due course of time he is sent to the

---

* Jahn, *Gedächtnissrede*, Leips. 1849, p. 11.

Gymnasium or grammar-school of the place. If he enters at the age of eight or nine, he passes through all six classes of a school of some 150 boys. Here he not only learns Latin and Greek with some Hebrew, but is also instructed in his own language and French, and receives regular lessons in geography, history, mathematics, and natural philosophy. I am only concerned with his classical training, which will be best inferred from an account of his studies during his last year in the first class*. He has read 450 lines of Homer's *Iliad*, half the *Œdipus Tyrannus* of Sophocles, and the *Euthyphro* of Plato; he has also been worked in Rost's Greek Grammar. In Latin he has read some odes of Horace and some orations of Cicero, and has been exercised in the theory of Latin style both out of Zumpt's Grammar, and out of one of the numerous exercise-books which they have in Germany. He has done some of Vömel's Greek exercises ; and has written Latin themes. But we hear nothing of his verse composition, except perhaps that he has volunteered some Latin Alcaics as the fruit of his private studies. Under the same head we find it recorded that he has read a good deal of Cicero and Livy, Horace's *Satires*, a little Plautus, some Homer, Xenophon, and Plato. And so, at the age of 16 or 17, he is sent to the University with some such character as this : " Egregie institutus, post examen pub-licum multa cum laude dimissus, Academiam Bonnensem petiit, philologorum studiis deditus." As this is the only real training, *as a scholar*, which our young philologer will have, it is worth while to inquire what it amounts to. He has acquired the faculty of writing tolerable Latin prose, and it must be admitted that the Germans gene-rally surpass us in this ; nor is the fact surprising, when

* These details are derived from an actual case.

we recollect that the Universities keep up, as we shall see, a practical demand for the accomplishment. In Latin verse, however, he has had no experience, and has probably never written a line of metrical Greek. Indeed his knowledge of quantity is very uncertain, and as in some *Gymnasiums* they are taught to pronounce Greek by the accent, the longs and shorts are as often wrong as right. The manner in which our student has read the few classical authors with which he is acquainted depends on the abilities and scholarship of his Rector, and it is to be remarked that in Germany nearly all the really good scholars remain settled as Professors at the Universities, and are not, as with us, as frequently found at the head of the public schools. If our young philologer has not received a scholarlike training at school, he will hardly make good his deficiencies at the University. He will there have the option of attending a great number of lectures, *publice, privatim,* and *privatissime,* when his occupation will be writing down for an hour at a time the dictations of the Professor. There will probably be a *Seminarium Philologicum,* in which some Professor will exercise a class in Latin writing and disputation, or preside at discussions on the text and interpretation of the classical writers. The whole curriculum is calculated to stimulate and assist private study, to give systematic information on the pet subjects of the leading Professors, and to prepare a young man for the profession or trade of learned book-making. After some years spent in this way, and perhaps diversified by occasional employment as a private tutor, he takes his degree as "Doctor in Philosophy" by a public disputation on certain theses appended to a Latin dissertation on some philological subject, which, if he is really an original man, may contain the germ of

11

his future literary labours.   If his first effort is favourably received, he is at once launched as a teacher and writer of books.   He must print something to obtain his *Habilitation,* and he must go on writing if he wishes to rise from the *Privat-docent* to the *Professor Extra Ordinem,* and so to ascend to the ordinary or regular Professorship.   Nor can his pen be allowed to rest even when he has obtained this ultimate object of his ambition.   He must publish books to keep his name before the world and attract pupils to his lecture-room.   And so from first to last he is a book-maker *ex rei necessitate.*   He acquires knowledge, not as a labour of love for the improvement of his own mind, but as fuel for his reputation and ammunition for the artillery of his literary displays.

While then the system of education pursued in Germany is less calculated than our own to produce finished scholars, the mode prescribed for the attainment of Professorships and the other educational positions, which abound in that country, furnishes a demand for literary production, which must lead to a vast amount of needless book-making.   The cases of Dr Parr and Professor Dobree, with others that might be named, show that in England a reputation for scholarship may exist independently of literary production and even without reference to the test of University distinctions.   This results from the diffusion of scholarlike acquirements in general society, and from the voice of general opinion, which connects the separate links of private circles.   In Germany, this social influence of scholarship is non-existent.   It is only as a *Gelehrte,* or writer on learned subjects, that a philological student can become distinguished ; and thus in the two countries the amount of scholarship and the number of learned books stand in a reciprocal ratio.   Though there can be no doubt that the German habit of book-making leads many men to write who have no real vocation for authorship, and thus deteriorates the learned literature of the country, it cannot be denied on the other hand that the facilities afforded for literary production have also their advantages. In this way, we are less likely to be deprived of the services of the few men in every age who are competent to instruct the world on these subjects. We do not run the risk in Germany, as we do in England, of losing all the critical and philological talent which was perhaps locked up in the life of a scholar, and having to content ourselves with recollections of his remarks, orally transmitted, or with scraps of corrections and interpretations derived from the margins of his books. Among so many millions of Germans, there is a fair proportion of men of genius or first-rate talent, and as they all write books, we have the best learning at our disposal.

And this brings me to the inquiry, without which this vindication of English scholarship would be incomplete—namely, what is really the relation between our learned writers and those of Germany, and what is the cause of the exaggerated view of the merits of the latter which I have had to combat? There can be no doubt that nearly all our best writers on classical literature for the last 20 years have been familiar with the philology of the Germans, and have derived great benefit from this widening of the field of contemporary knowledge, a benefit from which the Germans too often exclude themselves. And even those of our scholars, who are unacquainted with the German language, have been enabled, by means of translations, to read and appropriate the best books on learned subjects which the Germans have produced. There has been in fact a reaction since the termination of the last

11—2

European war. We paid too little attention to German learning before that time ; we now run into the opposite extreme, and seem to think that there is no learning out of Germany. We forget in point of fact that classical education has been so long established in England, and has produced such influence on the tastes, habits and character of Englishmen, that even when eminent writers on learned subjects, like Colonel Mure and Mr Kenrick, are indebted to the Germans, not only for a good deal of the materials of their learning, but also for a part of their education, they remain to the end distinguished by that knowledge of the world, acquaintance with political science[*], practical good sense, and facility of expression, which seem to be the essential property of our country-men, and are too generally wanting in German writers. It would have been eminently absurd, if we had not placed our mathematical studies on the advanced basis of the improved calculus, and had neglected the works of Lagrange and Laplace : but no one imagines that the countrymen of Herschel, Babbage, Adams, Rowan Hamilton, Hinds, Stokes, Hopkins, and Airy are inferior in mathematical knowledge to the teachers of the *École Polytechnique*. Why is this the case in regard to German philology? Why may we not take cognizance of Niebuhr, Böckh and Müller, without seeming to relinquish our own

---

[*] One of the most philo-teutonic of our scholars, Sir G. C. Lewis, writes thus in the Preface to his Translation of Böckh's *Public Economy of Athens,* p. xiii. : "It is much to be lamented that the author of this work, a man profoundly skilled in Grecian antiquities, and possessing very considerable powers of reasoning and discrimination, should not have added to these endowments a more ample portion of modern science : and that in his remarks and discussions he should exhibit few traces of those improvements in political philosophy which later ages have produced."

claim to rank as their equals? If this were the rule for
our guidance in estimating the literary merits of a particular nation at a particular time, we must, on the same
principle, consider the Germans, whose works have been
most immediately suggestive to us of late years, as mere
offshoots of an English school of philology, previously existing. For Niebuhr himself has pronounced F. A. Wolf
"the hero and eponymus of the race of German philo·
logers*," and it is universally admitted that Wolf was a
literary representative of Bentley. Indeed, a German
writer, who claims all that he can for his countrymen, has
not hesitated to avow, that historical philology, though it
is the heritage and the glory of German scholars, was the
discovery of Richard Bentley†, and the dissertation on
Phalaris must take rank before all the constructive or
reconstructive efforts of continental criticism. Our greatest obligation to modern German scholarship is the revival
among us of the spirit of Bentley; in this, no doubt, we
have been stimulated by the example of the great German
scholars—Wolf, Böckh, Niebuhr, C. O. Müller, Hermann,
Lachmann, and others—who have declared themselves his
disciples. And the general tone of German literature,
which, revived by Lessing, reached its culminating point
in Göthe, has produced a marked influence on Englishmen
of the largest minds and clearest discernment. But if we
try to trace backwards the mutual obligations of the two
countries, we shall always find the first entry to the credit
of England. Newton and Leibnitz, Young and Champollion, Rawlinson and Lassen, make contemporary, or
nearly contemporary discoveries; but in the great march
of· intellectual development, Occham precedes Luther,

* *Philol. Mus.* I. p. 176.
† Bunsen, *Ægypten,* I. Note 22.

Shakspere and Bacon are followed after a long pause by
German dramatists and philosophers, and more than half
a century passes away before Wolf and his school trim
once more and pass over to us the flickering torch of
Bentley.

The most obvious reason for the over-estimate of German
learning undoubtedly is because so many German commentaries and grammars are used in this country; and this is
because the classical student requires a considerable library,
and because German books are much cheaper than English.   The texts of the best classical authors can be settled in one country as well as in another; and if Germany
supplies a greater number who are stimulated by inducements to undertake this work, and can afford to live upon
its results, if the cost of compositors' work and paper is
infinitely less, and the publishers' capital less occupied by
books of political or general interest, we may expect, what
is the case, that more learned works will appear in Germany, and will appear at a lower price.   Accordingly,
they will either be imported or reprinted or accom-
modated by translation to the use of English students.
This is the simplest explanation of the respect in which
German editors seem to be held.   And money-making
speculations sometimes contribute to encourage this preference for foreign learning.   An English clergyman, who
died two or three years ago, found it answer his purpose
to employ one or more Germans to assist him in preparing
German school-books for the English press; and I have
seen a list of eighty or ninety works! with this gentleman's name on the title of each,   This was felt to be an
abuse, and evoked more than one expression of indignant
censure.   But it helps to explain the exaggeration which
I have been endeavouring to correct, and justifies the

steps which are being taken to provide the English student with classical texts edited by English scholars. Publishers in London and Oxford have commenced series of these manuals with or without notes, and the University of Cambridge has made some progress in a similar undertaking, which, I hope, will induce the Delegates of the Clarendon Press to inquire, whether there are not Oxford scholars quite as sound and accurate as Dindorf, who publishes Æschylus at an English press, without taking the trouble to ascertain what has been recently done for this poet by English scholars.

The erroneous views, of which Mr Horsman constituted himself the exponent, generally combine, as he did, with an extravagant exaltation of German scholarship an equally extravagant depreciation of German theology. On this subject I expressed my sentiments very fully some seven or eight years ago*. And while I admit that biblical criticism has been too little studied in England,—that, in fact, it is generally tabooed,—that it is pursued with great and important results in Germany, and that we have no books equal in comprehensive learning to the works of J. Müller, Nitzsch, Dorner, Lücke, Roth, Ewald, Gesenius, Ebrard, Lachmann, Hofmann, Winer, and de Wette, to say nothing of the writings of Schleiermacher, who is a host in himself, and of the numberless contributions to theological research in the volumes of the *Studien und Kritiken*, I must maintain that this deficiency or neglect has not arisen from any want of critical ability or accurate scholarship on the part of our divines, but is due entirely to the predominance of an ignorant and faithless timidity, which has long deterred those English clergymen, who have thought

* *Maskil le Sopher*, Cambr. 1848, pp. 48—50.

for themselves, from publishing what they knew would render them liable to eager misrepresentation. No one needs to be told, that, if an English divine brings to the criticism and interpretation of Scripture the fearless love of truth and liberty and plainness of speech*, which belongs alike to the true Christian and the true scholar, instead of receiving any reward, commendation, or encouragement, he is not only liable, but certain to have his words and motives misconstrued, and to be assailed with an utter renunciation of literary candour and with all the virulence of personal animosity. It would seem almost as though the foundations of religion were not to be sought in the word of God, but in certain opinions respecting the documents of Revelation held by the weakest or the wickedest of men—by those who would convert the religion of light and love into a creed of darkness and hatred. If we take even the most harmless and well-meaning of those who prefer "the letter which killeth to the spirit which giveth life," we shall find in this country a slavish subjection of the reason to the weak and beggarly elements of worldly dogmatism†, which, as manifesting itself in an enlightened and Protestant country, is perfectly astounding. The childish pietist clings to his *mumpsimus,* and will hear of no aids to the better understanding of holy writ, even though they present themselves in the honest shape of dictionary and grammar. We meet every day with representatives of the old lady of the French congregation at Berlin, who was horrified by

---

* 2 *Cor.* iii. 12: ἔχοντες οὖν τοιαύτην ἐλπίδα πολλῇ παρρησίᾳ χρώμεθα.

† *Col.* ii. 20: εἰ ἀπεθάνετε σὺν Χριστῷ ἀπὸ τῶν στοιχείων τοῦ κόσμου, τί ὡς ζῶντες ἐν κόσμῳ δογματίζεσθε; cf. *Col.* ii. 8, 14. *Gal.* iv. 3, 9.

the proposal to make a new version of the Psalms in French. "Bilden sie sich ein," she exclaimed to the proposer, "das französische besser zu verstehen, als der König und Prophet David?"—"Do you fancy you know more about French than David, who was a king and a prophet?" This is the spirit, in which the proposals made by Mr Heywood and others for an improved version of the Bible have been received by the old women of England and the writers who undertake to guide their opinions, and this task, which is absolutely necessary, is strenuously deprecated by those who consider it sacrilege to make any alterations in the established version, as though the labours, which were thought so beneficial some two hundred and fifty years ago, could not be resumed without positive sinfulness. This unreasoning terrorism has had its day. The degrading idolatry of an infallible literature is about to die the natural death of all Feti-chisms. *Mole ruit sua*—it is falling to pieces in consequence of its own excesses. And nothing has contributed more to the discredit, which it has brought upon itself, than the insolent folly, unscrupulous detraction, reckless dishonesty, and unchristian violence of the so-called religious periodicals; and it is felt that Christianity cannot consent to such a narrowing of its basis or accept the services of such advocates, unless it is to renounce all its characteristics. On the other hand, some recent publications have shown that there are pious clergymen, warmly and conscientiously attached to the Church, who have convinced themselves that true conservatism presumes the relinquishment of that which is felt to be untenable, and who can bring their critical talents to the illustration of the sacred text, without compromising any orthodox doctrine or weakening any real or solid buttress of the faith.

It is not a part of my business on the present occasion to pursue this important subject any farther. But in speaking, as I have done in these pages, of the functions proper to a University, I am naturally led to point out here that the position and duties of the Anglican divine are necessarily connected with the professional and academical character of the faculty to which he belongs. It is generally said that the Universities are made dependent on the Church: it would be more true to say that the ministry of the Church is, in theory at least, subordinate to the theological schools at the great Universities, and that, if so, the neglect of biblical learning in this country is not at all countenanced by the presumed privileges and obligations of the Anglican divine.

That the English clergyman is essentially a professional man, that his characteristic distinctions are academical rather than sacerdotal, is shown not only by the terms of his ordination, but by the general bearing of the articles which he subscribes, by the criteria of his social rank, and even by the prescriptions of his official costume, when ministering in the congregation. Let us consider these particulars separately.

(a) The articles refer every doctrine to Scripture, with the exception of the doctrine of the Trinity, which is considered as the necessary foundation of all faith, and which is laid down in the five articles preceding that which maintains the sole sufficiency of the Scriptures as a source of saving doctrine [14]. The reception of the creeds is made dependent on their scriptural warrants (*Art.* VIII.). The constitution of the Church and the sacraments rests only on the foundation of the word of God (*Art.* XIX.), and "it is not lawful for the Church to ordain anything that is contrary to God's word written, neither may it expound one place of Scripture, that it be repugnant to

another" (*Art.* xx.). If then Scripture is the only rule
of faith, and if the collective Church is not allowed to
deduce from it any arbitrary doctrine or contradictory
inferences, a certain liberty or latitude of interpretation
must be left to individual members of the Church; and
if there is any basis for scientific or methodical knowledge
on religious subjects, if in fact there is such a thing as
theology, and if the divinity schools of the old Universities are not a mere mockery and farce, it must be the
design and intention of a protestant Church to encourage
and promote theological learning, in order that some at
least may be competent to discuss the many questions on
which the Church cannot and does not presume to pronounce an arbitrary judgment.

(*b*) That professional or academical learning is regarded as the primary qualification of the Anglican clergy
may be inferred most distinctly from the criteria of their
social rank. The first subject in the realm, next to the
Royal Family, is the Archbishop of Canterbury; the next
place is occupied by the Lord High Chancellor or Lord
Keeper, being a baron, who is followed by the Archbishops
of York, Armagh, and Dublin, who thus take precedence
not only of all dukes, but also of those great officers who
take precedence of all peers of their own degree. Then
again the bishops, being barons, take precedence of all
barons. And from this it is concluded generally that a
clergyman ranks above any gentleman of his own degree.
Now it is obvious that the explanation of this rule or
convention must be sought in the relations of the two
personages who stand at the head of the list; and as
the Archbishop of Canterbury and the Lord High Chancellor are professional officers representing respectively the
faculties of divinity and law, we may conclude that they

are placed in this order, because the Universities from
time immemorial have counted divinity the first and law
the second of those faculties for which they grant degrees.
It is to be observed, that the precedence of the Lord Chancellor before the Archbishop of York is not of an earlier
origin than the reign of Charles the Second, and the previous state of things seems to be more in accordance with
analogy.   The division of the people into *clergy* and *laity*
and of parliament into *lords spiritual* and *temporal*, which
Sir E. Coke cites in explanation of the bishops' precedence,
does not account for the precedence of the primate and
chancellor; for as the position of the latter is clearly
professional and official, the former must owe his place to
considerations of the same kind.   The faculty of medicine,
which stands next in the academical scale, is not represented in the table of precedence, because this profession
has no place in the arrangements of our constitution in
Church and State; but Blackstone says that doctors in
the *three* learned professions rank before esquires, and at
the funeral of Lord Nelson in 1806 the knights bachelors
were immediately followed by "divines, physicians of the
deceased, esquires, gentlemen," no special provision being
made for doctors at law, who in all probability had no
representatives on such an occasion.   It is laid down by
the best authorities that deans, archdeacons, and rectors
have no rank as such, but that, *ceteris paribus*, even a
stipendiary curate, who was D.D., would take precedence
of any so-called dignitary, whose academical degree was
inferior.   As barons the bishops have a position of their
own.   But, in other respects and independently of social
inequalities, it cannot be doubted that the clergy take
rank among themselves from considerations of a professional or academical character.

(c) The canons not only recognise, but enforce the strictly academical character of our Church. In the 36th canon, which is especially subscribed by clergymen, the licence to preach, catechize, &c. by "one of the two Universities," is placed on the same footing as the licence by an archbishop or bishop. By the mere fact of granting degrees in theology, the Universities assume an active share in the doctrinal education of the country, and the terms, in which those degrees are conferred, imply an independent authority on the part of the bodies by which they are bestowed. The bachelor in divinity is empowered to expound all the apostolic epistles, and the doctor to profess and teach all theology; a commission which must have had some importance at the time when our Church was reconstituted, whatever may be its value now. The minister's relation to his University is openly exhibited to the eyes of the congregation by the distinctive features of his prescribed attire. Instead of the tippet which marks the equality of priesthood in the Romish Church, English clergymen are ordered by the 58th canon to wear upon their surplices "such hoods as by the orders of the Universities are agreeable to their degrees." Even the bishop, who wears no hood, is led in conformity with an invariable practice to obtain from one of the Universities the degree of doctor in divinity, and though this may be only a form at the present day, it indicates the original understanding that theology was a science and could not be taught authoritatively or rebuked when erroneous except by its duly qualified professors. In some Colleges at Cambridge it is still required by the statutes, that all M.A. Fellows should proceed in due course to the degree of B.D., and according to the old system of the University, which considered all doctors as professors or teachers of their faculties, all M.A.'s, who were designed for the clerical profession, were required to seek instruction from the doctors in divinity in their own University *.

(d) But the Church has not merely acquiesced in the hope that the Universities will do their duty and provide means and encouragements for the proper cultivation of theological learning. A promise that he will devote himself to these studies is exacted from the Anglican priest at his ordination. As the terms of this pledge are perhaps unknown to the majority of laymen, and seem to be forgotten or perhaps insufficiently appreciated by very many of the clergy, it may perhaps be as well to make a few remarks on the subject. The deacon, who is not necessarily a preacher or expounder of Scripture, and whose duty it rather is " to read holy Scriptures and Homilies in the Church," is not bound to a special course of study in this respect. He is merely asked " Do you unfeignedly believe all the canonical Scriptures of the Old and New Testament?" That is, he is required, in the sense of the sixth article, to receive the canonical Scriptures as his only rule of faith. The priest, however, receives from the bishop not the New Testament only, but the whole Bible with the words: " Take thou authority to preach the Word of God;" and his declaration with respect to the Scripture is more closely borrowed from the phraseology of the sixth article, which speaks of the Scriptures less as a rule of faith than as furnishing or including the materials of religious doctrine: he declares himself persuaded "that the holy Scriptures *contain sufficiently* all doctrine required of necessity for eternal salvation through faith in Jesus Christ;" and says that he has determined by God's grace " out of the said Scriptures to

* See Peacock, *On the Statutes of the University of Cambridge*, p. 12.

instruct the people committed to his charge, and to teach
nothing as required of necessity to salvation, but *that
which he shall be persuaded* may be concluded and proved
by the Scriptures."   He also promises that he will endeavour, the Lord being his helper, to "be diligent in prayers,
and in reading of the holy Scriptures, and *in such studies
as help to the knowledge of the same,* laying aside the study
of the world and of the flesh."   Any one who will pay
attention to the wording of these solemn promises, must
see that it is the bounden duty of the English priest to
regard and use the Scriptures as containing the materials
of his religious doctrine, which he must derive from the
Bible by independent investigation and learned research.
It can hardly escape the notice of any candid and intelligent person, that as the Scriptures are written in Hebrew
and Greek, "such studies as help to the knowledge of the
same" must include an unlimited amount of grammatical
and philological training ; and, as the sacred books belong
to the domain of ancient literature, criticism, in its most
refined and advanced condition, must be at least as applicable to these books as to the classical writings of Greece
and Italy.   Consequently, the ordination vow is but imperfectly fulfilled, if it is not absolutely and intentionally
violated, by those who have never made one attempt, since
they received orders, to acquire or improve a knowledge of
the original languages of Scripture, or to cultivate their
reasonable faculty of original interpretation ; and it is set
at nought or forgotten by those who disparage these and
similar studies, or declaim against the dangers of what
they call the rationalistic spirit of scientific criticism.
Again, it must be obvious that the obligation to teach
nothing as required of necessity to salvation but that
which the minister himself " shall be persuaded may be

concluded and proved by the Scriptures" is quite inconsistent with the position maintained by some, that an attempt to ascertain the real meaning of Scripture by independent investigation of the original texts and the publication of criticisms and interpretations, which are, according to our own persuasion, conclusively true, however much they may be at variance with the preconceived opinions of others, is a liberty denied to the Anglican minister, who can only teach according to stereotyped formularies. On the contrary, as we are pledged to the prosecution of the studies which are essential to the proper understanding of the Scriptures, and are personally responsible for the use of our own judgment in the doctrine which we deduce from the written Word, it cannot be said that we are the mere instruments or mouth-pieces of a predetermined and minute system of theology. Within the broad limits of our articles we are left to the results of our own researches. Our guiding-star is the caution suggested by St Paul in the *locus classicus* on this subject, namely, that the able or sufficient minister of the New Testament is a minister "not of the letter, but of the spirit; for the letter killeth, but the spirit giveth life*." What we have to avoid is that servitude to isolated texts half understood, which our twentieth article so expressly deprecates, even when it is put forward on ecclesiastical authority. We must endeavour to appropriate the general spirit of the Bible—that spirit which gives both life and liberty; for as the Apostle says: "The Lord is that Spirit, and where the Spirit of the Lord is, there is liberty†." And in seeking to extract the spiritual sense of Scripture, which is always contained in the Bible though sometimes far below the surface, where it has remained hid for gene-

---

* 2 Cor. iii. 6.   † *Ibid.* verse 17.

rations like the undiscovered gold of California, we must reject with disdain and indignation the slavish doctrine, with which the liberty of the Christian scholar is so often fettered, that "there is nothing new in religion." It has been well remarked that "novelty may be considered as an indication of the genuine Protestant feeling" with which a divine investigates the meaning of Scripture; for "to affirm that progress may be made in mental, moral, physical, but not in spiritual science, is a thought worthy of the dark ages*."

That in a Church thus connected with the Universities, and in a ministry thus pledged to the Protestant right and duty of a free use of the judgment in interpreting the Scriptures, theology is regarded as an unfettered academical faculty, must be quite obvious to all who are willing to reflect. And those of the clergy who respect themselves and their office must adopt the words of the late Bishop Marsh †: "As *our* Liturgy and Articles are avowedly *founded* on the Bible, it is the special duty of those who are set apart for the ministry to *compare* them with the Bible and see that their pretensions are *well* founded. But then our *interpretation* of the Bible must be conducted *independently* of that, of which the truth is to be *ascertained* by it. Our interpretation of the Bible, therefore, must not be determined by *religious system;* and we must follow the example of our Reformers, who supplied the place of tradition by *reason* and *learning*." If we relinquish this right and duty we really fall below the standard of research conceded by the Church of Rome to its ministers and theologians.

* Desprez, *The Apocalypse fulfilled,* Pref. p. xiv.

† Quoted by Sir William Hamilton, *Discussions on Philosophy,* &c. p. 487.

Notwithstanding the slavery to which the Romish Church
binds its satellites, freedom of theological investigation is
permitted in all details, provided the articles of faith
decreed by the Church are not impugned. We are told
by Möhler, the great authority of the Romish Church in
Germany, that "the Church does not trouble herself with
all the particulars which claim the attention of the scientific interpreter; she does not regard it as a duty, and
therefore does not include it within the sphere of her
rights, to define *e. g.* when, by whom, and for what purpose the book of Job was composed, and so forth. Just
as little does she explain the separate words and verses,
their coherence with one another, or the connexion between considerable portions of a sacred book. Antiquities,
in the general compass of the word, do not fall within the
province of her interpretation. In short, her explanation
extends only to the doctrines of faith and morals (*ihre
Erklärung erstreckt sich nur auf die Glaubens- und Sittenlehre*)*". Again he observes: "no one who belongs to
the Catholic Church pledges himself to anything except
her doctrines of faith and morals (*zu ihrer Glaubens- und
Sittenlehre*). As she pronounces her sense of holy Scripture only in this reference, and, indeed, only in general
terms, the learned interpreter also is bound by his confession as a Churchman to nothing farther; and a wide
field remains open to him in which he may exercise his
talents, his exegetic skill, his philological and antiquarian
knowledge, and employ them profitably for the improvement of science†." The cases here referred to by Möhler

* J. A. Möhler, *Symbolik.* Fünfte Auflage, Mainz, 1838, I.
Buch. v. Capitel, § 42, p. 382.

† *Ibid.* p. 385. I need hardly mention that, with all this liberality, the Church of Rome, as represented by Möhler, makes reser-

belong to the number of those in which attempts have been made to cramp the critical scholarship of English divines, not only by extracting dogmatical inferences from the practical formularies of the Church, but even by making the opinions and presuppositions of individuals and sub-sections a criterion of the doctrines and interpretations which ought to be held by all. And if this tendency is not quelled and rebuked, as it is likely to be, if the Church in which Jeremy Taylor pleaded for a liberty of prophesying some two hundred years ago, is to be confined by trammels, not imposed on the Romish priests, who are taught that matrimony is a sacrament and denied to the clergy, but the cup a sacrament and denied to the laity, and who are obliged to receive on bended knees and with real or feigned gratitude every new dogma framed by the Pope and his conclave, then we are taking on our necks a yoke which our fathers were not able to bear, and our boasted Protestantism is no longer a comfortable reality but merely a distressing delusion.

To return, however, to my more immediate subject; although, as I have shown at some length, we are decidedly superior to the Germans in the educational results of our classical studies—that is, in scholarship—and though we are not in all departments of classical learning,—or in the literary results of these studies—so inferior to our brethren on the continent, as Mr Horsman and others maintain, it is still desirable that the equilibrium between scholarship and learning should be more exactly maintained; and that while we recognise the importance of keeping up our scholarship, we should take steps for the more direct and

vations, to which German Protestants, at all events, would not give place by subjection—no, not for an hour.

regular encouragement of the learning, which ought to be its ultimate result and development.

If I were making suggestions for the improvement of the Schools and Universities of Germany, I should be disposed to insist on the importance of their adopting to a considerable extent our system of classical education. And I know that those Germans, who are best acquainted with the practical working of our higher education, would agree with me in this. In a private letter, which I received some years ago (9th June, 1850) from an eminent German scholar at that time residing in England, the following passage occurs : "I, of course, also subscribe to your opinion of its being desirable that the classical studies at the University should be raised by an increased demand, in the University Examinations, for *scientific knowledge;* although, at the same time, I do not know, if I were to make proposals for the improvement of the German University system, whether one proposal would not be, to raise, in the final examinations of our Universities, the demand for *practical skill*, chiefly with regard to the moral effects produced by the development of that faculty. The fact that, as now matters stand, the English system of classical education—and even of education in general— produces perhaps too little *knowledge*, and the German too little *skill*, seems to me to be the more worth noticing, as it may be said to be connected with the general difference of character between the two nations." A very similar view has been stated in print by Dr L. Wiese. He says* : "English and German education exhibit the contrast between skill (*Können*) and science (*Wissen*), practice and knowledge. The knowledge of the English

* *German Letters on English Education*, translated by W. D. Arnold. London, 1854, p. 59.

scholar is limited to a narrower circle than that of the
German, but he will generally be found to move in it
with greater accuracy; his knowledge lies in a narrower
compass, but generally serves more as a practical power to
him." Dr Wiese is also perfectly conscious that the advantage which he concedes to us is a purely educational
result, and he remarks very justly: "all that a school can
teach, beyond a certain small stock of knowledge, is *the
way to learn*. It is a lamentable misconception of that
most important maxim to suppose that a liberal education
can have any other end in view than to impart and exercise power to be used in after life*." As the business of
the University begins where that of the school ends, the
inference from these admissions on the part of eminent
Germans plainly is that they require, as I have shown, a
better school system, and we a more comprehensive method of University teaching and examination.

That the classical studies of the University of Cambridge in particular admit of improvement in regard to
this very opposition between knowledge and skill, or between learning and scholarship, is admitted by those who
have obtained the highest honours under the existing
system. Dr Whewell quotes† a very decided expression
of opinion to this effect from a correspondent, who appears, from internal evidence, to be Lord Lyttelton, one
of the most accomplished *scholars* κατ᾽ ἐξοχήν, whom
Cambridge has of late years produced. He justly attributes the defectiveness of the Cambridge classical system
to the total absence of all demand, in the *University* examinations, for any scientific and well-founded *knowledge*
on any classical subject whatever, not excluding language.

* *Ibid.* p. 76. See also above, p. 15.
† *Of a Liberal Education*, § 316.

He tells us that in his time, i. e. less than twenty years ago, "what was required, and of course what was produced, was not *knowledge*, but *skill*. At best," he says, " it was a sort of empirical knowledge, wholly confined to the languages of Greek and Latin. No scientific knowledge of ancient history, philosophy, antiquities, or philology was of the least importance. If a few questions appeared on such matters, they were wholly overbalanced and made insignificant by the preponderance of *skill* in writing the three languages, in all possible combinations; and it is a fact, that any one might get anything, up to the Chancellor's Medal, without even a tolerable knowledge of such subjects; for I did it."

There will be no difficulty in indicating the practical arrangements by which we may combine the grammatical knowledge, which we already possess and exhibit at Cambridge, with the encouragement of a wider study of the subject matter of the Greek and Latin authors, and of those general branches of philology, philosophy, and literature, which are most intimately connected with a profitable pursuit of classical learning.

As the accurate scholarship, which distinguishes this country, is undoubtedly a result of the number and value of the prizes and emoluments, which our great Universities offer as encouragements for eminent proficiency*, a first step towards giving classical learning, as distinguished from classical scholarship, the stimulus which it requires, would obviously be to make success, in some, at least, of these examinations, dependent on the learning, or literary talents of the competitors. It is unnecessary that I should here dilate on the small amount of direct reward, which is given in this country, to literature in general, and clas-

* Above, p. 154.

sical learning in particular.   But of course it is obvious,
that, independently of other considerations, there are more
inducements in Germany than in England for a man to
devote himself to a learned or literary life.   Professorships, privy-counsellorships, pensions, paid memberships
of scientific societies, to say nothing of personal decora-
tions, are the necessary consequence of admitted eminence
in any department of higher authorship.   Such rewards,
as are incidentally attained by learned men in this country, would be wrongly construed as a direct patronage of
letters.   They fall chiefly under the head of church patronage ; and though bishoprics, deaneries and stalls have
been given occasionally to men, whose chief claim to public
notice has been classical learning or scientific eminence,
it is well known that the real cause of the elevation has
been, in every case, parliamentary influence, or private
predilection, or some such connexion as that of pupil and
tutor.   All that the scholastic or scientific reputation of
the individual contributes to the result may be summed
up in the statement, that such qualifications are alleged to
justify in the eyes of the public a selection generally made
on other grounds, less openly avowed.   Waiving, however,
on the present occasion, any discussion of the questions,
which have often been proposed of late years, whether
there ought not to be some civil order of merit necessarily
attainable by eminent scholars and mathematicians, whether learned men, as such, should not be rewarded independently of church patronage, whether such positions as
the masterships of public schools ought not to be given
away by more public and responsible bodies than the
trustees to whom these appointments are confided, whether steps ought not to be taken to provide that the Head
of a College should necessarily be the most eminent man
in the society (as indeed he often is), whether there should

not be a central committee of education, consisting of the
most eminent University men, and endowed with certain
privileges, emoluments and patronage,—waiving all these
questions and others of the like description, I confine myself to a few practical suggestions respecting the steps
which might be taken at Cambridge, with a view to a
more accurate adjustment of the balance of learning and
scholarship in the examinations already existing in this
University.

Remembering that a competitive test is not merely
the means of ascertaining the completeness of a student's
previous training, but also a standard of relative fitness
for ulterior pursuits, it might be as well to allow the
undergraduate competitions to have, as is now the case, a
retrospective reference, or to be tests of skill already
acquired; but to make the examination for final honours
in classics a standard and guarantee of the student's fitness for the successful prosecution of that learning, which
is proper to the University as distinguished from the
school. With this view, I would suggest that the University scholarships, the composition prizes, and all the
distinctions which are open to undergraduates, should
continue to be, as they now are, the tests and the rewards
of that accurate acquaintance with the classical languages,
which distinguishes the University of Cambridge. No
alterations would be required in regard to those objects
of competition, unless perhaps some other species of composition could be substituted for the Greek Sapphic Ode,
which has already created a collection of nondescript
poems far outnumbering all the genuine remains of the
writers in this metre. School-boy excellences of the highest kind would be called forth by these examinations, as
is now the case, and the rewards would be at least adequate to the performances of the candidates. But the

final honours of the University—the first class of the Classical Tripos and the Chancellor's Medals—should not be awarded to any man who did not evince, in addition to the power or skill of translating the 'best authors and writing in imitation of them, a perfect familiarity with ancient geography, history, and biography; a competent knowledge of ancient mythology; an intimate acquaintance with the public and private life of the ancients; and a well-grounded study of philosophical and comparative grammar. It might be expected too that such candidates would be at home in the literary history of Greece and Rome, and that questions connected with ancient art would not find them altogether unprepared. In this way we should test their aptitude for the prosecution of those studies, which give to classical learning its greatest interest and value, and should combine the skill which we have with the knowledge which we want.

In order, however, to make these improvements as effectual as possible, it would be necessary not only to introduce some modifications in the detail of the examinations themselves, but also to make provision for the careful selection of examiners, and to increase the present staff of philological teachers in the University.

With regard to the Classical Tripos Examination itself, it would, I think, conduce very much to the value of the distinctions awarded, if this list of honours contained only the names of those who should pass the examinations with very considerable credit. It is not necessary that there should be a third class*; second-rate scholars should be arranged in alphabetical order, and all inferior

---

* The *Tripos* is not so called because it has *three* classes, but from the *stool* or *tripos*, on which the bachelor of the day sat before the Proctors during the disputations on Ash-Wednesday (Peacock, *on the Statutes*, Appendix, p. x.).

candidates should be passed over in silence. With regard to the first class, I quite agree with Mr Blakesley that it would be advantageous to revive the bracket system at Cambridge, and to make it available for the classical no less than the mathematical Tripos. The following is Mr Blakesley's proposal* :

"A few years back the examination for Mathematical Honours was divided into two parts. At the termination of the first, the names of the competitors were suspended on a pillar in the Senate-House, arranged in certain classes which were called the Brackets. The principle of the arrangement was, that the parties included in each bracket were substantially possessed of the same amount of knowledge : that all of them were superior to any person whose name appeared in a lower bracket, but inferior to all those comprised in the higher. The number of these brackets was left entirely to the option of the Examiners, as was also the number of names included in each. Some brackets contained fifteen or twenty names, some only one,—and (I cannot be quite sure, but I think,) now and then there was an empty bracket, or some other symbol, to indicate that there was a considerable difference between two contiguous batches of competitors. The parties included in each individual bracket had the option either of demanding a further examination, or resting their ultimate position in the List of Honours upon the judgment of the Examiner based upon the grounds already in his possession. Subsequently this practice was abolished, and the examination was continued without any interruption to the end, when the List of Honours appeared in the form in which it now stands in the University Calendar. Now it appears to me that in making this change, the University took exactly the wrong step. If it had taken

* *Where does the Evil lie?* pp. 28—31.

the opposite course, remained contented with the indication which these brackets afforded of the relative merits of the competitors, and refused to gratify the morbid emulation which could not be satisfied without a more minute subordination, a vast deal of the evil which is at present complained of would have been obviated. For it is precisely the minute subordination in question which makes Private Tuition (so far as it is prejudicial) in request. When the speed is equal, the riding of the jockey is what determines the race. And since the change in question, the List of Honours assumes exactly this character. Not the *difference* between the competitors, but their mere *order*, is exhibited. All that the world can see is that there was an arithmetical difference between the value of *A*'s performances and that of *B*'s; but what the ratio of this difference to the whole value of either is, remains much more in the dark than would have been the case if the classification by brackets (the names within each bracket being alphabetically arranged) had been made final*. By the change, we did our best to substitute the love of Excelling for the love of Excellence as a motive

* "For instance, let us suppose the first eight Wranglers to be classed in the following different ways in different years:

A	A	A	A	A
B	B	B	B	B
C	C	C	C	C
D	D	D	D	D
E	E	E	E	E
F	F	F	F	F
G	G	G	G	G
H	H	H	H	H

how much more ground would be furnished for a substantially correct opinion as to the intrinsic merit of any one of the eight, than our present mode of recording their rank will supply?"

to exertion, and we are now reaping the fruits of our act. It is not easy all at once to change the current of feeling which has long set in one direction; but I believe that if we correct the false step then made, we shall prepare the way for a healthier view of Academical distinctions, and consequently for a pursuit of them as earnest but less anxious than at present. My proposition, then, with reference to this particular part of the question, would be, that the Examiners both for Mathematical and Classical Honours should have unlimited discretion as to the number of brackets they might think fit to employ; but should be instructed to arrange the names in each bracket alphabetically, as the final result of the examination*."

With regard to the classical tripos in particular, it appears to me that the encouragement of literature and learning, as distinguished from mere scholarship, would be promoted, if the first few names in the classical list, as

---

* "The arguments against the present mode of arranging the List of Honours will apply even more strongly against the same principle applied to the Ordinary Degrees. I hope that, at no long distance of time, an effectual check will be put on the fatuous ambition which requires the exhibition of differences here, where all distinction is out of the question. Two, or at the most three, classes, of which the lowest should be a small one, and comprise the same kind of candidates as the second class at the Previous Examination, are all that in a mere examination of qualification can be justified on any obvious principle that has a claim to be recognised; for such, I conceive, is not the one which would make examinations serve the purpose of an University or Collegiate Police. The mode of arrangement here, as well as in the Examination for Mathematical Honours, rests entirely (if I am not mistaken) with the Proctors and Moderators for the time being, and requires no Grace of the Senate for its alteration, if this should be thought by those officers desirable. Such an alteration would effectually extinguish the worst form of Private Tuition in a very few years."

determined by examination, were always left in an alphabetical bracket, except in rare cases of great superiority on the part of one candidate, if those whose names were thus placed at the head should be required to produce severally essays or theses on classical subjects chosen by themselves, and if the best of these essays were rewarded with the honour of being printed at the expense of the University. These essays, which might bear an outward resemblance to those which German students write as exercises for their first degree, would show the originality and compass of a young man's erudition; and when we remember what has been done in this way in Germany we need not doubt that many first-rate *opuscula* would be submitted to the judgment of the examiners. There need be no limitation as to the choice of subjects—the emendation and explanation of difficult passages, the discussion of antiquities or art, new combinations in comparative philology, literary history, and criticism, and a variety of other topics, might be handled with success; and in many cases an impulse would be given for further researches in the same field, and the thesis, which was crowned by the approbation of University examiners, might also contain the germ of some capital work which would bring honour to the University itself. That such expectations are not chimerical might be shown by examples: C. O. Müller's *Æginetica* was a degree-exercise; so was Lepsius' treatise on the Eugubine tables; and more than one of our own scholars has published, while still a junior B. A., the first of a series of works which have obtained for him an European reputation. At all events there seems to be no good reason to doubt that we should occasionally have *ouvrages couronnés* quite as valuable and interesting as the duplicate essays on Menander, which have been recently published by Guillaume Guizot and Benoît, and have attracted so much notice.

Classical learning would be still farther encouraged if a complete acquaintance with one or more standard works on Classical Philology were required in addition to the general examination in Greek and Latin literature. This has been more than once urged by Dr Whewell, and I once saw a formal proposal for introducing this element into the classical examinations at Oxford.

If any one objects to the plan proposed by Mr Blakesley, that there is in such a bracket at the head of the tripos an extinguisher for the highest kind of emulation, that in such a plan there is no first man,

νικᾷ δ' ὁ πρῶτος καὶ τελευταῖος δραμών,

I would say, in addition to the general argument on which he relies, that the alphabetical first-class at Oxford, though half-yearly, is found to be a sufficient stimulant for all practical purposes, and that the history of Cambridge men shows us that in very many cases no injustice would have been done and no discredit reflected on examiners, if those who appear in the second or some lower place in the tripos had been bracketed for the highest honours of their year. No doubt in many cases the Senior Wrangler and Senior Classic or Medallist have proved themselves the foremost men in the subsequent business of life. But there are also many cases in which the names most familiar in learning and science, or at least in the management of the University, will not be found at the head of either tripos, and the second place has been a common location for those whose subsequent career has been most eminent. It would have been no disadvantage to any one if Herschel, Peacock, and Babbage had been bracketed in the Calendar as they are in the mathematical literature of Cambridge;

and though Porson, Maltby, Butler, Tindal, Parke, Pollock, Thirlwall, Blomfield, Airy, Kennedy, R. L. Ellis, Stokes, Adams, and others, are first in literature or science, or professional eminence, as they were in academical competition, we must not forget that a place second to none, if not in the world's calendar, at least in University repute, has been assigned to Copley, Shadwell, Monk, R. W. Evans, Whewell, Melvill, Malden, Bowstead, Praed, Hymers, C. Merivale, Blakesley, Shilleto, W. H. Thompson, D. F. Gregory, and others, whom the examiners, no doubt justly and in accordance with the data immediately before them, placed below one or more of their competitors; nor can there be any good reasons for establishing, with great trouble, minute differences, and occasional doubts, an order of merit which is so often neutralised by a subsequent career.

An adjudication of distinctions in classical learning, like that which I have proposed, would require a careful and systematic selection of examiners; but, as it appears to me, a very simple machinery would effect all that is necessary. With regard to the examinations at entrance and for the ordinary B. A. degree, through which all students would have to pass, I have already suggested a modified revival of the general regency of junior M. A.'s. The work to be done, if it included, as I think it ought, a good deal of *vivâ voce**, would require many examiners,

---

* I am decidedly of opinion that all examinations, which, like those for the East Indian Civil Service and those for Matriculation and Ordinary Degrees, are retrospective or educational tests, ought to be, to a considerable extent, oral, public, and conducted by a considerable staff of examiners; and the necessity for this is enhanced, exactly in proportion as the test refers to language rather than to processes of calculation or mathematical analysis. Besides, if we

and it would not involve any qualifications beyond those
which every M. A. ought to possess.   The publicity too
of the scrutiny, which I propose, would check any tendency to abuse arising from a multitude of examiners. But
the examinations for honours, and I will here speak of
classical honours only, would not call for the appointment
of more than the present number of examiners; for as the
candidates would not be numerous in the first instance,
and would be soon reduced by the elimination of the least
worthy, and as no *vivâ voce* trial would be required in a
case where the results to be tested would be literary rather
than educational, four examiners would be amply sufficient, provided always that they were fully competent to
the responsible office of undertaking to select the best
scholars of the year.   To determine this last point, I
would propose that the present system, which leaves the
nomination of examiners to the Colleges in a certain rota-
tion, should be abolished; that all those who are willing to
examine for the classical tripos should send in their names
to the Board of Classical Studies, and that the Board
should select four of these to be submitted for election to
the Senate.   I entertain a strong conviction that many
scholars of large experience and well-grounded reputation
would be induced to offer their services, and I am equally
sure that the Board would not fail to make such a selection
as would meet with the approbation of the University at
large.

In order to carry out fully the effort to add a larger
apparatus of learning to our undoubtedly accurate scholar-

wish to select fit persons for employments, in which it is more important that the agent should be ready and self-collected than that
he should be profoundly learned, we cannot neglect the moral inqui-
sition, which is involved in a good *vivâ voce* ordeal.

ship at Cambridge in particular, it would be desirable not
only to modify the examination for classical honours in
the manner which I have suggested, but also to increase
the machinery of linguistic teaching which is now available at the University. And, with this view, we should
have not only to increase the professional staff, but also to
prescribe and define the functions of existing professors.

The philological teachers at present employed by the
University of Cambridge are the regius professors of Greek
and Hebrew and two professors of Arabic. The duties of
the regius professor of Greek do not require any definition;
and as long as the office is held by the accomplished and
estimable person, who now fills the chair, the University
will derive the maximum of benefit from this royal foundation. As examiner and lecturer and by his general influence on the classical studies of the University, Professor
Thompson has earned a title to an eminent place among
the successors of Porson; and I trust that he will return
in safety from his journey to Greece, with fresh inspiration
derived from the scenes on which his own Plato used to
gaze, and that Cambridge will long enjoy the benefit of
his profound and accurate teaching. Of the lectures of
the present Hebrew Professor I cannot speak from personal knowledge, but I observe from the public notices
that he undertakes Sanscrit and Gothic in addition to
Hebrew. I do not for a moment question his ability to
give instruction in these languages, but it appears to me
that the regius professor of Hebrew ought to be *par
excellence* the biblical scholar and interpreter of the University. His appointment as an *ex officio* examiner for
classical competitions of the highest kind shows that his
presumed starting-point is general learning. And I
am sure that he might not only find quite enough to

13

occupy his time in a manly and enlightened survey of the whole domain of biblical criticism, but also that he might make this the most generally interesting, as it is confessedly the most important, province of learned research. Sir Thomas Adams's professorship of Arabic is properly an office for teaching the Semitic languages in general, with the exception of course of Hebrew, which belongs to the biblical interpreter. The professor, says the Calendar, "must be well skilled (*probe eruditus*) in the Oriental languages, especially the Arabic." At the time when this professorship was founded (1632) the study of Arabic had been revived or rather created by Erpenius and Golius, and the Oriental languages referred to were those which Pococke, Walton, and Castell soon afterwards studied with so much effect, namely, Arabic, Syriac, Æthiopic, &c. A general survey of this family of languages, not irrespective of the new discoveries in the ancient Himyaritic, Babylonian, and Assyrian languages, would furnish full occupation for an accomplished professor. The details of the Arabic in particular might be left to the Lord Almoner's Reader, and Professor Preston has proved himself as competent as any man in England to deal with all questions relating to this copious literature.

With regard to the augmentation of this staff of linguistic teachers, it appears to me necessary that we should create new professors of Latin, Sanscrit, and English. The first of these professorships has been pronounced necessary by the University Commissioners, and Mr Clark has suggested the creation of professors of English and comparative philology*. I will describe the functions

---

* *Cambridge Essays,* p. 302 : "it is not a little remarkable that the Commissioners have not included, in the subjects for which they

which I conceive to belong to the three professorships
which I have proposed, and will give some reasons why
I think the two professorships of Sanscrit and English
more desirable than one for comparative philology in
general. It would, I conceive, be the business of a Latin
professor, not only to explain the forms of the language
and the ethnography, on which Latin etymology, more
than any other, depends for its basis and its starting-
point, but also to investigate the history of the Romans, to
examine their political, social, military, legal, and religious
usages, to illustrate their literature, to show its bearing
on modern culture, and to dissect and elucidate the Romance languages, which, as I have said elsewhere*, are so
deserving of the attention of all those, whose ancestors,
in part or wholly, adopted them, and which lend a new
interest to the study of the Latin language, their immediate parent. We do not want a Latin professor to give
elementary instruction in a language which ought to be
learned at school. And it was well ordered in the old
statutes that Latin grammar should not be taught in any
College in the University, except to the *choristers* in
Trinity, St John's, and King's Colleges, such lessons
being only fit for mere boys. But it would not be too
much to say that Latin philology, in ıs wider sense, is
almost an untouched field; and independently of the
special subjects, which invite discussion, there are many
even of the best authors who still desiderate an enlightened and comprehensive interpretation. The reasons, which I have already alleged, for a professed study of
Sanscrit in this country, render it absolutely necessary

recommend the creation of new professorships, either the English
language or comparative philology."

* *Varron.* p. xix. 2nd Edit.

13—2

that, at Cambridge as well as Oxford, we should have an authorised exponent of the best knowledge on this subject. The eminent Sanscrit scholars to be found at Oxford (as worthy coadjutors of Professor Wilson I might especially mention Mr Monier Williams and Mr Cowell) are a proof that these studies find a congenial soil in the midst of our old seminaries of liberal education; and though we have lost, in the late Dr Mill, a Cambridge Pundit at least equally conspicuous by his knowledge and abilities, still, if the tree retains its sap,

> uno avulso non deficit alter
> Aureus, et simili splendescit virga metallo.

Of the functions of an English professor it is scarcely necessary to speak. He would survey the whole literature from its cradle to its present maturity. The Anglo-Saxon, Old Norse, and other cognate languages would furnish him with materials for his philological lectures; the great English poets, especially those who mark epochs, like Chaucer, Shakspere, and Milton, would supply the theme for his literary discussions, which might be varied also by investigations into the varying characteristics of our prose style, from the stately atticism of Hooker, the pedantic patchwork of Andrews, the learned imagery of Jeremy Taylor, the classic grandiosity of Milton, and the quaint verbiage of Sir T. Brown, to the simple energy of Swift, the balanced periods of Bolingbroke, the sustained eloquence of Burke, and the dashing rhetoric of Macaulay. Our professor might at one time teach like Kemble, at another time like Trench, at another time like Donne, at another time like Latham, at another time like Dyce, at another time like Jeffrey; or if he could not compass so many qualifications, we should be well content to have among us, for his own sake, the author of *English Past*

and Present. Now all philology, which pretends to be
scientific, must be comparative, or must rest on the comparison of cognate idioms. I do not think, therefore, that
we should need a special professor of the science which
belongs to all genuine linguists. All that need be done
would be expected especially from the professors of Greek,
Latin, Arabic, Sanscrit, and English. Or if we confine
ourselves to the Indo-Germanic branch, in which comparative grammar has found its first suggestions and most
satisfactory inductions, the professors of Sanscrit and English would deal with the Indian and Teutonic elements—
the two extremes as well as starting-points of the whole
field of inquiry.

As I have already said, professors may excite curiosity
and stimulate intelligent study. They cannot teach alone.
They do not prepare students for examination. They do
not impart accurate scholarship [15]. Private tuition must
exist alongside of the professorial expositions. And I
trust that the restoration of the University, as a corpora-
tion or community, independent of all particular colleges,
will greatly increase and improve the agency of the private tutors. I trust that we shall find at Cambridge, in
still greater numbers, those, who will not only read for an
hour a day with a varying number of pupils, but who will
also devote themselves to the mental and moral development of the young men committed to their care, who will
be in the truest sense of the terms *Gouverneurs, Tutores,*
παιδαγωγοί, not only preparing the ambitious for successful competition in the great public examinations, which
will every day become more important, but also encouraging the backward and diffident, making good
the defects of early training, exalting the minds of the
young by instructive association with matured ability and

established moral worth, and pointing out with familiar friendliness the folly and danger of idleness, extravagance, and vice. We shall then no longer hear complaints of cramming and jockeying for particular examinations, and the private tutor will be one, who deserves the highest remuneration, because he really devotes the largest portion of his time to the teaching of those committed to his almost parental care.

As a final contribution to the increase of classical learning at Cambridge, I would suggest the establishment of an "Historical and Philological Society*," of which the board of classical studies, augmented by the new language professors, and certain eminent men coopted for that purpose, would form the acting council or committee, and to the discussions of which any member of the University would be admitted, as in other societies, by the payment of an annual fee. To encourage study in the members, it would be advisable to have two classes, which might be called first and second, or *fellows* and *associates* respectively; and an admission to the first class might be made conditional on the production of some essay read before the society and pronounced by the council worthy of the higher diploma. The *Journal of Classical and Sacred Philology* shows that we already possess at Cambridge the life and learning necessary for the successful working of such a society as I propose and recommend.

A more active cultivation of the various applications of philology, as a result and development of our classical scholarship, is not only required by the full progression of our University system. It is also calculated to produce

* The relation between associations of this kind and Universities is discussed by J. Grimm in his paper *über Schule, Universität, Academie*, Berlin, 1850; see especially p. 31.

the most desirable effect on those school-studies, on which our scholarship depends; for it is only by this agency that we can retain, what we have in the classical accomplishments of our higher classes, and, at the same time, carry out those reforms in the system of our boy-teaching, which the spirit of the age requires, and which the experience of the most enlightened men has pronounced to be of paramount necessity. Many of those who are least disposed to underrate the value of a classical and grammatical training, and who would be most unwilling to substitute multifarious sciolism for the discipline of accurate knowledge, feel nevertheless that the whole period of boyhood and youth ought not to be given up to studies in which only a few can obtain marked distinction, and which still fewer will prosecute to the end of their lives. If, however, English boys are to be as good classical scholars as they now are at eighteen or nineteen, but are to bestow on other employments a large portion of the time which they now devote to these studies, there is only one way in which the two objects can be attained, namely, by an increase in the philological learning of the country and by an improvement in the method of our school-teaching. This is a subject to which I have paid considerable attention; it is one on which I have more than once expressed my opinion; and I shall conclude this essay with a brief exposition of the conclusions at which I have arrived.

When we speak of ten years spent in merely classical studies, we refer generally to the period between the eighth and eighteenth years of a boy's life. In most cases the pupil begins Latin when he is eight years old. With some the Latin accidence is made a child's book; and I have seen it stated by one eminent scholar that he commenced Latin with one of his children when he was

only five. But is it necessary to begin even at eight, if
we wish the boy to be a well-drilled classic at eighteen?
In answer to this I need only repeat what I have said on
a former occasion. "In my opinion, boys should not
begin to learn Latin until they begin to learn Greek;
and I think that from the tenth to the twelfth year, according to the capacity of the boy, should be the period of
initiation. In Latin learning, as in other things, we may
safely use the caution of Archidamus: σπεύδοντες σχολαί-
τερον ἂν παύσαισθε. And I think that half the time spent
in learning Latin with the aid of Greek will produce more
real effect than if we commenced the solitary study of
Latin at a very early age and carried it on even for ten
years. In general, I would increase the proportion of
classical and mathematical ,training as a boy advances,
and would bestow the earlier years of his school-training
on those general subjects which in the old days of grammar-schools were never learned at all. But in any case,
I would teach no grammar except according to the soundest
rules of scientific philology; and as the ultimate object of
classical training is to give the *many* a habit of methodically arranging their thoughts, and to make the *few* who
are capable of it, good philologers in the highest and fullest
sense of the term, I can acquiesce in no grammar, even for
beginners, if it does not contain glimpses of the true system of linguistic philosophy to which the latter will finally
be brought, or if it misleads even the humblest student,
by teaching him facts which are unsustained by evidence,
and principles which are contrary to the inductions of
modern science."

As early as the time of Milton it was felt that the
time expended on Greek and Latin was occasioned mainly
by the faultiness of the teaching. "We do amiss," says

our learned poet, "to spend seven or eight years merely in scraping together so much miserable Latin and Greek, as might be learned otherwise easily and delightfully in one year." It cannot be denied that no little mischief has been done, and no little discredit brought upon the old system of classical education by an inability or unwillingness to recognise the difference between first-rate and ordinary scholarship, both in the teachers of our schools and in the composers of our school-books. For the last few years a better state of things has been in full operation; but till quite lately one could hardly think without indignation of the number of Dr Blimbers and country clergymen who, with no academical pretensions, undertook to prepare young men for the Universities, or of the common run of educational manuals poured forth wholesale by men, who did not scruple to use the scissors of the appropriator or the pen of the copyist. With improved grammars, and teachers qualified by a proper philological training to use them effectually, the highest classical scholarship, which classical learning can require as its basis, might be learned in from four to six years, according to the abilities of the pupils. A good school-education, according to the plan which I endeavoured to carry into practice, as far as the obsolete arrangements of a grammar-school allowed me to do so, should begin with those common subjects of instruction, which all require and which involve only a trifling exercise of the boyish mind, and should ascend gradually to those studies, which the University undertakes to bring to their ultimate developments. All boys must learn to read and write; and the Civil Service examinations have recently proved that these essential accomplishments are not so much attended to as they ought to be. All boys should learn the properties of common objects, the outlines of physical geography, and the geography and history of their own country. All boys should learn to exercise their memory and store it with poetical passages culled from their vernacular literature. This is not the superficial cramming, which I have deprecated in a former part of this essay. It is the mere basis of all liberal teaching, as well as of teaching in general; and might be learned at home or in some district school, quite as well as in any endowed gymnasium. If parents would be content to teach their children during the first seven years of their life to *repent, believe,* and *obey* *, to love and listen to advice, and so to pass from an affectionate reverence for their earthly protectors to that higher piety which looks to a Father in heaven † ; and if, in addition to this, they would take such measures as would ensure the development of their bodily growth and strength and health, I cannot think that the children would need any other discipline. Then at seven or eight they might begin to read and write, and learn the other matters which I have specified, until the age of· ten or twelve, according to the bodily and mental advance of the child. Then, and not before, let him learn the first beginnings of grammar and arithmetic; and I will answer for it, that his progress will be more rapid, under good tuition, than if he had been stumbling on for three or four years of previous discipline in these subjects alone. In the great majority of cases, the proper business of a liberal education would begin at twelve, and a really good school, receiving its pupils at this age, and finding them already grounded in the neces-

---

* How the Church Catechism contains a complete manual for this kind of teaching I have shown in a little book entitled: " *The three treacherous Dealers,*" Lond. 1854.

† *Ibid.* p. 77.

sary elements of general instruction, would be able to propose to them three periods of departure or epochs of progress, corresponding to the usual subdivisions in the upper half of an English public seminary. The scale of teaching might be so arranged that, (1) those who left school at the age of fourteen or fifteen, after passing through the fourth form, or third class from the top, would be adequately educated for one of the ancillary professions, which cannot leave time for the completion of a liberal discipline; (2) those who left school at fifteen or sixteen, after passing through the fifth form or second class, would be properly prepared for the army, for the navy, for the military colleges, or for the civil service; and (3) those who passed through the sixth form or highest class would be ready at eighteen or nineteen to compete, according to their abilities, for the highest prizes in classics or mathematics, which are proposed to the undergraduates at Oxford and Cambridge.

This is the plan which I proposed many years ago to the trustees of the grammar-school, with which I was connected, and which I carried out as far as the obsolete machinery of the institution allowed me a free agency in the matter. Something very similar was more recently suggested in an elaborate form by an Oxford clergyman, with whom I am personally acquainted. And this writer, while he fully recognises the importance of classical studies, agrees with me in thinking that our scholarship would not be deteriorated, but rather improved, by such a postponement of its first beginning as that which I have recommended. He says*: "it is evident that in such a scheme of instruction every thing we now teach would

* *School of the Future*, by the Rev. Foster Barham Zincke, Lond. 1852, pp. 77, 78. See also pp. 68, 69.

find its appropriate place. In saying this, I have more particularly in view our present classical studies. I think that the number of those who study to good purpose the literature of Greece and Rome would not be diminished; that some of the difficulties which attend this study would be removed; and that its real advantages would be better understood. Should the very reasonable outcry, now beginning to make itself heard, against the manner in which almost every thing is being sacrificed to a long, aimless, and inefficient system of classical instruction, issue in the neglect of all classical studies, it would be a very undesirable result. With schools, however, of the kind I am endeavouring to describe in these pages, and supposing at the same time certain changes, which such schools for the people would force on in our higher schools and universities, the probability is that we should have many more really good classical scholars than at present; men who would study the monuments of the ancient literature with far more enlarged views than those with which they are at present regarded in our grammar-schools and colleges, and with far more fruitful results."

I have now discussed briefly, but, I hope, distinctly, the propositions which I stated at the beginning of this essay. If I have succeeded in explaining and enforcing my views, which, as I have shown, are shared in many points by the most eminent of those English and continental writers, who have written on education in general and liberal education in particular, we have close at hand the means of making our classical studies all that they ought to be; we may thus retain our scholarship, and increase our learning, and, without neglecting the pressing requirements of the present age, claim for the old foundations of our academical discipline, not only the place which has always belonged to them, but even functions of increasing importance and daily widening influence. For the performance of what is necessary the critical opportunity has presented itself. Now, when the work of University Reform, commenced at Oxford, is about to be completed at Cambridge, when we have just inaugurated a system of competitive examinations for the appointments which used to be dispensed by partiality or corruption, and when the subject of educational training in all classes of the community has assumed a recognised importance, which it never had before, now is the time for explaining to the impatient utilitarian that the old method of teaching is not merely a costly apparatus for the creation of learning which is not wanted by the state or by individuals; now is the time to show that, if classical education is not already all that it might be, we are prepared to remove all that is faulty in our own University system, and to adopt all that is worthy of adoption in the practical working of other institutions. And I am full of hope that we shall pass through the period of change with increased conviction of the fact, that classical scholarship and classical learning are not the professional training of a limited number of book-makers, but a general cultivation of that which is most godlike in man—his speech and reason, his taste and imagination ;—that they furnish us with means to all the highest ends of life; that they cannot be dispensed with, until the titles of "gentleman" and "scholar" have lost their combined significance, until the English language and literature have ceased to be what they are, and until the tone and habits of our higher society have succumbed to some sentence of degradation.

LONGER NOTES AND AUTHORITIES.

———•———

NOTE 1, p. 4.

THE following extracts from Professor Amos's *Report of the Class of English Law in the University of London*, for the Session 1828-1829, will show the extent of the legal studies, which I commenced at the age of fourteen and pursued for three years, and the value of the certificate, which I obtained together with the late Solicitor-General for Ireland and two other gentlemen at that time practising as Conveyancers or Special Pleaders:

" This assembly has already been informed, in the general statement read by the secretary, of an important circumstance relative to this class, which is, the number of the students. This has exceeded the most sanguine expectations of the members of the council. The words ' English Law ' still remain affixed on the door of a little lecture-room, which, it was originally conceived, would be adequate to our use, but which we outgrew in the first week of the course. And, although we are now only completing our first session, the class of English law amounts, in number, to a-hundred-and-forty-four.

" The attendance of the class in the lecture-room has been exceedingly numerous, every evening, without a single exception, from the beginning of the course to the end.

" The development of the principles of English law, from the importance of the subject, has produced among the students, in the hours of lecture, an universal earnestness of attention, which cannot fail to have made a strong impression upon all who have witnessed it, and to have excited their admiration.

" It will be proper to notice, that a Society for discussing legal subjects has been established by the students themselves. The meetings of the society are held in a room within the University, appropriated to its use. The professor has nothing to do with these meetings; but he cannot forbear expressing his commendation of the questions which he has seen, from time to time, announced for discussion at them; and which, as is provided by the rules of the society, relate exclusively to subjects of Jurisprudence, and English Law.

" The judicious measure, adopted by the council, of instituting prizes, for the distribution of which we are now assembled, has, I am convinced, been productive of effects highly beneficial. It has held forth an additional incentive to reading and reflection, by affording, what, in legal studies, is of incalculable importance,—an immediate prospect of gaining credit, through the means of a public examination, for the extent and precision of the knowledge the student may have acquired. I am persuaded also, that the competition which has preceded the adjudication of the prizes, has, to many of the students, given more self-knowledge of their intellectual powers and defects, than they could have acquired in any other way; and which they will doubtless turn to great advantage in their subsequent studies.

" The questions proposed for the examination of the Students, it will be found, have reference to every department of the law indiscriminately. For it has been a principal object of the course, to invite and enable the student, of whatsoever department, to look abroad beyond the circumscribed limits marked out by the practice of the particular office to which he has attached himself, and to survey the general structure of the law of the country, and the mutual dependency of its parts. An attempt has not been made to communicate that minuter information, and technical expertness in the various branches of the profession, which no single individual would be competent to teach, and which, I conceive, can be acquired nowhere so well as in the offices of practitioners.

" Two prizes and two certificates will be granted. But, I trust I may be allowed to state, that in the papers of many of those gentlemen who are not about to receive these testimonials of honor, have been evinced the most promising germs of future excellence.

" The number of prizes and certificates may appear small; but it is to be observed, that, owing to the practical avocations of many of the students, and much diversity in their situation and views, only an eighth part of the class has submitted to this public examination. And when it is considered how little can be accomplished, in the study of the law, by the most highly-gifted mind, and most unremitting industry, within the compass of a single year, this University ought to be *scrupulous in the extreme* about conferring legal fame on any individual who has not exceeded, in a striking manner, the ordinary standard of legal proficiency. We owe this to the public;—we owe this to ourselves; and I, at least, will never subscribe a certificate upon any other understanding."

The mere fact, as stated in the *London University Calendar*, that the person, who obtained the highest Greek prize in the session 1829-30, received one of the four legal certificates in the previous year, though perhaps somewhat singular, is of no general interest; but it becomes important in the particular case, when, as a professed philologer, he undertakes the defence of classical and general, as distinguished from professional, education. Every such argument is liable to be met with the objection that the advocate is pleading for the only form of training with which he is acquainted and that he exaggerates the benefit which he has derived from the studies of his youth, pursued, as they were, to the exclusion of all other reading, discipline, or experience. Now it so happens that this is not my case. And whatever I may now think of the mistake committed by my friends, when they sent me to study for the bar, while still a mere boy, and without a sufficient amount of "that liberal training, which can be obtained at public schools and universities; which opens, invigorates and enriches the mind, and should precede the special education, which must qualify a man for his special career, whether at home or abroad" (*Times*, 18 Oct. 1855); whatever I may now think of this mistake, for mistake it was, and however much I may regret the loss of three precious years spent in a study, which I was not destined, after all, to make the business of my life,

14

it cannot be doubted that the experience, which I thus gained at my own expense, has placed me in a position of peculiar advantage, in regard to the vindication of the old basis of University teaching, which I have undertaken in the present essay. Having passed through the course of study indicated in Professor Amos' Report, having read all the best text-books in English law, and having debated the knottiest points in the law of real property with a society of young men, some of whom have since risen to the highest eminence in their profession or in the literary world, and having received a certificate of proficiency in the first examination of English law-students, ever held in this country, it would have been most unnatural that I should, at the age of seventeen, return to the studies of boyhood, if I had not quite convinced myself that such studies were essential to the object of my ambition—a career of legal and oratorical distinction. Nor was mine a case in which the groundwork of a classical education had been neglected. My school, as I have said in the text, was a good one, it numbered some sixty boys, and I had not only been at the head of it for two years, but had done all the work of the Charter-house, and was prepared to go through that school, according to the plan which existed in Dr Russell's mastership. It was not therefore the usual modicum of Greek and Latin of which I felt the want. I was led to the conviction that I ought to be well acquainted with Demosthenes, Thucydides and the dramatists; with Cicero's oratorical works; with Quintilian; and with Livy and Tacitus. I remember too that an admirable paper by De Quincy, which appeared about that time in *Blackwood's Magazine*, inspired me with a desire to study logic and rhetoric in the Greek of Aristotle. Nor did I neglect geometry and algebra; for one of my first cares was to engage a mathematical tutor. I conceive therefore that I have earned a special right to maintain, without any imputation of prejudice, that a general education, and especially a study of classical literature, is necessary to the English barrister, and if so, *à fortiori* to the clergyman and man of letters. I have heard of instances, in which eminent lawyers have endeavoured to acquire late in life the knowledge for which I felt the necessity when it was still possible to remedy the defect. Not to mention those who are still living, the late Mr Sheil, with whom I was well acquainted, used to speak to me of his diligent study of Greek and of the value which he attached to it, although his early training in a Roman Catholic seminary had not given him a fair start in this branch of learning. Professor Amos, whose words I have quoted above, though himself an eminent mathematician, has written a book strongly recommending the cultivation of classical scholarship (*Four Lectures on the Advantages of a Classical Education,* Lond. 1846); and if he does not enter very profoundly into the discussion of the subject, or perhaps fully recognise all its significance, he insists, at all events, on the necessity of a classical education for lawyers, and takes care to mention that "all the present high judicial functionaries have received a classical education," and that "eleven of them have been fellows of colleges." It has for some years been the practice, I believe, in more than one Inn of Court to require candidates for admission to pass an examination in Greek and Latin. And I trust, that the improvements, which are about to be made in the education of English lawyers as such, will make provision for that basis of liberal training, which will otherwise be wanted, perhaps when it is too late to make good the deficiency.

Note 2, p. 20.

It may be interesting to some readers to see the terms in which the old basis of a liberal education was advocated at the inauguration of the University of Sydney, by the Principal, the Rev. John Woolley, D.C.L., late Fellow of University College, Oxford. He said in the course of his oration :—

"But, it may be asked, by what right do we arrogate to the chairs already founded amongst us the proud title of the faculty of arts? By what authority do they claim an exclusive or even pre-eminent value as the disciplinal method of education? To this question an answer must be returned. It is not enough to plead the suffrage of philosophers and educators throughout the civilised world : not even enough to exhibit the result of these, in comparison with more novel and popular systems. We acknowledge indeed, and accept our position as the youngest daughter of the family of learning : we are not rash to assay weapons other than those whose temper has been proved in many a conflict with ignorance and presumption : we hear with respect the counsels, and follow in the footsteps, of those who have already won the height which we are setting out to climb. But we follow neither implicity nor as unconvinced. The ceremonies of this day's inauguration, so far as they are retained from ancient academic ritual, the habits which we wear, our statutory and customary observances, are not adopted only because they preserve the traditions of our fathers, because they link us to the venerable procession of scholars in the days of old, because in them we seem to claim the kindred and inherit the spirit of the mighty dead ; but, also, because we believe that the GOD who, not in vain, had clothed the soul with a body, and made the senses interpreters and ministers of thought, and given to the outward world its mysterious hold and mastery upon our fancy, has designed and commanded us by the right use of material symbols to bring our souls and bodies into harmony, and attune our faculties to the work in which they are engaged. And thus we vindicate our proposed undergraduate course, not more from authority than common sense ; and in the vindication our only difficulty arises from the abundance and multiplicity of our materials. To enter in detail upon a theme so varied would ill become this place and occasion ; even to indicate in passing the topics of the argument will exercise the patience of my hearers. I will try to do so with all briefness. I say, then, generally, that the judgment of our founders, in appointing for their disciplinal course the study of philology, especially in the classical languages, with logic and mental philosophy on the one hand, and on the other mathematics and the elements of physical science, is supported, were the evidence of experience as doubtful as it is decisive, by the *reason of the case*. A liberal education is one which

cultivates and develops in their due and harmonious proportion what the Romans called 'humanitas,' all those faculties
and powers which distinguish man from the inferior creatures.
This end it accomplishes in two ways; (1) by the appropriate
and healthful exercise of those faculties; (2) by introducing
them to those objects, in the observation of which they will
hereafter be engaged; in other words, a good education must
induce a habit of patient, connected, vigorous, independent
thinking, and must afford a general prospect of the most important objects of thought, the world within us, and then
the world without, both in our relations to our fellowmen, and
the constitution of the physical creation. How the second of
these purposes, the opening, that is, of an extensive and many-
sided range of thought, is effected by the studies you recommend, we need scarcely to be told. We know that mathematical
science is the queen and guardian of all those pursuits which
investigate or apply the laws of nature ; the progress, nay even
the continuance of the meanest among the latter, ever keeps
pace with the cultivation of the former. And to take the lowest
ground : the mechanical arts, those which assuming scientific
truths, deduce from them discoveries which directly enhance
the luxury of life, but indirectly are most powerful agents in
promoting the moral and social progress of mankind ; all these,
in a thousand ways, are indebted to the abstracted studies of
the solitary recluse; and even the stability of moral and social
relations depends not a little upon a Galileo or a Newton. We
know, again, that the languages of Greece and Rome are the
master-keys which unlock the noblest modern tongues of
Europe, and, with the increased power of understanding our
brethren's speech, enlarge our sympathies and realise our fra-
ternity ; that as the disunion of the nations was the consequence
of misunderstanding, so the growth of fellow-feeling, what the
Greeks beautifully call συγγνώμη, the thinking with others,
the identifying of our minds with theirs, may prepare the
restoration of ' concord and unity.' We know that in their
rich and graceful literature, the model of all most perfect since,
they provide appropriate nutriment to the noblest faculties of

our nature; poets, historians, philosophers, with their keen
and delicate sense of the beautiful, their vigorous and versatile
intellect, their life of intense activity and ceaseless energy of
thought, not from books and theoretic rules, but fresh from
nature's inspiration and the school of experience, created those
masterpieces in every kind, to understand and emulate which
is daily more and more the noblest exercise of taste, of moral
judgment, even of scientific research. We have learnt, lastly,
that philology is the primary element of sciences, which, like
ethnology, trace back the stream of time to its fountain-head,
and disclose to our view the mysterious cradle of our race and
the history of our gradual alienation. These topics, however
important and interesting, I the more readily pass over, because in the works of one whose name is justly honoured in
this University they are doubtless familiar to many here*. And
if we pass to the higher purpose of education, if we ask in
what manner philology and mathematics conduce to mental
vigour and self-relying thought, the reply is not more difficult.
Singly powerful, but partial and one-sided, they form, united,
a perfect discipline of reflexion. How, except through mathematical habit, should we attain that power of abstraction, of
sustained attention, of patient reasoning long drawn out; every
link in the chain so essential, that the slightest error invalidates
and breaks the whole? Mathematics is the discipline of
necessary reasoning; philology of the probable and contingent.
Speech is the vehicle and outward form of thought, as the body
to the soul; as in the features of the face we love to read the
character of the mind, so in the analysis of speech is involved
the observation of the facts of thought; and in the marvellous
languages of Greece and Rome, with their minutely delicate
inflexions, their profound and subtle syntax, their all-sufficing
apparatus for expressing the variations of ideas, we possess, as
it were, an authentic and stereotyped record of mental operations
in the most intellectually gifted peoples of the earth. Thus,

* The terms of this antipodean reference were perhaps suggested by the fact that
Mr Stuart A. Donaldson, M.L.C., is one of the sixteen Fellows of the Senate who
constitute the Body Politic and Corporate of the University of Sydney.

whether we analyse the formation of words, and, comparing the members of a common family, or tracing the changes of meaning in a single term, investigate the association and connexion of ideas, or, in the laws of syntactical arrangement develop the fundamental principles of inward discourse, we are by healthy but not painful effort practised to turn the mind back upon itself, to learn the rudiments of our internal being, to place our feet upon the threshold of that holy portal which bids us, as the end of all knowledge, to make acquaintance with ourselves."

Note 3, p. 27.

The mediæval meaning of the word *universitas* is more intimately connected than is generally supposed with that of the classic adjective *universus*, a word which has never been adequately examined by the writers on Latin synonyms. The few, who have thoroughly studied the Latin language, are aware that some of the commonest words derive their primary signification from the phraseology of the *agrimensores* and of the *scriptores gromatici* who belonged to this school ; and even the modern German verb *orientiren*, " to put oneself or any one else in the right direction," may, perhaps, have originated in a similar method of settling the points of the compass with a view to land-surveying. (See Campe, *Wörterb. z. Erkl. u. Verdeutschung der u. Spr. aufgedrungenen fremden Ausdrücke*, p. 451). Now among the words thus used by the Romans to denote the directions of the *viæ* and *limites*, or main lines and cross lines in laying out an estate or district, the word *vorsus* or *versus*, both as a simple substantive and as forming the termination of compound adjectives, plays an important part. We are told that it is both Tuscan and Umbrian (Front. *de Limit.* II. p. 30, ed. Blume.), as denoting the 100 feet square which was the first element in land-surveying. That *verto* was a Tuscan verb, is shown by the fact that *Vertumnus* was the name of a Tuscan god, and that *Nortia* or *Nursia*, who corresponds to *A-tropos*, must mean *Ne-vortia*, " the unturning Goddess of Fate" (*Varron.* pp. 146, 149). Going still farther

we find *verto* in the Sanscrit *vrĭt*, which corresponds to the
meaning of *verto, versor,* and *werden,* and in compounds signifies "to go," or, with *punar* after it, means *redire, revertor.*
By itself then the *versus* is the integral part of the area; but
the lines forming right angles in the *vorsus* and in the whole
area were termed *prorsi,* i. e. *pro-versi limites* when they followed the main direction, but *trans-versi,* when they crossed it
(*Hygin.* p. 167, 17, &c.). In the same way, the adverb *prorsus*
would denote entirely straightforward and consistent action, and
rursus = re-versus would imply retrogression, or motion backwards, in the same horizontal line; similarly, *sursum = su-
versum* would imply motion upwards, and *de-orsum = de-versum*
its vertical opposite. According to this, *uni-versus* must signify
parallel motion or parallel direction, whether it be *prorsus* or
rursus, whether *sursum* or *deorsum ;* and the primary distinction between *universus* and its synonym *cunctus = conjunctus*
consists in this, that, while the former implies that there is
merely a community of direction and object in the individuals
composing the entirety or totality referred to, the latter denotes
their external and tangible union or conjunction at a particular
time ; so that there is an implication of durable or permanent
consent in the *universi,* whereas the *cuncti* are joined only for
a single and specified act. There are, no doubt, cases, in which
universus and *cunctus* seem to be convertible terms. This
results from the fact that it may be a matter of indifference
whether we say that a number of men did something "all in
a body" (*cuncti*), or that they acted "by common consent," i. e. all
going in the same direction (*universi*). We have the former in
Nep. xiv. 5: "Datames magnam invidiam aulicorum excepit, qui
illum unum pluris quam se *omnes* fieri videbant ; quo facto
cuncti ad eum opprimendum consenserunt." We have the latter
in Cic. *de Off.* ii. 7. § 26 : "Phalaris non ex insidiis interiit, non
a paucis, ut hic noster, sed in eum *universa* Agrigentinorum
multitudo impetum fecit." In the same way it may appear
that *universus,* which denotes the community of consent, purpose, and direction, may be used as a convertible term for *totus,*
which signifies that all the parts are so combined that they are

regarded as forming a new unit. Thus we have in Cicero *de Fin.* IV. 2. § 3 : " Nec exspectes dum ad *omnia* dicam; *universa* enim illorum ratione cum *tota* vestra confligendum puto." This promiscuous use of the words is only apparent, and their real distinction is easily shown ; for their opposites are neces- sarily different ; and *omnes, cuncti, totus,* and *universus* must be as capable of discrimination, as *unus* or *aliquot, dispersi, pars,* and *singuli* or *unusquisque,* to which they are respectively opposed. We have three of the synonyms used together in Cic. *Deiot.* IV. 11 : "Maxime perturbatus est, ut audivit con- sules ex Italia profugisse, *omnesque* consulares, *cunctum* sena- tum, *totam* Italiam esse effusam," where it is signified that not *some,* but *all* the consulars, not the senators previously *dis. persed,* but the *collected body* of the senate, not a *part,* but the *whole* of Italy, had shared in the panic. For *universus* we may turn to Cæs. *B. G.* VII. 76 : "Tanta *universæ* Galliæ consensio fuit, ut neque beneficiis neque amicitiæ memoria moverentur,' where it is distinctly implied that every single individual in Gaul concurred in this effort to recover their liberty. And that there is actually this difference between *universus,* as de- noting the community with express reference to the individuals of which it is composed, and *omnis,* as indicating only the sum of a plurality of persons or things, is clearly shown by the following passages; Cic. *de Officiis* III. 6 : " *Unum* debet esse *omnibus* propositum, ut eadem sit utilitas et *unius cujusque* et *universorum.*" While therefore *omnes,* like πάντες (cf. *quanti*), denotes " all as many as there are," while *cuncti* denotes " all conjoined or united for a particular purpose and at a particular time," and while *totus* implies that a new unit is formed, which must be broken up again, if it is to be regarded as separable into constituent parts, we see that *universus* has express refer- ence to the community, as consisting of separate members regu- larly and continually united. And this is our idea both of the *universe* and of the *university.*

The etymology of *omnis* and *totus* has a particular interest as illustrating the German affinities of the ancient Italians ; for while the former, an adjective in *-is* from *omn = o-min,* points

at once to the old German *eo-man=je-mand* or *jeder-mann*,
totus, which appears in old Umbrian as *tuta* or *tota,* "a city,"
is obviously connected with the O. N. *thiod,* A.S. *theod,* Goth.
thiuda, Lith. *thauta,* (Pott. *Etym. Forsch.* ii. 563), all signifying
"people," i. e. a collected mass, regarded as a new unit. This
adjective is also interesting as having taken the place of *omnis*
in some of the Romance languages; for while *ogni* for *omnis* is
retained in Italian to signify "every man," which was the original meaning of *omnis,* we have, for all other senses, in Italian
toto, in Spanish *todo,* and in French *tous.* The same pheno-
menon is observable in the German *all* (Gr. ὅλϜος, old Latin
sollus for *solvus,* cf. *salvus,* Sanscrit, *sarva*), in which, as Grimm
says, the idea of *omneity* (*allheit*) has gradually developed
itself from that of *totality* (*ganzheit*). The word *ganz* itself
compared with *genesen* concurs still more closely with the original idea of " all," ὅλϜος and *salvus.*

That the idea of a community of purpose, continually existing and recognised, which flows ftom the classical meaning
of *universus,* was actually involved in the mediæval term *universitas,* is clearly shown by the following extracts from Ducange. Thus in the Gloss. Lat. Gr. we have "*universim*=
ὁμοθυμαδόν ;" "*universitas* nude pro incolarum urbis vel oppidi
universitas, idem quod *commune,* Statuta Arelat. MSS. art. 132:
*prout inter bonæ memoriæ dominum Barralum quondam patrem
nostrum et inter consilium et Universitatem Arelatis hactenus
existit incartatum;* et passim." "Nostris *Université* eodem
sensu. Lit. remiss. ann. 1385. in Reg. 126. Chartoph. reg. Ch.
227: *et autres malefices, que les Universitez, gens et habitans des
villes de Thoulouse, Carcassone,* &c. *ont commis.*" "*Universitas*
collegium canonicorum. Charta Werrici ann. 1178: *quia ad
nostram pertinet Universitatem rem gestam concedere nostrique
sigilli testimonio roborare.* Potest et de superiori dominio haud
male intelligi, Gall. *suzeraineté.*" In its academical sense, *universitas* is always used with direct reference to the classes and
persons of which it is composed; the following instances are
cited by Sir W. Hamilton (*Discussions, &c.* p. 480). Paris:
Bull, 1209: *doctorum et scholarium Universitas;* Oxford: Mat-

thew Paris, 1250: *Universitas scholarium;* Bull, 1300: *Universitas magistrorum doctorum et scholarium;* Cambridge, 1268: *Universitas scholarium;* Decree, 1276: *Universitas regentium et scholarium.*

That *universitas* exactly corresponds in its mediæval use to our word "community" is clearly shown by Ducange's gloss: "*Commune, communia, communio, communitas,* incolarum urbis aut oppidi universitas, domino vel rege concedente, sacramento invicem certisque legibus astricta."

Note 4, p. 41.

That the Elizabethan statutes were forced upon the University of Cambridge is shown by the following accounts of the proceeding. Mr Walsh says (*A Historical Account of the University of Cambridge,* Lond. 1837, pp. 8, 10):

"This insidious composition was issued by Elizabeth in 1570. To make use of Mr Farish's words, 'it completely revolutionised the whole order of things, by transferring a more than ordinary influence over all our deliberative proceedings into the hands of the masters of colleges.—The history of its promulgation is so singularly interesting, so replete with intrigue and cunning, that we are impelled to enter still farther into its detail. We do not find that the design of giving laws to the University, had its origin with Queen Elizabeth. It was hatched in the brooding mind of Whitgift, the Master of Trinity College, than whom no man was ever more versed in the art of hypocritical duplicity. It was Whitgift who first applied to Lord Burleigh for a code of statutes, for the prudent but ambitious purpose "of curbing many of the younger sort of fellows, and scholars, that were disobedient to the heads, &c." It was Whitgift, that, with the assistance of some of the "ancient and chief heads," first compiled them, and submitted them to Cecil for his approbation. Their sole and avowed object in this application was the acquisition of power. There exists an entertaining and instructive history of the proceedings of our Alma Mater, at that period, in some MS. papers preserved in the library of Corpus Christi College. They inform us, that these statutes of Elizabeth, on their first promulgation, were rejected by the senate with scorn; and that "the proctors and divers regents and non-regents met to consult in way of supplication to seek redress." What the result of that consultation was, we are informed by another paper in the same curious collection. A petition was prepared and signed by 164 regents and non-regents, and presented to Lord Burleigh. Supplicatory letters were also addressed by the aggrieved members to several persons of rank and distinction, whose influence tended in any way to promote the interests of the petition.—No alteration in the statutes, however, appears to have taken place. At that time it was perhaps dangerous to inquire into the prerogative of the Crown, and the authority of the tyrannical Elizabeth. The agitation of men's minds gradually died away, and a passive indifference succeeded. In the mean time, the indefatigable zeal of Whitgift and his colleagues was labouring to establish the new code, and to secure to the Heads of Houses the permanent exercise of this strange and exorbitant power.'—Hence it has been doubted by some very distinguished men amongst us, whether this second code of Elizabeth's be binding upon the University. Sir Vicary Gibbs and Mr Hargrave, however, when professionally consulted on the subject, gave it as their opinion, (August 30, 1804, and August 24, 1805,) 'that where the University has acted upon particular parts, it may so far operate as an acceptance of it.' This third [Tudorian] code is the one by which the University is professedly governed at the present day."

To the same effect Dr Peacock writes (*Observations on the Statutes of the University of Cambridge*, Lond. 1841, pp. 53—55): "The new statutes, proposing, as they did, such extensive changes in the constitution of the University, and in the distribution of power amongst the different classes of its members, created, when first received, nearly universal discontent, and as much opposition to them, as the arbitrary principles of the government of Elizabeth rendered safe or tolerable. Dr Whitgift was nominated and elected the first Vice-Chancellor under the new code, and was not disposed to mitigate the severity of harsh laws by their mild and considerate administration. He availed himself without scruple of the extraordinary powers which the new statutes gave him, to suppress the rebellious spirit which had manifested itself in nearly every college of the University, and in which resistance to the hierarchy and liturgy of the Church was combined with a very reasonable hatred of the bondage which the new law imposed on the great body of the senate: but neither his own commanding talents, nor the well-known favour of the Chancellor, could save him from the storm of obloquy and opposition, which he encountered. A petition, signed by 164 masters of arts and superior graduates, was addressed to the Chancellor, containing a very detailed statement of their objections to the new statutes, and of their complaints of the severe and somewhat tyrannical conduct of Dr Whitgift and the other Heads of Houses in carrying them into execution. This petition was referred by the Chancellor to the two Archbishops, and to the Bishops of London, Ely, and Bangor, together with Whitgift's reply to it, and, as might have been anticipated, the decision of the referees was unfavourable to the petitioners, who are accused of using 'disordered means in seeking subscriptions of names, without the licence of the Vice-Chancellor.' An angry and decisive letter from the Chancellor, addressed to the University, expressing the pleasure of an authority which could not safely be questioned, put a final stop to any further attempt to resist the reception of the new statutes."

Note 5, pp. 65, and 95.

The Vice-Chancellor begs leave to publish to the University the following Report, which he has received from the Board of Classical Studies appointed by Grace, *May* 3, 1854.

"The Board of Classical Studies begs leave to report to the Vice-Chancellor, that Tables showing the proportionate amount of marks assigned to the Candidates in each subject of Examination have been prepared by the Examiners of the Classical Tripos, for the three preceding years. A copy of one of these Tables is annexed to this Report.

" The Board views with satisfaction the result which appears to be established, that the places of the Candidates on the Tripos are in a great degree determined by the manner in which the papers of translation from Greek and Latin are performed.

" The Board observes with regret, that a large proportion of the Candidates fail to obtain any high number of marks for the Examination in History. It is possible that this result may have arisen from other causes than the want of attention to the subject on the part of the Candidates. The nature and extent of the subject render it difficult for even the best Candidates to exhibit anything like a complete knowledge. Some of the questions proposed occasionally require much of the whole time allowed for the paper in order to their receiving a satisfactory and complete answer ; and the attention of the best prepared persons may have been so much engaged by one portion of the paper, as to leave too little time to answer the remainder even when the requisite information was at hand. If the experience of future Examiners should appear to confirm this supposition, it will, in the opinion of the Board, become a point for consideration, whether the Candidates should not in their answers, be limited to a selection, at their own discretion, of a fixed number of the questions, complete answers to which should receive the whole number of marks assigned to the paper ; or whether some system of marking the answers, different to that at present employed, should not be devised by which the History Paper should receive a full share of influence on the final classification of the Candidates. It may however be observed, that under existing circumstances, the History Paper acts with considerable force as a disturbing cause in the assignment of places on the Tripos ; a fact, which the Board desires to make generally known, with the view of preventing the subject of History from being regarded with indifference by any of the Candidates.

"The Board is desirous of calling the attention of the University to an anomaly arising out of the recent legislation of the Senate in regard to Classical Honors. In the year 1857, and then upwards, the Classical Tripos will be open to all Students who are of the proper standing to be Candidates for Honors in the Mathematical Tripos of that year; and all persons who obtain Honors in the Classical Tripos, will be entitled to admission to the Degree of Bachelor of Arts. But in the absence of any provision to the contrary, persons who obtain their Degree in this way, will rank with the Bachelors of the succeeding year. They will pay higher fees on admission than those who graduate in the ordinary way; and, besides losing Academical standing, they may be in danger of losing Scholarships in their several Colleges. The Board is not prepared on the present occasion to recommend any method for the satisfactory removal of this anomaly, but it regards it as a question deserving the early attention of the Senate, more particularly as special subjects in Mathematics have been added recently, by Grace of the Senate, to the Previous Examination for this Class of Candidates to Classical Honors.

> W. H. THOMPSON, *Chairman.*
> W. H. BATESON.
> THOMAS FIELD.
> ARTHUR WOLFE.
> WILLIAM HAIG BROWN.
> W. M. GUNSON.
> H. VANSITTART.
> EDW. H. PEROWNE.

December 10, 1855.

Average per centage of full Marks obtained in	Latin Verse Composition.	Latin Prose Composition.	Greek Verse Composition.	Greek Prose Composition.	Latin Verse Translation.	Latin Prose Translation.	Greek Verse Translation.	Greek Prose Translation.	History.
By the First Class	59	66	62	66	70	72	75	73½	35
... Second Class	37	52	34	43½	63	56	54	52¼	21
... Third Class	24	37	14	27	47	41	43	39	10
Rejected Candidate	14	24	7	13	35	29	25½	25½	10

"This Table is calculated from the averages of the three years 1853, 1854, and 1855."

Note 6, p. 72.

The following passage from Bishop Law's Preface to his Translation of Archbishop King's *Essay on the Origin of Evil*, has been pointed out to me by a learned friend. It contains some good remarks on the origin and tendencies of an exclusive addiction to Mathematics at this University in the 18th century:

"But, enough of these trifling particulars, which have detained me from a more important point intended for this place, namely, surveying the too general turn of our University education. Having, therefore, about the time above-mentioned (1723), remarked some abuses in the training up of our youth, by beginning it with inculcating the dull, crabbed system of Aristotle's Logic, and at a time when they were least capable of applying that to any valuable purpose; by persisting to retain such an idle system, even after it was grown obsolete, and not rather laying some solid foundation in natural philosophy, with its modern improvements, or 'natural law,' as the whole doctrine of morals is now termed; which would be of constant use to these young disciples, in what way of life soever they might afterwards be engaged, and likewise help to settle

in them right notions of religion; which would, above all
things, tend to make them more sober-minded, and, consequently, more submissive to their superiors here, as well as
more happy in themselves for ever hereafter. Reflecting on
these absurdities which still prevailed in our public forms of
education, some of my friends were induced to seek a remedy,
by freeing their pupils from all that pedantic jargon, and introducing some better means to engage their attention, and
accustom them to a close, regular way of thinking, and thereby
prosecuting their future studies with greater accuracy and precision: to this end they called in the assistance of the mathematics, little then imagining, that, in a short time, these same
assistants, these comparatively meagre instruments, should, like
Pharaoh's lean kine, eat up all that was good and well-favoured
in the sciences themselves; that they should usurp the place of
those very sciences to which they were originally designed to
be subservient, and for which station they were sufficiently
qualified. But such became the common infatuation, that
these helps for conducting an inquiry through the whole
Cyclopædia, instead of continuing to perform such useful
offices, were, by the mere force of fashion, set up for a capital
branch of it, and the best part of our scholars' time spent in
speculating on these same instruments; which would, in any
other case, appear perhaps to be somewhat preposterous. However, these favourite speculations did not at first so far engross
all the thoughts of our young students, as not to admit some
points of a moral and metaphysical kind to accompany them;
which last held their ground for above twenty years; and,
together with Mr Locke's Essay, Dr Clarke went hand in hand
through our public schools and lectures, though they were
built on principles directly opposite to each other; the latter
of them founding all our moral knowledge on certain innate
'instincts,' or absolute ' fitnesses,' however inconsistent these
two terms may appear, the former being wholly calculated to
remove them: till, at length, certain flaws being discovered in
the Doctor's celebrated argument *à priori*, (on the truth of
which many minute philosophers had wholly pinned their

15

faith) his doctrine fell into disrepute, and was generally given
up ; but its downfall, at the same time, sunk the credit of that
whole science, as to the certainty of its principles, which
thereby received so great a shock as is hardly yet recovered.
This threw us back into a more eager attachment than ever to
its rival, the mathematics, which grew from henceforth into a
most important and most laborious study, being confined chiefly
to the deepest and most difficult parts of them, and taking up
the student's whole time and pains, so as to become incom-
patible with any other much more necessary studies, as will
appear below.   And here one cannot avoid stopping to lament
the notorious weakness of the human mind ; which, instead of
exerting its own native powers of examining and judging in
points of faith, is ever apt to shelter itself under some sorry
system of opinions, accidentally thrown in its way ; and through
mere indolence, or perhaps dread of that *odium theologicum*
which too often attends on each attempt toward any improvement, or what is called ' innovation,' (though it be no more in
reality than removing those innovations made by time, the
greatest of all innovators, according to Lord Bacon,) sits down
contented with its ancient state of ignorance and blind credulity,
willing to connive at all those gross and glaring absurdities
that have long beset it, and been suffered to continue in so
many learned and religious societies.   But it is hoped, that
most of these are already seen through, and will shortly be
discarded by the laudable endeavours of the University of
Cambridge in particular ; which is labouring to reform such
abuses, and restore its credit to the first degree in arts, and the
exercise preparatory to it, which was once the peculiar glory
of this place ; and whereupon not only the academical character
of each candidate, but likewise his success in life, does still
very much depend ; well aware that this long-desired piece of
reformation can never be secured effectually, but by a careful
and impartial distribution of those honours which usually
attend the said promotion,—a prospect whereof is found to be
the great object of ambition to many of these young men from
the very time of their admission into college : to this they often

sacrifice their whole stock of strength and spirits, and so entirely devote most of their first four years to what is called *taking a good degree*, as to be hardly good for anything else, least of all for a proper discharge of that important duty to which the greatest part of them were originally destined, and which ought to be the chief business of their future lives ; but to which, alas! they have hitherto been utter strangers. A sad truth! of which we are made very sensible in the mortifying office of examining such persons for holy orders."

Note 7, p. 117.

The importance of making Classical Scholarship the basis of all the applications of philology and criticism occurred to me at a very early period in my literary career, and the development of this leading idea has occupied the best years of my life. It is due to myself and to English scholarship, which is interested in the humblest efforts of those who have spent their lives in contributing to it, that I should here show that this mode of conducting philological researches has been disregarded or rejected by the Germans, or only adopted by them at a later period. The time may perhaps come, when it will be proper that I should detail the results of the system which I have endeavoured to carry out. On the present occasion it is sufficient to say that, early in 1839, I published a book, which expressly made classical scholarship the starting-point in a course of linguistic discovery ; that, in the course of that book, (§ 39) I called attention to the fact, that comparative philology had been pursued previously from the side of the oriental languages or of the German dialects, and that disadvantages had arisen from the circumstance, that no one of the great comparative philologers was a professed classical scholar ; and in the preface to the new edition I stated (p. ix.), that continued experience and reflexion had convinced me of the increased importance of the task, which I had first attempted—namely, the prosecution of comparative philology on the safe and ascertained basis of the old classical scholarship. And having proved this in regard to the Indo-Germanic languages, I have since extended an application of the same principles and processes to Semitic philology and criticism.

Now, in the first place, this mode of philologising has been disregarded on the continent. The great classical scholars have not taken the pains, or condescended to extend the field of their researches, by taking up comparative philology in its full extent and compass. Lobeck has candidly admitted that, as one life is sufficient only for Greek or Sanscrit taken separately, he would, if nature would double the period of his existence, bestow it in equal shares on the two languages (*Paralipomena*, p. 126, note 12). The feeling in the minds of some professed Greek scholars has been, that we do not yet know all that might be learned from the remains of Greek alone; nay, more, that we have not yet got together a complete collection of materials for acquiring this knowledge. And in January, 1837, the Imperial Academy of Sciences at St Petersburg published a scheme for a prize essay on the Greek dialects, from which all consideration of Sanscrit was to be excluded. It is worth while to print this prospectus as showing the views which were entertained on the continent:

"*Præmium literarium, quod imperialis Academia scientiarum Petropolitani sectio doctrinarum politico-historico-philologica in solemni consessu 29 Decembris, 1836, (10 Januarii, 1837) publice proposuit.* Inter reliquas Græcæ linguæ dialectos, Attica, uti par erat, diligentius excoli, et modo Atticistarum præceptis accuratius definita et ad proprie dictam Atticam dialectum revocata, modo ad ampliorem quendam Græciæ usum delapsa et communis facta, plurimis literarum monumentis illustrari cœpit. Sed quem ita principatum Atticus sermo inter gravissimas vitæ publicæ res gestas et per diuturniorem scriptorum omnis generis usum adeptus est, is maturius ipsas vocabulorum grammaticas formas ita attrivit, ut antiquioris linguæ conformatio hic magis quam alibi obscuraretur. Verum in expendendis linguarum formis, sive in unius indolem inquiras, sive plures cognatas inter se comparare instituas, ubique antiquissima linguæ facies, quæ paucissimas mutationes subiit, ante

omnia momentum habet. Ut itaque priorem linguæ Græcæ
conformationem paulo propius attingas, superstites reliquarum
dialectorum reliquias adire oportet, quæ minus excultæ cum in
inferiori quodam loco substitissent, ob id ipsum antiquiora re-
ligiosius conservarunt, Æolicam potissimum et Doricam dialectum, et in quas discrepantias, diversis temporibus et locis,
utraque rursus divisa est. Et cum scientiâ linguarum nuperrime de novo lætiora capere incrementa, subtiliusque tractari
cœpisset, et cognatarum imprimis linguarum comparatio, partim linguæ Sanscritæ et Zendicæ studio, partim accuratiori
Germanicarum dialectorum cognitione commendata, multorum
ingenia mirum quantum teneat, tempus hoc ipsum novam
eamque criticam præceptorum et exemplorum, quæ de dialectis
linguæ Græcæ cértiora nos doceant, collectionem suadere et jure
quodam suo flagitare ibi videtur. Paucæ, quæ præsto sunt,
antiquiores hujus generis collectiones, ut Maittairii a Sturzio
editum opus et quæ Schæfero debetur novissima Gregorii Co-
rinthii editio, si ordinem, quo materies disponitur, criticam
fidem et plenum notitiarum recensum spectas, non ab omni
parte satisfaciunt. Præstitum ibi tantum, quantum illa ætate
et cum illis quæ habebantur subsidiis præstari potuit, et ut
disciplinæ ipsius ratio et modus tum ferebat. Neque postea
quicunque Grammaticorum recentiorum principes dialectorum
doctrinam attigerunt, rem totam exhauriendam sibi sumserunt,
sed contenti, generalia præcepta dedisse aut uni alterive parti
facem prætulisse, angustioribus se limitibus volentes circumscrip-
serunt. Interim apparatus, unde novum dialectorum corpus
concinnari possit, ab omni parte in majus crevit. Recentioribus
enim temporibus plura Grammaticorum antiquorum opéra,
antehac inedita, in lucem prodierunt, aliis novæ editiones
novam lucem accenderunt, ex quibus omnibus non contem-
nenda subsidia doctrinæ de dialectis parari poterunt. Pluri-
mum porro haurire licebit e locupletissimo illo dialecticarum
formarum fonte, Inscriptionibus marmorum antiquorum, quibus tanto criticæ supellectilis apparatu, tam plene, accurate et
docte tractari nondum ante contigit. Sufficiat exempli loco
Inscriptiones Æolico-Bœoticas commemorasse, quæ Corpore

Inscriptionum, ab Academia Regia Berolinensi edito, numero
non paucæ · continentur. Novum hujusmodi monumentorum
thesaurum nuperrime Rossius, Inscriptionibus Naupliæ editis,
nobis reclusit. Quidquid denique hac nostra ætate ad opera
antiquiorum Græciæ scriptorum correctius exhibenda, Homeri
nominatim, Hesiodi, tum Pindari præ cæteris, et in recensendis
Lyricorum Græcorum fragmentis a VV. DD. laudabili studio
congestum est, id non sine emolumento perlustrabitur ab iis,
qui de dialectis bene mereri cupiant. Præterea multa illa in
linguis comparandis posita tentamina et felicioris in hoc genere
successus exempla haud rara ita acuerunt ingenia in dijudi-
candâ hâc philologiæ parte, ut vel leves, quæ viderentur,
dialectorum discrepantiæ diligentius et observarentur et eno-
tarentur, quibus olim parum aut nihil tribuť solitum ; quod
subtilioris judicii acumen etsi fieri potest, ut passim ultra
quam fas sit progrediatur, ei certe, qui modum servare certo
pede didicit, non parum præsidii suppeditare necesse est. Quid ?
quod linguæ Græcæ fasciculo, sine titulo et conclusione raptim
edito, cujus auctor, *Giese*, Berolinensis Seminarii eruditus
alumnus, docte et subtiliter generalia quædam de dialectis
capita, perpetuâ linguæ Sanscritæ ratione habitâ præmisit,
sed, immaturâ morte absumtus, opus, quod non vulgaria
sperare nos jubebat, inchoatum reliquit. De quo opere absol-
vendo cum jam desperandum videretur, præterea optandum
sane esset, hanc de Græcis dialectis disquisitionem institui,
Græcis tantum et Romanis ducibus, remotis omnibus, quæ e
linguâ Sanscritâ cupidius immiscerentur, restat desiderandum,
quod ab initio declaravimus. *Desideramus itaque plenum et
in artis formam redactum dialectorum linguæ Græcæ corpus,
summa cum fide ex ipsis fontibus haustum, diligenter sepositis
iis, quæ sola conjectura nituntur, compositum illud eum in finem,
ut ex his, arte critica comprobatis, reliquiis antiquissima, ad
quam redire concessum, linguæ Græcæ conformatio, qualis ubique
fuisse videatur, quam possit fieri clarissime ante oculos ponatur.*
In quem finem cum omnis labor proxime dirigendus sit, ratio
rei tractandæ inde omnium facillime dijudicari poterit. Linguæ
Latinæ antiquiores formas, tam arcte cum Æolicâ dialecto

conjunctas, an comparare simul placeat, et similia e lingua Græcorum hodiernâ, si certo fundamento stabiliri possunt, quod in Laconum dialecto a Thierschio egregie factum vidimus, in medium vocanda sint, unius-cujusque, qui scripturus sit, arbitrio permittimus. Sed disertis verbis declaramus, omnem aliam linguæ Sanscritæ aut ceterarum cognatarum linguarum conjunctionem alienam censeri et rejici, non quod ipsi existimemus, hac via nihil boni in rem redundaturum, sed quod nolimus, omnem hanc disquisitionem, ut cupidius et partium quodam studio institutam, suspectam reddi iis, qui plures fortasse nostræ opinionis non sint. Unum addimus, nos satis bene intelligere, hunc laborem non esse talem, qualem sibi quis nunc primum peragendum proponat, imo, qui illi tantum feliciter successurus sit, qui diu paratus, in re sponte suscepta, externo demum incitamento opus habeat, ut ultimam operi caro manum lætior adjiciat. Etsi lingua Latina ante omnes apta, qua utantur, qui de hoc argumento Scripturi sint; admittitur tamen et Rossica, et Germanica, et Gallica. Ceterum ut moris est, auctor nomen et patriæ mentionem obsignatæ committat tesseræ, quæ parem operi adjunctam habeat. Exhibendus est liber ante d. I (13.) m. Augusti a. 1839. Præmium operis, ab Academia comprobandi, est *centum et quinquaginta aureorum Holland.* decernendum in publico ejusdem anni consessu d. 29 m. Decembr. (d. 10. Januar. 1840)."

Printed in *Seebode's Neue Jahrbücher* VII. *Jahrgang* 20. *Band.* 3. *Heft.* p. 341.

It appears from this elaborate and able program, that the best classical scholars, even in St Petersburg, where Pallas and Adelung had created a craving for polyglot accomplishments, regarded comparative philology with some suspicion and distrust, even at the time, when I was engaged in making the bridge between the old and new methods of linguistic research. At this time I said in English, and Hamaker wrote in Dutch, that Buttmann would have substituted induction for conjecture, if he had not been placed in an age preceding, though by a few years only, the full establishment of comparative philology. C. O. Müller, who fully recognised the importance of this

alliance between things new and old*, and who, as the col-
league of J. Grimm, had every opportunity of knowing the
progress of linguistic science, was prevented by the wide compass of his own studies from entering upon this department;
indeed, he was not professedly so much a verbal scholar, as a
Sachkenner, or one who made it his business to be acquainted
with the contents of ancient books, and with the facts and
theories of history, geography, mythology and art, which
tended to their elucidation; and as such a *connoisseur* he has
been unrivalled in Germany as in England. His pupil Lepsius
started from a better basis of classical scholarship than any
other general philologer in Germany, and shows this in his
greater exactness and more finished skill in etymological criticism. Indeed, he has no equal in these respects. But Egypt-
ology has of late entirely absorbed his activity, and withdrawn
him from a full development of Müller's old Italian philology.

On the whole, then, it may be said, that the best classical
scholars in Germany have not, as such, formally engaged in the
prosecution of comparative grammar. The great comparative
philologists have started, like Grimm, from the Teutonic dialects, or like Pott, from the Lithuanian and Old Prussian,
or like Burnouf, from the Zend, or like Bopp, from the
Sanscrit compared with all these; or like Gesenius, Ewald,
and Fürst, from the Semitic dialects. And, while classical
scholarship is a very secondary matter with most of these
great etymologists, while a new school, as I have mentioned
in the text, is looking to Sanscrit for far-fetched explanations of words and things, which are obvious enough to the
classical critic; we find some instances in which the claims
of the old school of learning are not only disputed, but con-
temptuously rejected. For example, Ewald, whose overween-
ing self-confidence has been fostered by an exclusive pursuit of
Semitic and biblical philology, has thus answered my assertion,
"scientiam philologicam unam esse, et ad materiam qualem-

---

* Müller's appreciation of Comparative Philology is shown by his article on *escit*,
and by his reviews of Hartung, Kühner, and Grotefend, (*Kleine deutsche Schriften*,
Vol. I. pp. 375, 326, 354). See also his remarks in Vol. I. p. 12.

cunque adhiberi posse." He says (*Gött. Gel. Anz.* 1855, p. 157): "The author thinks that the labours of classical philologers may serve as an excellent pattern for Hebraists. This may be all right enough in England, as long as one has still to contend in that country for the first commencement of an improved Old Testament philology. But this can hardly be said of us Germans, who have made more progress. If we look back on the last 400 years (and such a comparison could not be made with reference to a still earlier period), history shows that the Bible, and especially the Old Testament, has evoked and stimulated the efforts of scholars and men of letters just as much as the classical writers. If this has been otherwise, thanks to the theologians, in many places, and particularly in England, and if classical philology has meanwhile made a great advance, which is gladly recognised, the very fact of the special difficulties suggested by biblical criticism has quite recently, and in Germany, furnished an additional inducement for seeking a sure foundation ; and this depends so entirely on a knowledge of the subject matter and involves the eradication of such a number of prejudices, that the borrowed aid of another department of science becomes quite inadmissible." Now I could give any number of instances to prove the position that, in spite of his genius and learning in his own field, Ewald is not a good philologer, even in Semitic matters, and not a good general critic, simply because he has not passed through the strict and wholesome discipline of the classical school. It will be quite sufficient to cite one example from the immediate subject of the above remarks. In his *Geschichte de Volkes Israels,* I. 315, he seeks a Semitic explanation for לֶמֶךְ, and the best he can find is תָּמַךְ. In December, 1853, I suggested that the word was not Semitic at all, but simply the Greek Λάμαχος. At the end of the same year he arrived accidentally at the same conclusion. He says (*Jahrb. d. Bibl. Wissensch.* VI. p. 2): "der mannesname Λάμαχος, *Gen.* V. 25, IV. 18, kehrt in Pisidien wider ; *C. Inscr.* n. 4379 m.: der frauenname Ἄδα, *Gen.* IV. 19, 23. vgl. XXXVI. 2, 4. ebenfalls in jenen gegenden ; *C. Inscr.* III. p. 333: dies zusammentreffen ist umso denkwürdiger da beider namen in Israel später sich nicht mehr finden." I could not wish for a more triumphant proof of the expediency of philologising from a classical basis. On the general question, Ewald ought to read what Lachmann has written in the preface to the second volume of his Greek Testament, pp. iii. iv.

I will now show briefly that the first professed attempt, which has been made in Germany, to pass by a direct road from classical to comparative grammar, was long subsequent to the adoption of this method in England. Giese's work on the Æolic dialect, and Kuhn's tract on the conjunction in -μι, both published in 1837, refer only to subordinate details. But, in 1845, the subject was taken up with some parade by Mr G. Curtius, who published in that year, at Berlin, a tract with the title: *Die Sprachvergleichung in ihrem Verhältniss zur classischen Philologie,* i. e. " Comparative grammar in its reference to classical philology ;" and in the following year, this was followed up by a larger treatise, entitled : *Sprachvergleichende Beiträge zur griechischen und lateinischen Grammatik,* i. e. " Contributions of comparative philology to Greek and Latin Grammar." Now in these treatises there is not the slightest allusion to the fact that, in 1839, there appeared at Cambridge, a book entitled, " Contributions (i. e. *Sprachvergleichende Beiträge*) to a more accurate knowledge of the Greek Language," and that this was followed, in 1844, by a corresponding book on Latin philology,—both books having been published at Leipsig as well as at Cambridge, and all the copies sent to Germany having found a ready sale. Besides this singular omission, it is remarkable that the preface to Mr Curtius' larger book, of 1846, is *mutatis mutandis* identical with that of the Cambridge work of 1839. For example, the latter begins with these words : " In writing this book, it has been my object to combine an investigation of general principles with an exposition of particular results." Mr Curtius says : " It is the object of this book to combine, as far as possible, the general study with the particular," (*das allgemeinere Studium mit dem besonderen möglichst zu vereinigen*). The remarks about Bopp, in p. ix., appear to me to be a poor imitation of what is said in § 39, of the English book. But the most striking feature of resemblance, is the following. In the second edition of his earlier treatise, published in 1848, we have a note referring to his larger treatise, p. 129, (published in 1846) where he suggests, as an original discovery, that the augment is a pronominal particle implying *distance* or *remoteness,* and where he compares the Sanscrit particle *sma* by means of which the present is converted into a preterite; and these remarks are brought forward in direct opposition to Bopp. In the English book of 1839, Bopp's theory is also confuted, and the following remark is added (§ 370): "in our opinion it (the augment) is the pronominal root $\acute{e} = \acute{a} = \acute{a}v\acute{a}$, which we find elsewhere as denoting *distance* or *remoteness*. We have seen how this idea of separation is connected with that of the first personal pronoun, and we shall thus understand how the separate particle *sa-ma,* which denotes completeness, or all between the *near* and the *here,* is used as a mark of past time in Sanscrit." Now, in the note of 1848, (p. 72) Mr Curtius appeals to an article by that excellent philologer, the late Mr Garnett, in the *Transactions of the Philological Society* (24 May, 1844), as an independent confirmation of his own original view. And that paper is professedly an argument in support of the theory propounded, in 1839, in a large book published and sold in Germany, as well as in England. I need say no more. It is not necessary to prove that the Germans copy from us and dissemble their obligations. It is quite sufficient to show that they are not only behind us in a great application of philology, but that, by not making themselves acquainted with our proceedings, they are in the same position as the English scholars of forty years ago, who were too proud to learn from their German contemporaries.

Note 8, p. 128.

It is somewhat remarkable that Ewald, who almost always allows himself to speak with undisguised contempt, and with overbearing arrogance, of English writers in his own department of learning, has been seriously and formally charged by our late eminent orientalist, Dr Lee, with deliberate "plagiarisms committed by him on the Hebrew Grammar" of that author (see *An Examination of the Grammatical Principles of Professor von Ewald of Tübingen*, Lond. 1847), who finishes the discussion with these words (Kitto's *Journal of Sacred Literature*, July, 1849, p. 160): "I am prepared to maintain that he is an unprincipled plagiary, and that it is his inability to purge himself from this charge, that has now induced him to take refuge in a tissue of unmeasured abuse." However this may be, there cannot be the least doubt that Ewald regards himself as a sort of infallible pope in Semitic and biblical literature, and, to say the truth, treats his own countrymen only a little better than the English, whom he so thoroughly despises. What has been said of his last work is applicable to all his writings. They are all distinguished by inordinate pretension to originality and ungenerous ignoring of the fruits of other labourers in the same field : "With the exception of the ancients, almost all the works cited as authorities are the author's own. He seems determined to owe everything to himself. He marches triumphantly through the country with the air of a discoverer, as if no one had set foot in it before, and boldly breaks up its surface, and erects arbitrary landmarks, as if there were not a trace of previous occupation" (*Nat. Rev.* No. I. p. 95). That his own countrymen are not disposed to submit to this absurd arrogance is shown by many severe rebukes which have been bestowed upon Ewald. For example, Tischendorf, in the *Prolegomena* to his Greek Testament, Ed. 2. p. LIV., answers one of Ewald's dictatorial criticisms, by calling it "a short specimen of the virtues of ignorance, negligence, and insolence." and winds up with the remark : "I am of opinion that critics of this kind would do a great service to criticism, if they would prefer to be silent and learn rather than to write or teach."

Not to speak however of an extreme case like Ewald's, it must be remarked that very many of the Germans write and speak as if classical learning and philological knowledge were confined to their own country ; whereas Englishmen willingly acknowledge the merits of their German contemporaries, and even in theology our peculiar prejudices do not always prevent us from doing them justice. Indeed, our candour is so great, that we are liable, as I have said in the text, to be construed as renouncing our own originality; and I am myself obliged to take this, the first opportunity that has occurred, of replying to the charge, that I have, in one case, done injustice to a distinguished English scholar by conceding too much to the counter-claims of a foreigner. In Mr Leitch's edition of the *Miscellaneous Works* of Dr Thomas Young, repeated reference is made to an article in the *Quarterly Review*, of which, with the exception of one short paragraph, I must take upon myself the literary responsibility. In the preface (p. v.) the editor remarks that, unlike M. Arago and many of Champollion's countrymen, he has "carefully avoided treating the discovery of the hieroglyphical alphabet as a national question ; and that in England generally it has not been regarded as such; for although Chevalier Bunsen has unjustly endeavoured to deprive an Englishman of the honour of having made what he, as well as his illustrious countryman, Niebuhr, pronounces the greatest discovery of modern times, he has found Englishmen sufficiently free from natural bias, as well as sufficiently uninformed, to back him in his attempt." And we are referred to a note in p. 255 where the following words occur in reference to the article in the *Quarterly :* " The critic has devised an allegory in illustration of what was respectively accomplished by Young and Champollion, the utter inapplicability of which is the more remarkable from the talent otherwise displayed in the article." Now I am quite prepared to rest the applicability of my allegory, as Mr Leitch calls it, on the account of the matter given by Dr Young himself, in the letter to Hamilton, which Mr Leitch has printed in p. 220. My words are as follows: " With regard to Young and Champollion, of whom it is the fashion to speak as rivals, we may be well content to leave to each of them his own share of the credit which they have both fully earned. The case between them seems to be this. A man, having laboriously travelled along a difficult road, in search of a definite object, and having on his way put aside many obstacles which might impede those who should follow him, is overtaken, at a place where the road divides, by a lightly-equipped traveller, who recalls him from the wrong road, which he had begun to follow, and points out, by his natural shrewdness, that the other way is most likely to lead him to his journey's end. The lightly-equipped traveller does not, however, follow the painful wayfarer for more than a few steps on the right road, and on that short journey is saved from tripping by the strong arm of his friend, who goes on patiently and stoutly till he has won the wished-for goal. Let us give the keen-sighted guide the praise which his ingenious sagacity deserves; but let us not, from national jealousy, seek to deprive the wayworn pilgrim of his higher meed of fame."

Now I contend that this is supported, even with an approach to the same metaphors, by the following words of Young himself: " Paris, 29th Sept. 1822. I have found here, or rather recovered, Mr Champollion, junior, who has been living for these ten years on the Inscription of Rosetta, and who has lately been making some steps in Egyptian literature, which really appear to be *gigantic*. It may be said that he found the key in England, which opened the gate for him, and it is often observed that *c'est le premier pas qui coute;* but if he did borrow an English key, the lock was so dreadfully rusty, that no common arm would have had strength enough to turn it; and, in a path so beset with thorns, and so encumbered with rubbish, not the first step only, but every step, is painfully laborious; especially such as are retrograde; and such steps will sometimes be necessary; but it is better to make a few false steps than to stand quite still." And he goes on to explain what Champollion had done. With this testimony from Dr Young himself, I will leave the reader to decide who is "ill-informed," Mr Leitch or I. That I am not disposed to undervalue my countryman's merits in this matter, may be inferred from what I have said in the *New Cratylus*, p. 47, namely, that " Young guided Champollion to the systematic examination of Egyptian hieroglyphics;" and that I do not " adopt Chevalier Bunsen's opinions with implicit faith," appears from the very page before that in which this comparison of Young and Champollion occurs, and from other passages in the review, in which I make sharp strictures on Bunsen's lax philology. I agree, however, with Mr Leitch, that Bunsen is not disposed to take a very high estimate of English learning; and he must be numbered among those of his countrymen, who, without the same opportunities of ascertaining the facts, seem to think that the best of us are only fit to assimilate German nutriment.

Note 9, p. 130.

That Mr Horsman was answered at the time, though not in the House of Commons, is shown by the following extracts from the *Report of the Anniversary of the Royal Literary Fund,* held on Wednesday the 3rd of May, 1854, that is, less than a week after the speech of the 27th of April. I happened to be called upon by the Chairman, Lord Mahon, to respond to the toast of " The Church," and the following appears to have been my speech: " My Lord,—My Lords and Gentlemen,—I beg to return you my best thanks for the honour you have done me in drinking my health in connexion with the toast which has just been proposed from the chair. Although I feel, and I say it quite unaffectedly, that in the presence of clergymen much older than myself, I am quite unworthy to return thanks for the toast, I feel at the same time that the Church of England is entitled to conspicuous acknowledgment on anniversaries like the present. I think that the Church of England is connected by a double,—by a special and a general, —relation with this charitable Institution. Whenever the hand of benevolence is stretched out to aid suffering humanity, I believe I may say, without fear of contradiction, that not only in their preaching, but in their practice, and with pecuniary contributions often abstracted from a scanty income, the clergy of the Church of England are never behind their Christian brethren of any denomination. But when the object is to relieve those who combine with poverty some amount of literary and scientific merit, the Church of England does stand

forward with peculiar zeal and earnestness of purpose; for I
hope I may be allowed to say, even in the presence of those
who do not belong to the same religious denomination, that
the Church of England does represent in a large measure the
literary and scientific eminence of this country; and with
regard to one department,—that of classical learning,—I feel
myself bound to put in a special claim for the Church of England and the Universities of this land, with which the Church
of England is closely connected. I am the more called upon
to do so because some attempts have been recently made to
disparage the scholarship of England in comparison with that
of another country. I am acquainted, by long familiarity, with
the classical literature of Germany, as well as with that of
England, and I express not my opinion only, but my conviction, when I say that there are more good, able, and accomplished scholars in this country than in any other in the world.
It may be true that there is a greater number of persons in
Germany who write on philology and classical literature, but
I think it would be for the advantage of classical literature,
and for the reputation of Germany, if there were fewer. Take
those tests which are applied in the examinations at our
Universities and Public Schools, and you will find that very
few of our brother scholars on the continent would be able to
meet them. If you have recourse to other standards of comparison, and appeal to the number of literary scholars as the
only materials for forming a judgment, I will say, in contradiction to a member of the House of Commons, that while
men of genius,—first-rate men,—are very few in any country,
there are as many in this country as in any country in the
world, and it is only among these that you will find the really
great scholars. And there is one advantage which English
scholars have over those of Germany. We take care to know
what they are doing in Germany, but I am sorry to say that
they treat what is going on here with some species of contemptuous indifference, and have scarcely any acquaintance with the
learning of England. On the whole then, I hope that if this
Society should feel disposed to bestow its liberality upon those

scholars of England who happen to be *poor*, it will not be deterred from doing so by any belief, however recommended, that in England we are all "*poor scholars.*"

Dr W. Smith followed a similar train of thought in acknowledging the toast of "The Writers on Classical Li erature," at a later period on the same evening. His remarks are reported as follows: "My Lords and Gentlemen, in rising to acknowledge this toast, I can truly say I am very sorry Dr Donaldson had been called upon before, as I feel that he would have been in every respect more worthy to reply to it than I am. I am conscious that I do not deserve the flattering terms in which the gentleman who has proposed this toast has mentioned my name; but one thing I can claim in common with the great scholars of this country, however slender my own merits may be, and that is a sincere love of classical literature, and an anxious desire to extend and promote its cultivation. I join with the gentleman who proposed the toast in expressing a hope, that the day is far distant when the study of classical literature will cease to be essential to the education of the English gentleman; and that whatever changes, in this reforming age, may be made in our Universities and public schools, classical literature will stand as the foundation on which everything else is based. For whether we regard the language as a means of sharpening the intellectual faculties, or the literature as a means of elevating and purifying the taste, it would be easy to show that no subject could take their place or accomplish the objects which they effect. But it would be improper in me, and discourteous to this assembly, to enlarge upon this subject. Those only are the detractors and opponents of classical literature who are ignorant of it. Is it not the fact, that our whole English literature is indissolubly bound up with classical literature, and that on almost every page it bears the impress of the great writers of antiquity? Their civilization may be said to be our civilization; their literature is our literature; their institutions and laws have moulded and modified our institutions and laws; and the life of the western nations of Europe is but a continuation of the

16

life of Greece and Rome. Therefore, my Lord, I rejoice that
classical literature still flourishes among us; and before I sit
down, I cannot help joining in the opinion expressed by Dr
Donaldson, that the classical writers have, on a recent occasion,
been treated with discourtesy and unfairness. No one can be
more ready than I am to admit the obligations which English
scholars are under to the great writers of Germany. To them
we owe a new school in literature, and from the time of Niebuhr to the present time they have produced a race of writers
of whom we may be proud, and who have greatly influenced
our scholarship. But at the same time it is a libel upon English scholars to represent them as mere borrowers from the
Germans, and as failing to produce any original works of
learning and research. I might easily refer to a long list of
living writers, who may challenge competition with the best
writers of Germany. I might mention in chronology, the Fasti
of Mr Clinton; in geography, the Travels of Colonel Leake;
in Greek literature, the History of Colonel Mure; in the interpretation of the ancient writers, the recent editions of Cicero
by Mr Long, of Horace by Mr Macleane, of Propertius by Mr
Paley, and of Herodotus by Mr Blakesley; in philology, the
new Cratylus and Varronianus of Dr Donaldson; in Roman
History, the work of Mr Merivale; and in Grecian History,
the incomparable works of Bishop Thirlwall and Mr Grote.
And in these works there is something which Germany does
not possess. If we take Mr Grote's work, combining as it
does the industry of a German professor and the learning of a
German scholar, with that knowledge of men, of events, and
of political institutions which distinguishes the English gentleman and the British statesman, there is a work which, without disparagement to our brethren on the Continent, and
holding them in all honour, no German professor could produce; a work which is an honour to its author and to the
literature of his country. But I feel, my Lord, that I am led
away from the toast. I will only say one word more. Throughout the whole classical literature of this country, there is one
excellence which has, perhaps, more than anything else, been

characteristic of English literature from the time of Chaucer to the present day,—I mean sound judgment and practical good sense. My Lord, I beg to return you my thanks on behalf of the classical writers of this country, and to assure you how much I feel the honour conferred on me by my name being coupled with this toast."

NOTE 10, p. 135.

This is perhaps sufficiently shown by the following extract from a recent notice in Gersdorf's *Leipsig Repertorium der deutschen und ausländ. Literatur:* "Schon die Dedication an Lepsius und dann die Præfatio lässt auf vertraute Bekanntschaft und nahe Verwandtschaft des gelehrten Vfs. mit deutscher Gelehrsamkeit schliessen. Bei näherer Einsicht in das Buch findet man nicht nur alle namhaften deutschen Interpreten von J. D. Michaelis und J. A. Ernesti an bis herab auf Ewald, Thenius, u. a. Zeitgenossen berücksichtigt, sondern man glaubt häufig einen deutschen Kritiker unserer Tage von der gemässigten Linken sprechen zu hören," (*i. e.* the dedication to Lepsius, and then the preface allows us to infer the learned author's intimate familiarity with and near relationship to German learning. On a closer inspection we not only find that due notice is taken of all eminent German interpreters, from J. D. Michaelis and J. A. Ernesti down to Ewald, Thenius and others of our contemporaries, but we often believe that we are listening to the words of a German critic of the moderate liberal party in our own days.)

NOTE 11, p. 153.

It is sufficient to mention the name of Dr B. H. Kennedy, of Shrewsbury, who is not only a most eminent scholar himself, but has sent forth from his own tuition a greater number of eminent scholars than any teacher in England. To the same class belonged Dr J. P. Lee, formerly master of Birmingham school, and now Bishop of Manchester. It is a proof of Mr Dickens's instinctive observation, that, amid his satirical censure

of all sorts of schools, he reserves an old grammar school
for exclusive commendation. As I am no longer a master of
one of these schools, I will venture to remark on the absurdity
of limiting the title of "a public school" to a few only of the
endowed Grammar Schools of England. They are all equally
"Grammar Schools," because they were founded for the purpose of teaching the classical languages; and they are all
equally "public schools," because they are not the results of
private enterprize, but are endowments held in trust for the
public good. "The broad distinction," says Dr Kennedy,
(*Sermon at Bath*, 28 Dec. 1853, note II. p. 19), "between a
public and a private school must be this, that the former is
endowed, and therefore perpetual; the latter, unendowed, and
therefore ephemeral;" and a public school, "in its generally
received sense, implies a school of liberal education open to the
whole community of the realm." In the first note to the same
Sermon, Dr Kennedy has remarked on the common error with
regard to the meaning of a "free Grammar School;" his explanation, which deserves general attention, is as follows :

"The term, Free Grammar School, is among those which
have ceased to convey their true meaning to the public ear.

"A. Ask what a 'Free School' is, and ninety-nine persons
in every hundred will tell you it means a school in which the
instruction is wholly, or in part, gratuitous. Johnson, in his
Dictionary, gives it so. Lawyers will state this as the legal
acceptation. And it is probable that many schools have been
founded, with the epithet *free* attached by their founders in
this sense.

"Yet nothing is more certain than that the Latin words
'Libera Schola,' in Edward's charters, had no such meaning.

"1. For in so solemn an instrument as a charter, if it were
intended to embody an important principle in the title of the
foundation, the term chosen would be one either of legal
validity, or of obvious and popular import.

"But it cannot be shown that, at the date of Edward's
charters, the word *liber* had ever borne the meaning *gratuitous,*

either in legal documents or in popular usage; either in classical or in mediæval Latinity.

"2. Again, had the words *Libera Schola* been the known and recognised description of a school in which instruction was to be given without fee or reward, the primary ordinances of such a school would never have contravened its fundamental character.

"But among the ordinances enacted in Elizabeth's reign, with royal sanction for the government of '*Libera Schola Grammaticalis Regis Edwardi Sexti*,' in Shrewsbury, we find the following:

"'Item: every scholar shall pay for his admission; viz. a lord's son, ten shillings; a knight's son, six shillings and eightpence; and a son and heir apparent of a gentleman, three shillings and fourpence; and for every other of their sons, two shillings and sixpence; and under those degrees above said, and born without the county of Salop, two shillings; and any under those degrees, and born within the county of Salop, twelve pence; every burgess's son, inhabiting within the town or liberties thereof, or of the Abby Forgate, if he be of abilitie, fourpence; the son of every other person there inhabiting, eightpence.'

"What, then, it may be asked, was the meaning designed by the term 'Libera Schola'?

"In answer to this question, three suggestions have been offered:

"1. A school of *liberal* education.

"2. A public school (*free* to the public of the realm).

"3. An unattached school, *i.e.* a school unattached to, and *free* from the jurisdiction of, any superior institution.

"This last we hold to be the strictly correct meaning of the term, but in it we believe the second meaning, 'public school,' to be implicitly conveyed; so that in our times the word *public* most correctly represents the ancient sense of *libera*.

"B. The term 'Grammar School' is of no ambiguous import. All well-read persons know that grammar, logic, and rhetoric, formed a course of study in the middle ages, which was called *Trivium* (three-ways); as geometry, arithmetic, astronomy, and music, constituted a second course, called *Quad-rivium* (four-ways). *Grammatica*, or Grammar (the literary science) implied the study of language and linguistic literature. A Grammar School is, therefore, by its constitution, a school of literature.

" As, however, the term '*free*' is not generally understood in its true sense, so the word '*grammar*' is popularly known in a meaning much narrower than that which it represents in Edward's charters. And thus, on the whole, the title ' Free Grammar School,' may be considered as one, of which the precise import is not comprehended by the community at large.

" Not only, however, has the term Free Grammar School ceased to convey its original meaning, but such schools have ceased, and must cease more and more, to be merely Grammar Schools, since the mathematical and physical sciences have been added to their course of studies. For these reasons it would seem proper to discontinue this title, and to designate chartered schools by the name of their founder and locality, in accordance with the precedent of ' King Edward's School, in Birmingham.' "

Note 12, p. 154.

It would be easy to adduce many proofs of the exact scholarship which English lads bring to the University from good schools. The following copy of Greek Iambics was written on the spur of the moment in the Pitt Scholarship examination for 1824, by the successful competitor, who was then a freshman, and is now one of the most eminent scholars in England. Professor Dobree was so pleased with its vigour and spirit that he had a few copies printed for circulation among his friends, and when I came up to Cambridge six years afterwards it was still recollected. I print it as it came into my hands; and I think it quite unnecessary to criticize it by saying that νοῦς is not an Attic form, or that it would have been as well to avoid making the first syllable of ἀβληχρός, short. As for βοήσουσι instead of βοήσονται a freshman might be well excused for not knowing the future of βοάω in 1824, seeing that

Blomfield, in the third edition of the *Agamemnon*, published in 1826, did not know that *ὀκούσεις* (v. 1406) was an impossible form; and, until John Wordsworth showed that it was the conjunctive (*Philol. Mus.* I. p. 233), it was generally supposed that *διαβοάσω* in Æsch. *Pers.* 640, was the future indicative.

ÍSAIAH XIV. 6—17.

ὁ πρὶν πρὸς ὀργὴν ξυντόνῳ πληγῇ λεὼν
πλήξας, ὁ πάντων πρὶν τυραννεύσας ἐθνῶν,
διώκεται νῦν οὐδ᾽ ὁ κωλύσων πάρα.
ἡδεῖα πᾶσαν εὐδία θέλγει χθόνα,
φλέγουσί θ᾽ ὕμνων παντόθεν τερπνῶν νόμοι,
πεῦκαι δ᾽ ἐπεγγελῶσιν, ὑψηλοῦ τέ σοι
κέδροι Λεβανῶνος, ἐκβοῶσί τ᾽ ἐμφανῶς,
" Οὐδεὶς ἐφ᾽ ἡμᾶς ὧδ᾽ ἀνέρχεται τανῦν
πελεκεῖ ξὺν ὠμῷ κατακεκρυμμένου σέθεν."
Ἅιδης ἔνερθέν σου χάριν κινούμενος
χαίρειν κελεύει πολλά, σόν τ᾽ ἰδὼν κάρα
ἅπαντ᾽ ἐγείρει σοι λεών, γαίας πρόμους,
ἐθνῶν ἄνακτας, ἐξαναστήσας θρόνων.
οὗτοι δ᾽ ἐροῦσιν εὐφιλῆ προσφθέγματα·
Ἆρ᾽ οὖν ἀβληχρὸς καὶ σὺ γεγένησαί ποτε,
ὁποῖα χἠμεῖς, καὶ σὺ δῆθ᾽ ἡμῖν ἴσος;
ἤδη μὲν ἐν τάφοισι σαὶ κεῖνται χλιδαὶ
καὶ τυμπάνων σῶν κέλαδος, ἐγκρύπτει δέ σε
σκώληξ ἐν ὀστοῖς σοῖς ὑποστρώσας λέχος.
Φεῦ! Φωσφόρ᾽, Ἠοῦς ἔκγον᾽, οἶ᾽ ἀπ᾽ οὐρανοῦ
πέπτωκας ἤδη πτώματ᾽ οὐκ ἀνάσχετα!
οἴοις πέπληξαι πλήγμασιν χαμαιπετής,
ὦ πρίν ποτ᾽ ἐθνῶν ἐκκεραυνώσας σθένος!
ἔφης γὰρ, οἶδ᾽, ἔφης ποτ᾽ ἀνοσίῳ φρενί,
" Εἰς οὐρανὸν βὰς ἀμὸν ὑψώσω θρόνον
Θεοῦ παλαιῶν ἀστέρων ὑπέρτερον."
ὅμως δ᾽ ἐς Ἅιδου, καίπερ ὧδ᾽ εἰπών, πεσεῖ,
κὰς πλεῦρα βαράθρου, χοἳ σ᾽ ἰδόντες ὄμμασι
βλέψουσ᾽ ἀκριβῶς, καί σ᾽ ἐρευνήσαντες εὖ
ὁμοῦ βοήσουσ᾽, " Ἆρ᾽ ὅδ᾽ οὖν ἀνὴρ ἔφυ

ὁ γῆν φοβήσας, πάνθ' ὁ συγκρούσας ἔθνη ;
ἆρ' οὖν ὅδ' ἀνὴρ οὐξερημώσας χθόνα,
πόλεις θ' ἁπάσας ἐξαϊπτώσας πυρί,
οὐδ' αἰχμαλώτων δεσμίους οἴξας δόμους ;"

As a specimen of the power of Latin composition possessed
by young Englishmen, I subjoin a copy of Galliambics written
by two undergraduate scholars of Trinity College, Cambridge,
and distributed among the guests at the Tercentenary Com-
memoration in December, 1846. The merits of the effort are
greatly enhanced by the success with which it imitates a somewhat difficult metre.

> Εἰπέ μοι τί τηνικαῦτα δρῶμεν, ὦ Κωμαρχίδη ;
> ἐμπιεῖν ἔμοιγ' ἀρέσκει.
>
> ARISTOPH. *Pax*, 1142.

Age, concitate cantus ; age, ludite, bibite ;
Hodie procax December venit : improba patrio
Venit hora more, lætis dolor exulat animis,
Fugit omnis ægritudo, male sollicita, procul ;
Neque displicet jocari, neque desipere pudet.
Breve Dî dedere vitæ spatium : nova soboles
Subit indies priori, cita tempora fugiunt,
Adolescit usque natus, genitorque minuitur,
Novaque ordinatur ætas trieteride decima :—
Decima at peragitur ætas hodie, undecima venit,
Deciesque decima nostræ celebrabitur hodie
Trieteris ædis, ævo neque subripitur honos.
Breve Nestori exprobramus, tria secula, senium,
Superatque nostra regem sapientia Pylium :
Agite, impedita myrto niteat coma viridi,
Hilarem explicate frontem : neque enim sine cyathis
Decus ædis ille nostræ colaphum hostibus adigit,
Metuendus Atticistis, grave Teutonis odium,
Neque poculis secundus, neque acumine metrico.
Age, barbitos morantem jubet ire celerius
Pateram, accinitque curvo grave tibia calamo,

Cava cymbalum per aulæ laquearia reboat,
Properantque jam cadentes typana excipere sonos.
Hodierna turba festis coit undique dapibus,
Teritur dies loquendo, vetus amphora Thasii
Pice solvitur Lyæi, neque mensa capit onus ;
Tenebras lucerna vincit : lepidos agite jocos ;
Opera invido renascens referet jubare dies,
Variis aget sodales nova lux itineribus :
Aquilonis ille regnum petet, usta loca gelu,
Petet hic plagas beatas super æquora pelagi,
Ubi vere sempiterno tepefacta viret humus,
Viret imputata vitis, vacuusque amat opera
Semeleii colonus latices bibere Dei,
Recubans odora in herba, tremulo prope resonat
Ubi murmure unda, terram foliis nemus operit.
  Nova dividet sodales redeunte face dies,
  Hodie omnibus bibendum est ; age, ducite cyathos.
Alii Camœna forsan studiis trahit animum,
Avidoque amore sunt quos Sophia usque retineat,
Sophia adprobanda paucis, Sophia invida Veneri,
Adamat quod Alma Mater genus in gremio alere :
Ibi desides solutis remorantur operibus,
Sua seque garrientes, iterare cata cohors
" Placet otium docendi, neque cœlibe melior
Homini petenda vita est, neque sit mihi pueros
Alere us;ue, turbam edacem, strepituque perimier,
Neque mane semper uxor nova munera rogitet."
  Cito dividet sodales redeunte face dies,
  Hodie omnibus bibendum est ; age, ducite cyathos.
Alii forum placebit, strepitant ubi rabulæ,
Scelerata turba, Dîs gens odiosa et hominibus ;
Redimendus ille nummis populo dabit operam,
Sibi protulisse testes catus undique veteres ;
Mera fraus, dolus meracus, male callidus agili
Dare verba utrinque lingua ; negat omnia pretio,
Pretioque se refellit, pretioque reticuit,
Bonus implicare nodos, neque solvere pigrior.

Nova dividet sodales reduci jubare dies,
    Hodie omnibus bibendum est; age, ducite cyathos.
Alius paterna agelli sola vomere subiget;
Subito ecce! gemma cui nunc rubet Indica digitis,
Syrioque odora nardo nitet in capite coma,
Ovium uncta tractat unctis modo vellera manibus,
Modo curat arva cœno, medicamine liquido
Renovat novale, multis enerve segetibus;
Nimios crepat calores, mala frigora, pluvias:
Ubi Granta rursum adultam revocat sibi sobolem,
Ibi bellus ille quondam, lepidissumus hominum
Redit inficetus, asper, male rasus, agricola.
    Nova dividet sodales reduci jubare dies,
    Hodie omnibus bibendum est; age, ducite cyathos.
Alium trahent honores: petet ille comitia,
Nivea toga, tabellis popularibus inhians,
Celebrique signa campo sua proferet; olidas
Avide manus prehendet, facili bene sapiens
Dare conjugi catellam, dare basia pueris,
Dare verba mox marito, ut suffragia tulerit.
Redimite flore crines; age, ducite cyathos:
Hodie domus frequentes nequit accipere epulas:
Variis aget sodales nova lux itineribus:
Quotus inde quisque tanget pede limina reduci?
Abigat hodierna curas, abigat mala; videat
Hodierna lux bibentes, hodiernaque juvenes:
Age, concitate cantus; age, ludite, bibite.

Note 13, p. 158.

In the Middle Ages it may be supposed that German writers of Latin verse were not inferior to those who cultivated this form of classical composition in the other countries of Europe. Two of the most familiar quotations of this kind are of German origin. The well-known line:

"Incidis in Scyllam cupiens vitare Charybdim,"

is addressed to Darius, (who, flying from Alexander, fell into the hands of his treacherous Satrap,) in a German poem called the *Alexandreis.* The equally hackneyed hexameter:

"Tempora mutantur et nos mutamur in illis,"

which was supposed, in spite of a false quantity and an inadmissible construction, to be of classical extraction, is a misquotation from a couplet by Casimir, which runs:

"Omnia mutantur, sed nos mutamur in illis;
Quæque sibi proprias res habet usque vices."

In the seventeenth century Heinsius and Scaliger obtained some distinction in Holland by their Latin verses; but from that time the accomplishment seems to have been dying out on the continent, whereas in England, from the time of Cowley and Milton, through the periods illustrated by the *Musæ Anglicanæ,* the *Musæ Etonenses,* and Vincent Bourne, down to the time of our fathers, when Mr Isaac Hawkins Browne's poem, *de Animi Immortalitate* reached its fourth edition (1811), and our own days when the universities and public schools are annually contributing to our collections of classical poetry, there has never been wanting the most decided proof of this permanent excellence of English scholarship. To show the style of versification which was thought wonderful in Germany in the days of Gray and Bourne, I subjoin a few lines taken at random from a book in two volumes, 8vo, with the following title: *Recentiorum Poetarum Germanorum Carmina Latina Selectiora ex Recensione M. Joannis Tobiæ Rœnickii.* Helmstad. MDCCXXXXVIII—MDCCLI. An English schoolboy of the fifth form would have avoided most of the errors which I have marked.

Et gravis et justus dolor est, qui pectora vestra
    Urit et ingenti vulnere læsa quatit.
Perditis hei geminos angusto tempore gnatos
    Tot passi miseras fortis in orbe vices.
Et quum jam vitæ restat pars ultima vestræ,
    Perpetuas lacrimas ultimus actus habet.
Doctus uterque bonas fuit haud vulgariter artes,
    Ingenii specimen doctus uterque dedit.

Amboque dilectos semper coluere parentes,
   Amboque supremum deperiere Deum.
Fastus et ambitio diræque libidinis æstus
   Non, veluti multos, *contaminavit* eos.
Sed pietas primis mentem formavit ab annis,
   Jussit et *ostensas* ætheris ire vias.
Jamque juventutis miras *academia* dotes
   Auxerat, a sale quæ nobile nomen habet.
Jamque Dei verbum facundo fluxerat ore,
   Ex patrio Christus quod tulit ore sinu.
Summaque spes aderat, fore mox, ut patria dulcis
   Illorum fida perfrueretur ope :
Hectica quum *phthisis* depascere corpora cœpit,
   Flammaque *febrilis* spem male sana tulit.
Sic natu major cœpto, qui labitur, anno
   Occidit et placida morte peremtus abest.
Alter jam sequitur, qui non distractus ab illo
   Quem coluit vivum, mortuus esse cupit.

Note 14, p. 170.

These principles were avowed nearly six years by the chief minister of the English Church.

Mr Maskell in a letter to the Archbishop of Canterbury, dated April 23, 1850, remarked : " It seems to me that *excepting the doctrine of the ever blessed Trinity*, I have no doctrines and no faith to teach as certainly the faith and doctrines of the Church of England. I may perhaps teach what I believe to be true ; but, as it seems, it is quite open to me, if I thought it to be right, and that I should be no less justified, to teach the opposite." The Archbishop answered (April 26) : " Your Bishop justly states that there are many subjects connected with an holy religion upon which we have no reason to expect the dogmatic teaching of the Church. Indeed, your second published letter complains of matters left undetermined, upon which the Church could not probably pronounce a decision, unless it were her office to reveal what is to be believed, rather than to teach what has been revealed." And in another letter

he says (April 27) : " Whether the doctrines, concerning which
you inquire, are contained in the Word of God, and can be
proved thereby, *you have the same means of discovering as myself,
and I have no special authority to declare.*" From this Mr Maskell concludes, in his last letter (April 27) : " I consent entirely
to your Grace's opinion that I am not authorised by the re-
formed Church of England to teach those doctrines in the terms
stated as being certainly true; I mean, authorised in such a
manner as would forbid and condemn my teaching the contrary.
In saying I take this to be your Grace's opinion, I venture to
conclude it to be so because, if I were authorised to teach distinctly a particular and defined statement of the truth as to
those doctrines, I cannot doubt but that your Grace would
readily have told me. So that it seems to be as I had supposed;
and I have no faith and no doctrines to teach on any subject—
except perhaps regarding the ever blessed Trinity—as containing the doctrines and the faith of the Church in which I am
a minister. In other words, if there is anything which I ought
to teach it is this, that the Church of England has no distinct
doctrine except on a single subject" (see *Times*, 1st May,
1850). Mr Maskell's premises are not the less correct because
he draws an erroneous conclusion from them.

Note 15, p. 197.

It so happens that I can cite a special proof of the fact that
even the best lecturers cannot impart accurate scholarship to
their hearers. In 1848 a translation of Plato's *Phædrus, Lysis,*
and *Protagoras* was published by a Cambridge B.A. who concludes his preface with acknowledging "the obligation that he
owes to the lectures on the *Phædrus* which were delivered in
Trinity College by the Rev. W. H. Thompson in the year 1844."
We may therefore infer, that, if points of scholarship are attended to in the version of the *Phædrus,* but neglected in the
other versions, the translator was indebted to his notes in the
former case, but had to rely on himself in the latter, and that
he could adopt Mr Thompson's renderings of the Greek without
perceiving the lesson in Greek which they involved. Now it is

well known to all really good Greek scholars that οὐ πάνυ does not mean, as it is so often rendered by those who are imperfectly trained, whether Germans or Englishmen, "not altogether," which admits that the thing may be so partially, but "altogether not," which contradicts the supposition that it can be so at all. Thus in Soph. *Œd. Col.* 142, the blind king describes himself as οὐ πάνυ μοίρας εὐδαιμονίσαι πρώτης, which Hermann renders *non primæ profecto sortis homo*, and which an English annotator has translated "not altogether of a condition to be congratulated on as the first," but which really means "not at all of an enviable condition, as I show you, for I should not otherwise be dependent on the guidance of a poor weak girl." To apply this to the case of the B.A. in question, in the *Phædrus*, p. 229 c, he translates οὐ πάνυ νενόηκα " I have *never* noticed it," and D : οὐ πάνυ εὐτυχοῦς ἀνδρός "*not at all* particularly enviable person ;" but in the *Protagoras,* p. 321 B, he renders ἅτε δὴ οὖν οὐ πάνυ τι σοφὸς ὢν ὁ Ἐπιμηθεύς, "forasmuch as Epimetheus was *not altogether* wise," where the whole passage shows that he was represented as not at all wise, but on the contrary as an absolutely silly person.

I have mentioned this example, not because the case is one of any great importance, but because it seems to me to prove distinctly the proposition in the text that lectures cannot make scholars. That they may furnish suggestions creative of studies, I know by my own case ; for if Rosen had not been a professor at the London University, and if I had not received, at second-hand, some of his lessons in Sanscrit and comparative philology, my attention might never have been directed to the studies which have formed the principal business of my life ; but all successful Cambridge men will agree with me in attributing the accuracy of their acquaintance with Greek and Latin to their own private studies either preceded or accompanied by the active and immediate instruction of a good schoolmaster or a good private tutor. In fact, what they learned in this way was drilled into them by a *repetent*—it matters not by what name he is called—who had sufficient opportunities of correcting their early errors and inaccuracies, and whose particular vocation it was to remember unceasingly the fact, that the idiosyncrasy of the pupil and the peculiarities of his mental constitution and previous acquirements require a careful diagnosis no less than the special cases, which are submitted to the skill and judgment of a medical practitioner. To teach a class without reference to the wants of the individuals of which it is composed is about as effective as to write one prescription for a room-full of patients. And yet this is constantly done in College lecture-rooms. My own conviction is that, which is more than once expressed in the text—namely, that while private or immediate tuition is required with reference to educational results, namely, scholarship as opposed to learning, professorial lectures and good libraries are the only auxiliaries required for the literary development of classical studies, namely, for classical learning properly so called. Consequently, the College lecture must approach more and more to private tuition if it would produce any effects educationally; it must approach more and more to the real professorial exposition, if it would contribute to the promotion of learned literature. In stating this view of the case, which seems to me sufficiently obvious, I have not made any direct allusion to other opinions on the subject; but I must not conclude this note without referring to Dr Peacock's very uncompromising asseveration that private tuition in the University of Cambridge "is an evil of the most alarming magnitude, not merely as occasioning a great and ruinous increase of the expenses of academical education, but as threatening to supersede the system of public instruction, both in the Colleges and in the University" (*on the Statutes*, p. 153). The arguments, by which this strong statement is supported, appear to me to be not altogether free from exaggeration. The practice of private tuition by resident graduates at large is much more in accordance with the constitution of the University than the College lectures, which Dr Peacock—I think erroneously—calls "public." In fact, as the Colleges monopolise the University, the College tutors and lecturers, appointed at the pleasure of the Masters and not always on grounds of superior qualification, monopolise the functions of private tutorship, which originally belonged to all the fellows. So that private tuition is not an innovation, but a spontaneous restitution of the primitive practice, originating in the revived conviction that instruction cannot be too immediate and individual. An increased attendance on the real professorial lectures of the University will be best effected, as I have mentioned in the text, by increasing the demand, in the final examinations, for learning as distinguished from scholarship, and, generally, for knowledge or science as distinguished from skill. But as long as the examinations, whether classical or mathematical, look strictly, or in a large measure, to educational results, as long in fact as the competitive tests are mainly retrospective, the aid of the private tutor must be sought at some time and in some form. When Dr Peacock fixes the " *average* annual expenditure of every student at the University for private tuition at £40," I think he makes the estimate much too high. But even if this were the case, it must be remembered that the payment, which is not more than a sufficient remuneration for the labour bestowed, is optional, and occasioned generally by a real want of the assistance which is thus procured ; whereas the College lectures, which are generally not wanted, or do not supply the wants of the undergraduates, involve a necessary payment of £10 a year from every pensioner in the University. This payment is no doubt very small; indeed it is quite inadequate as a remuneration for any real or sufficient instruction. And it is only by the appointment of a few Fellows to do the work of the whole Society, that anything like an income can be made from this source. It would therefore be very unreasonable to compare the charges of a private tutor with the fee of a College lecturer, who stands in the place of a large number of private tutors—namely, of the whole body of Fellows in his own College, who would otherwise act in that capacity. Dr Peacock also states that " a great majority of the persons to whom the duty of private tuition is intrusted are young men of very limited attainments, without experience, and perfectly incompetent to convey to their pupils any correct or enlarged views of the subjects which they teach." I believe that this description, so far as it is still apposite, applies mainly to those private tutors who establish and maintain themselves by the patronage of the College tutors. The really good private tutors, who are quite independent of such patronage, are generally men of great attainments, and as experienced in the business of teaching as the best of the College tutors themselves. In fact, many of them are assistant tutors in the great Colleges. But those who are in most repute are persons, who have made this mode of teaching the business of their lives. Some of the most successful of the mathematical tutors are married men living at Cambridge on this account, and the best known of the classical private tutors has carried on his present business for nearly 24 years. It is perhaps true that Dr Peacock's description of " the great majority of persons to whom the duty of private tuition is intrusted " was more applicable when he wrote in 1841 than it would be now ; and even then it was just as applicable to the College lecturers. So far as it is accurately drawn, it indicates a state of things which I should agree with him in deploring. All teaching to be adequate demands complete knowledge and matured experience : but most of all that in which the relation between the tutor and pupil is most immediate and familiar. The private tutor is properly a *pædagogus*, who prepares his pupil for the more public teaching of the professor, and fills up the interval between childish education and manly learning. Thus Varro says (*ap. Nonium*, v. 105) : " educit obstetrix, educat nutrix, instituit pædagogus, docet magister." In the same way we must understand St Paul's striking figure (Gal. iii. 24), that the law of the Jews was a *pædagogus* or " boy-leader " to bring its disciples to the higher teaching of Christ. And this relation between the nurse and the careful teacher is expressed in old high German, which calls the *pædagogus* by the name *magazogo* or *magazoho*, i. e. *qui filium ducit*, and the nurse by the feminine *magazoha*, i. e. *quæ filium educat* (Graff, *Sprachschatz*, v. 619). There is no reason why the Professor should not also be a private tutor, and this is constantly the case in Germany. For not only do the most eminent Professors give private *Stunden* or "hours" in the subjects which they profess,

17

but even receive young men of the better class as domestic pupils, entirely under their care. I have heard that Prince Albert stood in this relation to A. W. von Schlegel at Bonn, and the present King of Prussia had the advantage of receiving similar instruction from the great Niebuhr at Berlin. It would, I conceive, be a great advantage, if the old regulations were revived in the Colleges, and if College-tuition were entirely a system of private teaching and guiding. But whatever chance there may be of this, I hope that the changes, which are imminent, will increase the number of experienced graduates, who are willing to devote themselves to the personal teaching and superintendance of a small number of pupils. And if this should lead to a diminution of the class of private tutors described by Dr Peacock, I should see no reason to regret it. No one can be less disposed than I am to acquiesce in the belief that teaching is a business which requires no apprenticeship, and that the attainment even of the highest academical distinctions qualifies a young man to pass from the status of a mere learner to that of an instructor of others. Dr Peacock says that "the veriest tyro in classical or mathematical knowledge, when himself hardly fledged from the nursing care of a private tutor, will consider himself perfectly qualified to teach as far as he has been taught, though in the most imperfect and superficial manner, and thus becomes the instrument of propagating crude and inaccurate knowledge through successive generations of pupils." To this sort of private tuition I object as strongly as he does ; only I think that the case is worse when the young scholar is set to learn his business, as is too often the case, by presiding over a College lecture-room. As I have suggested in the text, the proper employment of the youngest graduates, if they continue to reside at Cambridge, would be to conduct the initial and other probationary examinations, which do not involve a large amount of knowledge and experience. Or if their tastes lie that way, the under-masterships in the public schools would enable them to make the first beginnings of an educational career under the guidance of some experienced instructor of youth. But I must not hesitate to avow my belief that if steps, like those which I have suggested in this book, were taken with a view to an increased demand for learning as distinguished from scholarship, the number of young men competent to teach would be greatly augmented, and the time of probation which must always intervene between the completion of one's own course of study and the commencement of an attempt to direct the studies of others, would be proportionally abridged. Be this as it may, I cannot suppose that any one, who is competent to form an opinion, will venture to gainsay the proposition, that, with reference to moral as well as intellectual results, the benefits which a really good tutor can confer upon his pupil must be in direct proportion to the amount of his time and attention, which are appropriated by the individual under instruction. This is implied in the fable which relates how Chiron taught Achilles in his solitary cavern, and the poet, who tells us how Hercules brought up Hylas, in order that he might make him as good a man as himself, dwells particularly on the fact that they were always together from morning to night (Theocr. XIII. 10—13). This mode of tuition would not be adopted in England by those who have an unlimited command of the means and opportunities of getting the best training for their children, —beginning with the Queen on the throne and the highest nobles of the land,—if it were not felt that the advantages to be secured are worth any price; and for those who can afford it, the only precaution required is that which has reference to the qualifications of the tutor, and his devotion to his business. If parents would attend to the guarantees of higher competency furnished by the Universities, and abandon the practice of sending their sons to persons, whose qualifications in scholarship are sometimes inappreciable, and whose ostensible business is the care of a parish, they would have less reason to regret their expenditure on this account.

For EU product safety concerns, contact us at Calle de José Abascal, 56–1°, 28003 Madrid, Spain or eugpsr@cambridge.org.